PENGUIN MODERN CLASSICS

Childhood, Youth, Dependency

'*Childhood, Youth and Dependency*, a trilogy of memoirs, should make Tove Ditlevsen as big a name here as she is in her native Denmark. Composed with artful clarity decades after the events they describe, but written with the immediacy of journal entries, these slim books are bright, fresh, funny, shocking, tense and vital' John Self, *The Irish Times*, Books of the Year

'Haunting, intense, elegant . . . a genius . . . Ditlevsen's portrait of Vesterbro in the Twenties has something of the same texture of Elena Ferrante's description of the poor Neapolitan neighbourhood in which her heroines grow up' Lucy Scholes, *Daily Telegraph*

'Sophisticated technique and scalpel-sharp prose. The term autofiction had yet to be coined when she wrote the trilogy (1967–71), but it is the only word that can adequately describe what she is doing. She looks the slimy and intolerable in the eye and burnishes it into cut glass. She's a writer who, like Jean Rhys, explores the seamy ambiguities of female abjection – with a voice whose power blasts through. The subjective truths she tells are about agency and passivity, narcissism and self-destruction, artistic idealism and psychological squalor . . . dazzling' Lucasta Miller, *Times Literary Supplement*

'Despite the darkness that haunts these three books, they shine with Ditlevsen's honesty and humanity . . . Her work, seemingly so simple, has the miraculous quality of a life perceived in perfect clarity. Despite the author's untimely death, *The Copenhagen Trilogy* is a powerful – and uplifting – testament of survival' Erica Wagner

'The simple declarative sentences of Natalia Ginzburg and the pervasive horror of a good fairy story . . . There is a disconnect between the dark matter of these books and the thrilling impact on the reader. They act as a manifesto for art, showing that literature is not the base metal: it is the process of alchemy, and the gold that results' John Self, *New Statesman*

'Compulsive autofiction . . . Mordant, vibrantly confessional . . . its evocation of a working-class woman's battle with masters, leashes and her own demons makes it a masterpiece in its own right' Liz Jensen, *Guardian*

'*The Copenhagen Trilogy* is as raw and poignant as Janet Frame's *An Angel at My Table*. Like that book, it radiates the clear light of truth and stands as the ultimate victory of a life that must have felt, in the living of it, like a defeat. Semi-miraculous, raw and poignant' Alex Preston, *Observer*

'The greatest Danish writer you've never heard of . . . The poignant *Copenhagen Trilogy* describes her progress from slum girl to literary prodigy, before her tragic descent into alcoholism and drug dependency . . . It captures the naivety, terror and rapture of her early life across a fast-changing palette of prose colours. The tones darken from her quizzical interrogation of adult follies in *Childhood* through the satirical larkiness of *Youth* to the junkie melodrama of *Dependency*' Boyd Tonkin, *Spectator*

'As in much of the best autofiction, the protagonist's weakness is counterpoised by the strength of her voice . . . [Ditlevsen speaks] beyond the cruel and disappointing figures she encounters to us, her readers, awaiting her in another time and another place' Lara Feigel, *Guardian*

Tove Ditlevsen (1917–78) was born in the working-class neighbourhood of Vesterbro in Copenhagen. Her first published work, the poetry collection *Girl-Soul*, came out when she was in her early twenties. She went on to write some thirty books, including novels, poetry, story collections and children's books, and for many years she had an agony-aunt column in a Danish family magazine. As a writer, she enjoyed fame and was much loved by readers, but her personal life was troubled. She struggled with alcohol and drug addiction and was admitted to psychiatric hospitals several times. She embarked on her brilliant autobiographical books *Childhood*, *Youth* and *Dependency* (1967–71) and the novel *The Faces* (1968) after a devastating period of depression and writer's block. Today she is celebrated as one of Denmark's most important twentieth-century writers.

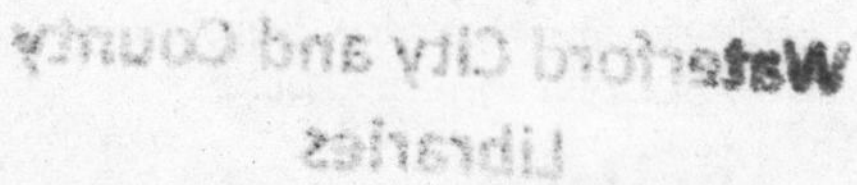

TOVE DITLEVSEN

Childhood, Youth, Dependency

The Copenhagen Trilogy

Translated by Tiina Nunnally and by Michael Favala Goldman

PENGUIN BOOKS

PENGUIN CLASSICS

UK | USA | Canada | Ireland | Australia
India | New Zealand | South Africa

Penguin Books is part of the Penguin Random House group of companies
whose addresses can be found at global.penguinrandomhouse.com

Childhood and *Youth* first published in Denmark as *Barndom* and *Ungdom* 1967
These translations first published in the USA by The Seal Press 1985
First published in Penguin Books 2019

Dependency first published in Denmark as *Gift* 1971
This translation first published in Penguin Books 2019

Published as a trilogy in Penguin Books 2020

003

Set in 11.28/14.34 pt Dante MT Std
Typeset by Jouve (UK), Milton Keynes
Printed and bound in Great Britain by Clays Ltd, Elcograf S.p.A.

A CIP catalogue record for this book is available from the British Library

ISBN: 978–0–241–45757–3

www.greenpenguin.co.uk

Contents

Childhood

I

In the morning there was hope. It sat like a fleeting gleam of light in my mother's smooth black hair that I never dared touch; it lay on my tongue with the sugar and the lukewarm oatmeal I was slowly eating while I looked at my mother's slender, folded hands that lay motionless on the newspaper, on top of the reports of Spanish flu and the Treaty of Versailles. My father had left for work and my brother was in school. So my mother was alone, even though I was there, and if I was absolutely still and didn't say a word, the remote calm in her inscrutable heart would last until the morning had grown old and she had to go out to do the shopping in Istedgade like ordinary housewives.

The sun broke over the gypsy wagon, as if it came from inside it, and Scabie Hans came out with bare chest and a wash basin in his hands. When he had poured the water over himself, he put out his hand for a towel and Pretty Lili gave it to him. They didn't say a word to each other; they were like pictures in a book when you quickly turn the pages. Like my mother, they would change in a few hours. Scabie Hans was a Salvation Army soldier and Pretty Lili was his sweetheart.

In the summer, they packed a bunch of little children into the green wagon and drove into the country with them. Parents paid one krone a day for this. I had gone myself when I was three years old and my brother was seven. Now I was five and the only thing I could remember from the trip was that Pretty Lili once set me out of the wagon, down in the warm sand in what I thought was a desert. Then the green wagon drove away from me and got smaller and smaller and inside of it sat my brother and I was never going to see him or my mother again. When the children came back home, they all had scabies. That's how Scabie Hans got his name. But Pretty Lili was not pretty. My mother was, though, on those strange and happy mornings when I would leave her completely in peace. Beautiful, untouchable, lonely, and full of secret thoughts I would never know. Behind her on the flowered wallpaper, the tatters pasted together by my father with brown tape, hung a picture of a woman staring out the window. On the floor behind her was a cradle with a little child. Below the picture it said, 'Woman awaiting her husband home from the sea'. Sometimes my mother would suddenly catch sight of me and follow my glance up to the picture I found so tender and sad. But my mother burst out laughing and it sounded like dozens of paper bags filled with air exploding all at once. My heart pounded with anguish and sorrow because the silence in the world was now broken, but I laughed with her because my mother expected me to, and because I was seized by the same cruel mirth as she was. She shoved the chair aside, got up and stood in front of the picture in her wrinkled nightgown, her hands on her hips. Then, with a clear and defiant little-girl voice that didn't belong to her in the same way as her voice did later in the day when she'd start haggling about prices with the shopkeepers, she sang:

Can't I sing
Whatever I wish for my Tulle?
Visselulle, visselulle, visselulle.
Go away from the window, my friend,
Come back another time.
Frost and cold have brought
The old beggar home again.

I didn't like the song, but I had to laugh loudly because my mother sang it to amuse me. It was my own fault, though, because if I hadn't looked at the picture, she wouldn't have noticed me. Then she would have stayed sitting there with calmly folded hands and harsh, beautiful eyes fixed on the no-man's-land between us. And my heart could have still whispered 'Mother' for a long time and known that in a mysterious way she heard it. I would have left her alone for a long time so that without words she would have said my name and known we were connected to each other. Then something like love would have filled the whole world, and Scabie Hans and Pretty Lili would have felt it and continued to be colored pictures in a book. As it was, right after the end of the song, they began to fight and yell and pull each other by the hair. And right away, angry voices from the stairwell began to push into the living room, and I promised myself that tomorrow I would pretend the wretched picture on the wall wasn't even there.

When hope had been crushed like that, my mother would get dressed with violent and irritated movements, as if every piece of clothing were an insult to her. I had to get dressed too, and the world was cold and dangerous and ominous because my mother's dark anger always ended in her slapping my face or pushing me against the stove. She was foreign and strange, and I thought that I had been exchanged at birth and she wasn't my mother at all. When she was dressed, she stood in front of the mirror in the bedroom, spit on a piece of pink tissue paper, and rubbed it hard across her cheeks. I carried the cups out to the kitchen, and inside of me long, mysterious words began to crawl across my soul like a protective membrane. A song, a poem, something soothing and rhythmic and immensely pensive, but never distressing or sad, as I knew the rest of my day would be distressing and sad. When these light waves of words streamed through me, I knew that my mother couldn't do anything else to me because she had stopped being important to me. My mother knew it, too, and her eyes would fill with cold hostility. She never hit me when my soul was moved in this way, but she didn't talk to me, either. From then on, until the following morning, it was only our bodies that were close to each other. And, in spite of the cramped space, they avoided even the slightest contact with each other. The sailor's wife on the wall still watched longingly for her husband, but my mother and I didn't need men or boys in our world. Our peculiar and infinitely fragile happiness thrived only when we were alone together; and when I stopped being a little child, it never really came back except in rare, occasional glimpses that have become even more dear to me now that my mother is dead and there is no one to tell her story as it really was.

2

Down in the bottom of my childhood my father stands laughing. He's big and black and old like the stove, but there is nothing about him that I'm afraid of. Everything that I know about him I'm allowed to know, and if I want to know anything else, I just have to ask. He doesn't talk to me on his own because he doesn't know what he should say to little girls. Once in a while he pats me on the head and says, 'Heh, heh.' Then my mother pinches her lips together and he quickly takes his hand away. My father has certain privileges because he's a man and provides for all of us. My mother has to accept that but she doesn't do it without protest. 'You could sit up like the rest of us, you know,' she says when he lies down on the sofa. And when he reads a book, she says, 'People turn strange from reading. Everything written in books is a lie.' On Sundays, my father drinks a beer and my mother says, 'That costs twenty-six øre. If you keep at it like this, we'll end up in Sundholm.' Even though I know Sundholm is a place where you sleep on straw and get salt herring three times a day, the name goes into the verse I make up when I'm scared or alone, because it's beautiful like the picture in one of my father's books that I'm so fond of. It's called 'Worker family on a picnic', and it shows a father and mother and their two children. They're sitting on some green grass and all of them are laughing while they eat from the picnic basket lying between them. All four of them are looking up at a flag stuck into the grass near the father's head. The flag is solid red. I always look at the picture upside down since I only get a chance to see it when my father is reading the book. Then my mother turns on the light and draws the yellow curtains even though it's not dark yet. 'My father was a scoundrel and a drunkard,' she says, 'but at least he wasn't a socialist.' My father keeps on reading calmly because he's slightly deaf, and that's no secret, either. My brother Edvin sits and pounds nails into a board and afterwards pulls them out with pliers. He's going to be a skilled worker. That's something very special. Skilled workers have real tablecloths on the table instead of newspaper and they eat with a knife and fork. They're never unemployed and they're not socialists. Edvin is handsome and I'm ugly. Edvin is smart and I'm stupid. Those are eternal truths like the printed white letters on the baker's roof down the street. It says, '*Politiken* is the best newspaper'. Once I asked my father why he read *Social-Demokraten* instead, but he just wrinkled his brow and cleared his throat while my mother and Edvin burst into their paper-laughter because I was so incredibly stupid.

The living room is an island of light and warmth for many thousands of evenings – the four of us are always there, like the paper dolls up on the wall behind the pillars in the puppet theater my father made from a model in *Familie Journalen*. It's always winter, and out in the world it's ice cold like in the bedroom and the kitchen. The living room sails through time and space, and the fire roars in the stove. Even though

Edvin makes lots of noise with his hammer, it seems like an even louder sound when my father turns a page in the forbidden book. After he has turned many pages, Edvin looks at my mother with his big brown eyes and puts the hammer down. 'Won't Mother sing something?' he says. 'All right,' says my mother, smiling at him, and at once my father puts the book down on his stomach and looks at me as if he'd like to say something to me. But what my father and I want to say to each other will never be said. Edvin jumps up and hands my mother the only book she owns and cares about. It's a book of war songs. He stands bending over her while she leafs through it, and though of course they don't touch each other, they're together in a way that excludes my father and me. As soon as my mother starts to sing, my father falls asleep with his hands folded over the forbidden book. My mother sings loudly and shrilly, as if dissociating herself from the words she sings:

> Mother – is it Mother?
> I see that you have wept.
> You have walked far, you have not slept.
> I am happy now. Don't cry, Mother.
> Thank you for coming, despite all this horror.

There are many verses to all of my mother's songs, and before she reaches the end of the first one, Edvin starts hammering again and my father is snoring loudly. Edvin has asked her to sing in order to avert her rage over my father's reading. He is a boy and boys don't care for songs that make you cry if you listen to them. My mother doesn't like me to cry, either, so I just sit there with a lump in my throat and look sideways down at the book, at the picture of the battlefield where the dying soldier stretches his hand up toward the luminous spirit of his mother, who I know isn't there in reality. All of the songs in the book have a similar theme, and while my mother is singing them I can do whatever I want because she's so completely absorbed in her own world that nothing from outside can disturb her. She doesn't even hear it when they start to fight and argue downstairs. That's where Rapunzel with the long golden braid lives with her parents who haven't yet sold her to the witch for a bunch of bluebells. My brother is the prince and he doesn't know that soon he'll be blind after his fall from the tower. He pounds nails into his board and is the family's pride and joy. That's what boys are, while girls just get married and have children. They have to be supported and they can't hope for or expect anything else. Rapunzel's father and mother work at Carlsberg, and they each drink fifty beers a day. They keep on drinking in the evening after they've come home, and a little before my bedtime they start yelling and beating Rapunzel with a thick stick. She always goes to school with bruises on her face or legs. When they get tired of beating her, they attack each other with bottles and broken chair legs and the police often come to get one of them – and then quiet finally falls over the building. Neither my mother nor my father likes the police. They think Rapunzel's parents should be allowed to kill each other in peace if they want to. 'They're doing the big shots' work,' my father says about the police, and my mother has often talked about the time the police came and got her father and put him in jail. She'll never forget it. My father doesn't drink and he's never been in jail, either. My parents don't fight and things are much better for me than for them when they were children. But a dark edge of fear still invades all my thoughts when things have gotten quiet downstairs and I have to go to bed. 'Good night,' says my mother and closes the door, and goes into the warm living room again. Then I take off my dress, my woolen petticoat and bodice, and the long black stockings I get as a Christmas present every year. I pull my nightgown over my head and sit down on the windowsill for a minute. I look into the dark courtyard way down below and at the front building's wall that's always crying as if it has just rained. There are hardly ever lights in any of the windows because those are the bedrooms, and decent people don't sleep with the light on. Between the walls I can see a little square scrap of sky, where a single star sometimes shines. I call it the evening star and think about it with all my might when my mother has been in to turn off the light, and I lie in my bed watching the pile of clothes behind the door change into long crooked arms trying to twist around my throat. I try to scream, but manage only a feeble whisper, and when the scream finally comes, the whole bed and I are both sopping wet with sweat. My father stands in the doorway and the light is on. 'You just had a nightmare,' he says. 'I suffered from them a lot when I was a child, too. But those were different times.' He looks at me speculatively, and seems to be thinking that a child who has such a good life shouldn't be having nightmares. I smile at him shyly and apologetically, as if the scream were just a foolish whim. I pull the comforter all the way up to my chin because a man shouldn't see a girl in her nightgown. 'Well, well,' he says, turning off the light and leaving again, and in some way or other he takes my fear with him, for now I calmly fall asleep, and the clothes behind the door are only a pile of old rags. I sleep to escape the night that trails past the window with its train of terror and evil and danger. Over on Istedgade, which is so light and festive during the day, police cars and ambulances wail while

I lie securely hidden under the comforter. Drunken men lie in the gutter with broken, bloody heads, and if you go into Café Charles, you'll be killed. That's what my brother says, and everything he says is true.

3

I am barely six years old and soon I'll be enrolled in school, because I can read and write. My mother proudly tells this to everyone who bothers listening to her. She says, 'Poor people's children can have brains too.' So maybe she loves me after all? My relationship with her is close, painful, and shaky, and I always have to keep searching for a sign of love. Everything I do, I do to please her, to make her smile, to ward off her fury. This work is extremely exhausting because at the same time I have to hide so many things from her. Some of the things I get from eavesdropping, others I read about in my father's books, and still others my brother tells me. When my mother was in the hospital recently, we were both sent to Aunt Agnete's and Uncle Peter's. That's my mother's sister and her rich husband. They told me that my mother had a bad stomach, but Edvin just laughed and later explained to me that mother had 'ambortated'. A baby had been in her stomach, but it had died in there. So they had cut her open from her navel down and removed the baby. It was mysterious and terrible. When she came home from the hospital, the bucket under the sink was full of blood every day. Every time I think about it, I see a picture in front of me. It's in Zacharias Nielsen's short stories and depicts a very beautiful woman in a long red dress. She's holding a slim white hand under her breast and saying to an elegantly dressed gentleman, 'I'm carrying a child under my heart.' In books, such things are beautiful and unbloody, and it reassures and comforts me. Edvin says that I'll get lots of spankings in school because I'm so odd. I'm odd because I read books, like my father, and because I don't understand how to play. Even so, I'm not afraid when, holding my mother's hand, I go in through the red doorway of Enghavevej School, because lately my mother has given me the completely new feeling of being something unique. She has on her new coat, with the fur collar up around her ears and belt around her hips. Her cheeks are red from the tissue paper, her lips too, and her eyebrows are painted so that they look like two little fish flicking their tails out toward her temples. I'm convinced that none of the other children has such a beautiful mother. I myself am dressed in Edvin's made-over clothes, but no one can tell because Aunt Rosalia did it. She's a seamstress, and she loves my brother and me as if we were her own children. She doesn't have any herself.

When we enter the building, which seems completely empty, a sharp smell strikes my nose. I recognize it and my heart stiffens because it's the already well-known smell of fear. My mother notices it, too, because she releases my hand as we go up the stairs. In the principal's office, we're received by a woman who looks like a witch. Her greenish hair perches like a bird's nest on top of her head. She only has glasses for one eye, so I guess the other lens was broken. It seems to me that she has no lips – they're pressed so tightly together – and over them a big porous nose juts out, its tip glowing red. 'Hmm,' she says without introduction, 'so your name is Tove?' 'Yes,' says my mother, to whom she has hardly cast a glance, let alone offered a chair, 'and she can read and write without mistakes.' The woman gives me a look as if I were something she had found under a rock. 'That's too bad,' she says coldly. 'We have our own method for teaching that to children, you know.' The blush of shame floods my cheeks, as always when I've been the cause of my mother suffering insult. Gone is my pride, destroyed is my short-lived joy at being unique. My mother moves a little bit away from me and says faintly, 'She learned it by herself, it's not our fault.' I look up at her and understand many things at once. She is smaller than other adult women, younger than other mothers, and there's a world outside my street that she fears. And whenever we both fear it together, she will stab me in the back. As we stand there in front of the witch, I also notice that my mother's hands smell of dish soap. I despise that smell, and as we leave the school again in utter silence, my heart fills with the chaos of anger, sorrow, and compassion that my mother will always awaken in me from that moment on, throughout my life.

4

In the meantime, there exist certain facts. They are stiff and immovable, like the lampposts in the street, but at least they change in the evening when the lamplighter has touched them with his magic wand. Then they light up like big soft sunflowers in the narrow borderland between night and day, when all the people move so quietly and slowly, as if they were walking on the bottom of the green ocean. Facts never light up and they can't soften hearts like *Ditte menneskebarn*, which is one of the first books that I read. 'It's a social novel,' says my father pedantically, and that probably is a fact, but it doesn't tell me anything, and I have no use for it. 'Nonsense,' says my mother, who doesn't care for facts, either, but can more easily ignore them than I can. Whenever my father, on rare occasions, gets really mad at her, he says she's full of lies, but I know that's not so. I know every person has their own truth just as every child has their own childhood. My mother's truth is completely different from my father's truth, but it's just as obvious as the fact that he has brown eyes while hers are blue. Fortunately, things are set up so that you can keep quiet about the truths in your heart; but the cruel, gray facts are written in the school records and in the history of the world and in the law and in the church books. No one can change them and no one dares to try, either – not even the Lord, whose image I can't separate from Prime Minister Stauning's, even though my father says that I shouldn't believe in the Lord since the capitalists have always used Him against the poor.

Therefore:

I was born on December 14, 1918, in a little two-room apartment in Vesterbro in Copenhagen. We lived at Hedebygade 30A; the 'A' meant it was in the back building. In the front building, from the windows of which you could look down on the street, lived the finer people. Though the apartments were exactly the same as ours, they paid two kroner more a month in rent. It was the year that the World War ended and the eight-hour day was instituted. My brother Edvin was born when the World War began and when my father worked twelve-hour days. He was a stoker and his eyes were always bloodshot from the sparks from the furnace. He was thirty-seven years old when I was born, and my mother was ten years younger. My father was born in Nykøbing Mors. He was born out of wedlock and he never knew who his father was. When he was six years old, he was sent out as a shepherd boy, and at about the same time his mother married a potter named Floutrup. She had nine children by him, but I don't know anything about all of these half brothers and half sisters because I've never met them, and my father has never talked about them. He cut off ties with everyone in his family when he went to Copenhagen at the age of sixteen. He had a dream of writing and it never really left him completely. He managed to get hired as an apprentice reporter with some newspaper or other, but, for unknown reasons, he gave it up again. I know nothing of how he spent the ten years in Copenhagen until, at twenty-six, he met my mother in a bakery on Tordenskjoldsgade. She was sixteen, a salesgirl in the front of the shop where my father was a baker's assistant. It turned out to be an abnormally long engagement that my father broke off many times when he thought my mother was cheating on him. I think that most of the time it was completely innocent. Those two people were just so totally different, as if they each came from their own planet. My father was melancholy, serious, and unusually moralistic, while my mother, at least as a young girl, was lively and silly, irresponsible and vain. She worked as a maid at various places, and whenever something didn't suit her, she would just leave. Then my father had to go and get the servant's conduct book and the chest-of-drawers, which he would drive over on a delivery bicycle to the new place, where there would be something else that didn't suit her. She herself once confided to me that she'd never been at any job long enough to have time to boil an egg.

I was seven years old when disaster struck us. My mother had just knit me a green sweater. I put it on and thought it was pretty. Toward the end of the day we went over to pick up my father from work. He worked at Riedel & Lindegaard on Kingosgade. He had always worked there – that is, for as long as I'd been alive. We got there a little too early, and I went and kicked at the mounds of melting snow along the curb while my mother stood leaning against the green railing, waiting. Then my father strode out of the gate and my heart began to beat faster. His face was gray and funny and different. My mother quickly went up to him. 'Ditlev,' she said, 'what's happened?' He looked down at the ground. 'I've been fired,' he said. I didn't know the word but understood the irreparable damage. My father had lost his job. That which could only strike others, had hit us. Riedel & Lindegaard, from which everything good had come until now – even down to my Sunday five øre that I couldn't spend – had become an evil and horrible dragon that had spewed out my father from its fiery jaws, indifferent to his fate, to us, to me and my new green sweater that he didn't even notice. None of us said a word on the way home. I tried to slip my hand into my mother's, but she knocked my arm away with a violent motion. When we got into the living room my father looked at her with an expression heavy with guilt. 'Well, well,' he said, stroking his black mustache with two fingers, 'it'll be a long time before the unemployment benefits give out.' He was forty-three and too old to get a steady job anymore. Even so, I remember only one time when the union benefits ran out and welfare came under discussion. It happened in whispers and after my brother's and my bedtime, because it was an indelible shame like lice and child support. If you went on welfare, you lost your right to vote. We never starved, either, at least my stomach was always full of something, but I got to know the half-starvation you feel at the smell of dinner coming from the doors of the more well-to-do, when for days you've been living on coffee and stale pastry, which cost twenty-five øre for a whole school bag full.

I was the one who bought it. Every Sunday morning at six o'clock my mother woke me up and issued her orders while well hidden under the comforter in the marriage bed next to my father, who was still sleeping. With fingers that were already stiff from the cold before I reached the street, I grabbed my school bag and flew down the stairs that were pitch-dark at that time of day. I opened the door to the street and looked around in every direction and up at the front building's windows, because no one was supposed to see me perform this despicable task. It wasn't proper to take part in the school meals at the Carlsbergvej School, the only social-service institution that existed in Vesterbro in the 1930s. The latter, Edvin and I were not allowed to do. For that matter, it wasn't proper, either, to have a father who was unemployed, even though half of us did. So we covered up this disgrace with the craziest lies – the most common of which was that Father had fallen off a scaffold and was on sick leave. Over by the bakery on Tøndergade the line of children formed a winding snake along the street. They all had bags with them and they all jabbered on about how good the bread was at that particular bakery, especially when it was freshly baked. When it was my turn, I shoved the bag up on the counter, whispered my mission and added aloud, 'Preferably cream puffs.' My mother had expressly told me to ask for white bread. On the way home I stuffed myself with four or five sour cream puffs, wiped my mouth on my coat sleeve, and was never discovered when my mother rummaged in the depths of the bag. I was never, or rarely, punished for the crimes I committed. My mother hit me often and hard, but as a rule it was arbitrary and unjust, and during the punishment I felt something like a secret shame or a heavy sorrow that brought the tears to my eyes and increased the painful distance between us. My father never hit me. On the contrary – he was good to me. All of my childhood books were his, and on my fifth birthday he gave me a wonderful edition of *Grimms' Fairy Tales*, without which my childhood would have been gray and dreary and impoverished. Still, I didn't hold any strong feeling for him, which I often reproached myself for when, sitting on the sofa, he would look at me with his quiet, searching glance, as if he wanted to say or do something in my direction, something that he never managed to express. I was mother's girl and Edvin was father's boy – that law of nature couldn't be changed. Once I said to him, 'Lamentation – what does that mean, Father?' I had found the expression in Gorky and loved it. He considered this for a long time while he stroked the turned-up ends of his mustache. 'It's a Russian term,' he said then. 'It means pain and misery and sorrow. Gorky was a great poet.' I said happily, 'I want to be a poet too!' Immediately he frowned and said severely, 'Don't be a fool! A girl can't be a poet.' Offended and hurt, I withdrew into myself again while my mother and Edvin laughed at the crazy idea. I vowed never to reveal my dreams to anyone again, and I kept this vow throughout my childhood.

5

It's evening and I'm sitting as usual up on the cold windowsill in the bedroom and looking down at the courtyard. It's the happiest hour of my day. The first wave of fear has subsided. My father has said good night and has gone back to the warm living room, and the clothes behind the door have stopped frightening me. I look up at my evening star that's like God's benevolent eye; it follows me vigilantly and seems closer to me than during the day. Someday I'll write down all of the words that flow through me. Someday other people will read them in a book and marvel that a girl could be a poet, after all. My father and mother will be prouder of me than of Edvin, and a sharp-sighted teacher at school (one that I haven't had yet) will say, 'I saw it already when she was a child. There was something special about her!' I want so badly to write down the words, but where in the world would I hide such papers? Even my parents don't have a drawer that can be locked. I'm in the second grade and I want to write hymns because they're the most beautiful things that I know. On my first day of school we sang: 'God be thanked and praised, we slept so peacefully'; and when we got to 'now lively like the bird, briskly like the fish of the sea, the morning sun shines through the pane', I was so happy and moved that I burst out crying, at which all the children laughed in the same way as my mother and Edvin laugh whenever my 'oddness' brings forth my tears. My classmates find me unceasingly, overwhelmingly comical, and I've gotten used to the clown role and even find a sad comfort in it, because together with my confirmed stupidity, it protects me against their peculiar meanness toward anyone who is different.

A shadow creeps out from the arched doorway like a rat from its hole. In spite of the dark, I can see that it's the pervert. When he's certain that the way is clear, he pushes his hat down on his forehead and runs over to the pissoir, leaving the door ajar. I can't see in, but I know what he's doing. The time is past when I was afraid of him, but my mother still is. A little while ago, she took me to the Svendsgade Police Station and, indignant and trembling with rage, told the officer that women and children in the building weren't safe from his filthiness. 'He scared my little girl here out of her wits,' she said. Then the officer asked me whether the pervert had bared himself, and I said no with great conviction. I only knew the word from the line 'thus we bare our heads each time the flag is raised'. He had really never taken off his hat. When we got home, my mother said to my father, 'The police won't do anything. There's no law or justice left in this country.'

The door opens on its screeching hinges and the laughter and songs and curses break through the solemn silence in the room and inside of me. I crane my neck to get a better look at who's coming. It's Rapunzel, her father, and Tin Snout, one of her parents' drinking companions. The girl is walking between the two men, each with an arm around her neck. Her golden hair shines as if reflecting the glow from some invisible streetlamp. Roaring, they stagger across the courtyard, and a little later I can hear their ruckus out on the stairway. Rapunzel's real name is Gerda, and she is almost grown-up, at least thirteen years old. Last summer, when she went with Scabie Hans and Pretty Lili in the gypsy wagon to mind the smallest children, my mother said, 'I guess Gerda has got herself more than just scabies on this trip.' The big girls said something similar in the trash-can corner in the courtyard, where I often find myself on the outskirts. They said it in a low voice, giggling, and I didn't understand any more than that it was something shameless and dirty and obscene, something about Scabie Hans and Rapunzel. So I got up my courage and asked my mother what really had happened to Gerda. Angrily and impatiently she said, 'Oh, you goose! She's not innocent anymore, that's all.' And I wasn't any the wiser.

I look up at the cloudless, silken sky and open the window in order to be even closer to it. It's as if God slowly lowers His gentle face over the earth and His great heart beats softly and calmly, very close to mine. I feel very happy, and long, melancholy lines of verse pass through my soul. They separate me, unwillingly, from those I should be closest to. My parents don't like the fact that I believe in God and they don't like the language I use. On the other hand, I'm repelled by their use of language because they always employ the same vulgar, coarse words and expressions, the meanings of which never cover what they want to say. My mother starts almost all of her orders to me by saying, 'God help you, if you don't . . .' My father curses God in his Jylland dialect, which is perhaps not as bad, but not any nicer to listen to. On Christmas Eve we sing social democratic battle songs as we walk around the tree, and my heart aches with anguish and shame because we can hear the beautiful hymns being sung all around in the building, even in the most drunken and ungodly homes. You should respect your father and mother, and I tell myself that I do, but it's harder now than when I was little.

A fine, cool rain strikes my face and I close the window again. But I can still hear the soft sound of the hallway door as it's opened and closed far below. Then a lovely creature slips across the courtyard as if held upright by a delicate, transparent umbrella. It's Ketty, the beautiful, spiritlike woman from the apartment next to ours. She has on silver high-heel shoes under a long yellow silk dress. Over it she has a white fur that makes you think of Snow White. Ketty's hair is black as ebony, too. It takes only a minute before the arched doorway hides the beautiful sight that cheers my heart night after night. Ketty goes out every evening at this time, and my father says that it's scandalous when there are children around, and I don't understand what he means. My mother doesn't say anything, because during the day she and I are often over in Ketty's living room drinking coffee or hot chocolate. It's a wonderful room, where all the furniture is red plush. The lampshades are red, too, and Ketty herself is pink and white like my mother, although Ketty is younger. They laugh a lot, those two, and I laugh with them even though I seldom understand what's so funny. But whenever Ketty starts to talk to me, my mother sends me away because she doesn't approve of that. It's the same with Aunt Rosalia, who also likes to talk to me. 'Women who don't have children,' says my mother, 'are always so busy with other people's.' Afterwards she puts Ketty down because she makes her old mother live in the unheated room overlooking the courtyard and never lets her come into the living room. The mother is called Mrs Andersen; and, according to my mother, that's 'the blackest lie', since she's never been married. It's a great sin then to have a child – I know that. And when I ask my mother why Ketty treats her mother so badly, she says it's because the mother won't tell her who her father is. When you think about something that terrible, you really have to be grateful you have the proper relationships in your own family.

When Ketty has disappeared, the door to the pissoir opens cautiously, and the pervert edges sideways like a crab along the wall of the front building and out the door. I had completely forgotten about him.

6

Childhood is long and narrow like a coffin, and you can't get out of it on your own. It's there all the time and everyone can see it just as clearly as you can see Pretty Ludvig's harelip. It's the same with him as with Pretty Lili, who's so ugly you can't imagine she ever had a mother. Everything that is ugly or unfortunate is called beautiful, and no one knows why. You can't get out of childhood, and it clings to you like a bad smell. You notice it in other children – each childhood has its own smell. You don't recognize your own and sometimes you're afraid that it's worse than others'. You're standing talking to another girl whose childhood smells of coal and ashes, and suddenly she takes a step back because she has noticed the terrible stink of your childhood. On the sly, you observe the adults whose childhood lies inside them, torn and full of holes like a used and moth-eaten rug no one thinks about anymore or has any use for. You can't tell by looking at them that they've had a childhood, and you don't dare ask how they managed to make it through without their faces getting deeply scarred and marked by it. You suspect that they've used some secret shortcut and donned their adult form many years ahead of time. They did it one day when they were home alone and their childhood lay like three bands of iron around their heart, like Iron Hans in Grimms' fairy tale, whose bands broke only when his master was freed. But if you don't know such a shortcut, childhood must be endured and trudged through hour by hour, through an absolutely interminable number of years. Only death can free you from it, so you think a lot about death, and picture it as a white-robed, friendly angel who some night will kiss your eyelids so that they never will open again. I always think that when I'm grown-up my mother will finally like me the way she likes Edvin now. Because my childhood irritates her just as much as it irritates me, and we are only happy together whenever she suddenly forgets about its existence. Then she talks to me the way she talks to her friends or to Aunt Rosalia, and I'm very careful to make my answers so short that she won't suddenly remember I'm only a child. I let go of her hand and keep a slight distance between us so she won't be able to smell my childhood, either. It almost always happens when I go shopping with her on Istedgade. She tells me how much fun she had as a young girl. She went out dancing every night and was never off the dance floor. 'I had a new boyfriend every night,' she says and laughs loudly, 'but that had to stop when I met Ditlev.' That's my father and otherwise she always calls him 'Father', just as he calls her 'Mother' or 'Mutter'. I get the impression there was a time when she was happy and different, but that it all came to an abrupt end when she met Ditlev. When she talks about him it's as if he's someone other than my father, a dark spirit who crushes and destroys everything that is beautiful and light and lively. And I wish that this Ditlev had never come into her life. When she gets to his name, she usually catches sight of my childhood and looks at it angrily and threateningly, while the dark rim around her blue iris grows even darker. This childhood then shivers with fear and despairingly tries to slip away on tiptoe, but it's still far too little and can't be discarded yet for several hundred years.

People with such a visible, flagrant childhood both inside and out are called children, and you can treat them any way you like because there's nothing to fear from them. They have no weapons and no masks unless they are very cunning. I am that kind of cunning child, and my mask is stupidity, which I'm always careful not to let anyone tear away from me. I let my mouth fall open a little and make my eyes completely blank, as if they're always just staring off into the blue. Whenever it starts singing inside me, I'm especially careful not to let my mask show any holes. None of the grownups can stand the song in my heart or the garlands of words in my soul. But they know about them because bits seep out of me through a secret channel I don't recognize and therefore can't stop up. 'You're not putting on airs?' they say, suspiciously, and I assure them that it wouldn't even occur to me to put on airs. In school they ask, 'What are you thinking about? What was the last sentence I said?' But they never really see through me. Only the children in the courtyard or in the street do. 'You're going around playing dumb,' a big girl says menacingly and comes up close to me, 'but you're not dumb at all.' Then she starts to cross-examine me, and a lot of other girls gather silently around me, forming a circle I can't slip through until I've proved I really am stupid. At last it seems clear to them after all of my idiotic replies, and reluctantly they make a little hole in the circle so I can just squeeze through and escape to safety. 'Because you shouldn't pretend to be something you're not,' one of them yells after me, moralistic and admonishing.

Childhood is dark and it's always moaning like a little animal that's locked in a cellar and forgotten. It comes out of your throat like your breath in the cold, and sometimes it's too little, other times too big. It never fits exactly. It's only when it has been cast off that you can look at it calmly and talk about it like an illness you've survived. Most grownups say that they've had a happy childhood and maybe they really believe it themselves, but I don't think so. I think they've just managed to forget it. My mother didn't have a happy childhood, and it's not as hidden away in her as it is in other people. She tells me how terrible it was when her father had the D.T.'s and they all had to stand holding up the wall so that it wouldn't fall on him. When I say that I feel sorry for him, she yells, 'Sorry! It was his own fault, the drunken pig! He drank a whole bottle of schnapps every day, and in spite of everything, things were a lot better for us when he finally pulled himself together and hanged himself.' She also says, 'He murdered my five little brothers. He took them out of the cradle and crushed their heads against the wall.' Once I ask my Aunt Rosalia, who is mother's sister, whether this is true, and she says, 'Of course it's not true. They just died. Our father was an unhappy person, but your mother was only four years old when he died. She has inherited Granny's hatred of him.' Granny is their mother, and even though she's old now, I can imagine that her soul can hold a lot of hatred. Granny lives on the island of Amager. Her hair is completely white and she's always dressed in black. Just as with my father and mother, I may only address her in an indirect way, which makes all conversations very difficult and full of repetitions. She makes the sign of the cross before she cuts the bread, and whenever she clips her fingernails, she burns the clippings in the stove. I ask her why she does this, but she says that she doesn't know. It was something her mother did. Like all grownups, she doesn't like it when children ask about something, so she gives short answers. Wherever you turn, you run up against your childhood and hurt yourself because it's sharp-edged and hard, and stops only when it has torn you completely apart. It seems that everyone has their own and each is totally different. My brother's childhood is very noisy, for example, while mine is quiet and furtive and watchful. No one likes it and no one has any use for it. Suddenly it's much too tall and I can look into my mother's eyes when we both get up. 'You grow while you're asleep,' she says. Then I try to stay awake at night, but sleep overpowers me and in the morning I feel quite dizzy looking down at my feet, the distance has grown so great. 'You big cow,' the boys on the street yell after me, and if it keeps on like this, I'll have to go to Stormogulen where all the giants grow. Now childhood hurts. It's called growing pains and doesn't stop until you're twenty. That's what Edvin says, who knows everything – about the world and society, too – like my father, who takes him along to political meetings; my mother thinks it will end in both of them being arrested by the police. They don't listen when she says things like that because she knows as little about politics as I do. She also says that my father can't find work because he's a socialist and belongs to the union, and that Stauning, whose picture my father has hung up on the wall next to the sailor's wife, will lead us into trouble one day. I like Stauning, whom I've seen and heard many times in Fælled Park. I like him because his long beard waves so gaily in the wind and because he says 'comrades' to the workers even though he's Prime Minister and could allow himself to be more stuck-up. When it comes to politics, I think my mother is wrong, but no one is interested in what girls think or don't think about such things.

One day my childhood smells of blood, and I can't avoid noticing and knowing it. 'Now you can have children,' says my mother. 'It's much too soon, you're not even thirteen yet.' I know how you have children because I sleep with my parents, and in other ways you can't help knowing it, either. But even so, somehow I still don't understand, and I imagine that at any time I can wake up with a little child beside me. Her name will be Baby Maria, because it will be a girl. I don't like boys and I'm not allowed to play with them, either. Edvin is the only one I love and admire, and he's the only one I can imagine myself marrying. But you can't marry your brother and even if you could, he wouldn't have me. He's said that often enough. Everyone loves my brother, and I often think his childhood suits him better than mine suits me. He has a custom-made childhood that expands in tune with his growth, while mine is made for a completely different girl. Whenever I think such thoughts, my mask becomes even more stupid, because you can't talk to anyone about these kinds of things, and I always dream about meeting some mysterious person who will listen to me and understand me. I know from books that such people exist, but you can't find any of them on my childhood street.

7

Istedgade is my childhood street – its rhythm will always pound in my blood and its voice will always reach me and be the same as in those distant times when we swore to be true to each other. It's always warm and light, festive and exciting, and it envelops me completely, as if it were created to satisfy my personal need for self-expression. Here I walked as a child holding my mother's hand, and learned important things like an egg in Irma costs six øre, a pound of margarine forty-three øre, and a pound of horse meat fifty-eight øre. My mother haggles over everything except food, so that the shopkeepers wring their hands in despair, declaring she'll drive them to wrack and ruin if this keeps up. She's so wonderfully audacious, too, that she dares to exchange shirts that my father has worn as if they were brand new. And she can go right in the door of a store, stand at the end of the line and yell in a shrill voice, 'Hey, it's my turn now. I've certainly waited long enough.' I have fun with her and I admire her Copenhagen boldness and quick-wittedness. The unemployed hang around outside the small cafés. They whistle through their fingers at my mother, but she doesn't give them the time of day. 'They could at least stay at home,' she says, 'like your father.' But it's so depressing to see him sitting idly on the sofa whenever he's not out looking for work. In a magazine, I read this line: 'To sit and stare at two fists that our Lord has made so magnificently skilled.' It's a poem about the unemployed and it makes me think of my father.

It's only after I meet Ruth that Istedgade becomes a playground and permanent hangout for me after school until dinner time. At that time I'm nine years old and Ruth is seven. We notice each other one Sunday morning when all of the children in the building are chased out into the street to play so the parents can sleep late after the week's drudgery or dreariness. As usual, the big girls stand gossiping in the trash-can corner while the little ones play hopscotch, a game I always make a mess of because I either step on the line or touch the ground with my swinging leg. I never understand what the point is and find the game terribly boring. Somebody or other has said that I'm out, and resignedly I'm leaning against the wall. Then quick footsteps pound down the front building's kitchen stairway, which leads out into the courtyard, and a little girl emerges with red hair, green eyes, and light brown freckles across the bridge of her nose. 'Hi,' she says to me and grins from ear to ear, 'my name is Ruth.' I introduce myself shyly and awkwardly, because no one is used to new children making such a cool entrance. Everyone is staring at Ruth, who doesn't seem to notice it. 'Want to run and play?' she says to me, and after a hesitating glance up at our window I follow her, as I will follow her for many years, right up until we've both finished school and our profound differences have become apparent.

Now I've got a friend and it makes me much less dependent on my mother, who of course doesn't like Ruth. 'She's an adopted child and nothing good ever comes of that,' my mother says darkly, but she doesn't forbid me to play with her. Ruth's parents are a pair of big, ugly people who themselves could never have brought something as lovely as Ruth into the world. The father is a waiter and drinks like a fish. The mother is obese and asthmatic and hits Ruth for the slightest reason. Ruth doesn't care. She shakes off the claws, roars down the kitchen stairs, shows all of her shining white teeth in a smile, and says gaily, 'That bitch, I wish she'd go to hell.' When Ruth swears it isn't ugly or offensive because her voice is so crisp and fine, like the little Billy Goat Gruff. Her mouth is red and heart-shaped with a narrow, upturned upper lip, and her expression is as strong as that of the man who knew no fear. She is everything that I'm not, and I do everything she wants me to do. She cares as little as I do for real games. She never touches her dolls and she uses her doll buggy as a springboard when we put a plank on it. But we don't do that very often because the landlady comes running after us or we're told to stop it by our watchful mothers who have much too good a view from the windows. Only on Istedgade are we away from any supervision, and that's where my criminal path begins. Ruth accepts sweetly and good-humoredly that I'm not prepared to steal. But then I have to distract the clerk's attention from her tiny, quick figure that indiscriminately grabs things while I stand there asking when they expect to get bubblegum in the store. We go into the nearest doorway and share the plunder. Sometimes we go to stores and endlessly try on shoes or dresses. We select the most expensive one and politely say that our mother will come in to pay for it if they would kindly put the goods aside for the time being. Even before we get out the door, our delighted giggles break loose.

Throughout the whole long friendship, I'm always afraid of revealing myself to Ruth. I'm afraid that she'll discover how I really am. I make myself into her echo because I love her and because she's the strongest, but deep inside I am still me. I have my dreams about a future beyond the street, but Ruth is intimately tied to it and will never be torn away from it. I feel as if I'm deceiving her by pretending that we're of the same blood. In a mysterious way I am indebted to her; together with fear and a vague guilty feeling, this burdens my heart and colors our relationship in the same way it will color all close and lasting relationships later in my life.

The shoplifting comes to an abrupt end. One day Ruth has pulled off a coup by swiping a whole jar of orange marmalade inside her coat. Afterwards, we eat ourselves sick on it. Completely stuffed, we throw the rest into one of the garbage cans, which is so full that it can't be closed. So we jump up and sit on the lid. Suddenly Ruth says, 'Why the hell does it always have to be me?' 'The receiver is as bad as the thief,' I say, terrified. 'Yes, but still . . .' grumbles Ruth, 'you could do it once in a while.' I can see the reasonableness in her demand and promise uneasily to do it next time. But I insist it has to be very far away, so on Søndre Boulevard I pick out a dairy store that looks suitably deserted. Ruth cautiously opens the door and sails in, followed by her long shadow, which could very well be her own slumbering conscience. The shop is empty and there's no window in the door out to the back room. On the counter there's a bowl full of twenty-five-øre chocolate sticks in red and green foil. I stare at them, pale with excitement and fear. I lift my hand, but it's held back by invisible powers. I shake all the way down to my feet. 'Hurry up,' whispers Ruth, who is keeping an eye on the back room. Then the hand-that-can't-steal reaches up to the bowl, grabs some of the red and green dancing before my eyes, and knocks the whole pile over behind the counter. 'Idiot,' hisses Ruth, and races off just as the back door bangs open. A pale woman comes rushing out and stops, astonished, when she sees me standing there like a pillar of salt with a piece of chocolate in one upraised hand. 'What's the meaning of this?' she says. 'What are you doing here? Oh, look, now the bowl is broken!' And she bends down and picks up the pieces, and I don't know what to do, since the world hasn't crashed around me after all. I wish that it would happen now, right there. All I feel is a boundless, burning shame. The excitement and the adventure are gone; I'm just an ordinary thief, caught in the act. 'You could at least say you're sorry,' says the woman as she goes out with the shards of glass. 'Such a big, clumsy oaf.'

All the way down by Enghavevej, Ruth is standing laughing so hard she has tears in her eyes. 'You're such a blithering idiot,' she manages to say. 'Did she say anything? Why didn't you get out of there? Hey, do you still have the chocolate? Let's go to the park and eat it.' 'Do you really want to eat it?' I ask in disbelief. 'I think we should throw it under a tree.' 'Are you crazy?' Ruth says. 'Good chocolate?' 'But Ruth,' I say, 'we'll never do it again, will we?' Then my little friend asks me whether I'm becoming a goody-goody, and in the park she stuffs the chocolate in her mouth right before my eyes. After that the stealing expeditions stop. Ruth doesn't want to do it alone. And whenever my mother sends me out shopping, I always barge into the store with unnecessary noise. If, after that, it still takes a while for the clerk to come, I stand far away from the counter with my eyes on the ceiling. But my cheeks still flush red when the woman appears, and I have to control myself to keep from desperately turning my pockets inside out in front of her so she can see they're not full of stolen goods. The episode increases my guilt feeling toward Ruth, and also makes me afraid of losing her prized friendship. So I show even greater daring in our other forbidden games, such as trying to be the last one to run over the tracks in front of the train under the viaduct on Enghavevej. Sometimes I'm toppled over by the air pressure from the locomotive, and I lie on the grass embankment for a long time, gasping for breath. It's reward enough when Ruth says, 'Good God! That time you just about kicked the bucket!'

8

It's fall and the storm rattles the butcher's signs. The trees on Enghavevej have lost nearly all of their leaves, which almost cover the ground with their yellow and reddish-brown carpet that looks like my mother's hair when the sun plays in it, and you suddenly discover it's not totally black. The unemployed are freezing, but still standing erect with their hands deep in their pockets and a burned-out pipe between their teeth. The streetlamps have just been lit, and now and then the moon peeks out between racing, shifting clouds. I always think there is a mystical understanding between the moon and the street, like between two sisters who have grown old together and no longer need any language to communicate with each other. We're walking in the fleeting dusk, Ruth and I, and soon we'll have to leave the street, which makes us eager for something to happen before the day is over. When we reach Gasværksvej, where we usually turn around, Ruth says, 'Let's go down and look at the whores. There are probably some who have started.' A whore is a woman who does it for money, which seems to me much more understandable than to do it for free. Ruth told me about it, and since I think the word is ugly, I've found another in a book: 'Lady-of-the-evening'. It sounds much nicer and more romantic. Ruth tells me everything about those kinds of things; for her, the adults have no secrets. She has also told me about Scabie Hans and Rapunzel, and I can't comprehend it, since I think Scabie Hans is a very old man. And he has Pretty Lili, besides. I wonder whether men can love two women at once. For me the grownups' world is still just as mysterious. I always picture Istedgade as a beautiful woman who's lying on her back with her hair near Enghaveplads. At Gasværksvej, which forms the boundary between decent people and the depraved, her legs part, and sprinkled over them like freckles are the welcoming hotels and the bright, noisy taverns, where later in the night the police cars drive by to pick up their scandalously intoxicated and quarrelsome victims. That I know from Edvin, who is four years older than me, and is allowed to be out until ten o'clock at night. I admire Edvin greatly when he comes home in his blue Danish Youth shirt and talks politics with my father. Lately they're both very outraged over Sacco and Vanzetti, whose pictures stare out from the poster displays and the newspaper. They look so handsome with their dark foreign faces, and I also think it's too bad they're going to be executed for something they didn't do. But I just can't get as excited about it as my father, who yells and pounds the table whenever he discusses it with Uncle Peter. He's a Social Democrat like my father and Edvin, but he doesn't think that Sacco and Vanzetti deserve a better fate since they're anarchists. 'I don't care,' yells my father furiously and pounds the table. 'Miscarriage of justice is miscarriage of justice, even if it concerns a conservative!' I know that's the worst thing you can be. Recently, when I asked whether I could join the Ping Club because all the other girls in my class were members, my father looked at my mother sternly, as if I were a victim of her subversive influence in political matters, and said, 'There, you see, Mutter. Now she's becoming a reactionary. It will probably end with us subscribing to *Berlingske Tidende*!'

Down by the train station life is in full swing. Drunken men stagger around singing with their arms around each other's shoulders, and out of Café Charles rolls a fat man whose bald head strikes the pavement a couple of times before he lies still at our feet. Two officers come over to him and kick him emphatically in the side, which makes him get up with a pitiful howl. They pull him roughly to his feet and push him away when he once again tries to go into the den of iniquity. As they continue down the street, Ruth puts her fingers in her mouth and sends a long whistle after them, a talent I envy. Near Helgolandsgade there's a big crowd of laughing, noisy children, and when we go over there I see that it's Curly Charles, who is standing in the middle of the road, putting the steaming horse droppings in his mouth. All the while he's singing an indescribably filthy song that makes the children scream with laughter and give him shouts of encouragement in the hope he'll provide them with more entertainment. His eyes roll wildly. I find him tragic and horrifying, but pretend he amuses me because of Ruth, who laughs loudly along with the others. Of whores, however, we see only a couple of older, fat women who energetically wiggle their hips in an apparently vain attempt to attract the favors of an audience driving slowly by. This disappoints me greatly, because I thought all of them were like Ketty, whose evening errands in the city Ruth has also explained to me. On the way home, we go through Revalsgade, where once an old woman who owned a cigar store was murdered. We also stop in front of the haunted house on Matthæusgade and stare up at the fourth floor window where a little girl was murdered last year by Red Carl, a stoker my father worked with at the Ørsted Works. None of us dares go past that house alone at night. In the doorway at home, Gerda and Tin Snout are standing in such a tight embrace that you can't tell their figures apart in the dark. I hold my breath until I'm out in the courtyard because there's always a rancid stench of beer and urine. I feel oppressed as I go up the stairs. The dark side of sex yawns toward me more and more, and it's becoming harder to cover it up with the unwritten, trembling words my heart is always whispering. The door next to Gerda's opens quietly as I go by, and Mrs Poulsen signals me to come inside. According to my mother, she's 'shabby-genteel', but I know that you can't be both shabby and genteel. She has a lodger who my mother contemptuously calls 'a fine duke' even though he's a mailman and supports Mrs Poulsen just as if they were married; they have no children, however. I know from Ruth that they live together as man and wife. Reluctantly, I obey the command and step into a living room exactly like ours except that there's a piano that is missing many keys. I sit down on the very edge of a chair and Mrs Poulsen sits on the sofa with a prying look in her pale blue eyes. 'Tell me something, Tove,' she says ingratiatingly. 'Do you know whether many gentlemen come to visit Miss Andersen?' I immediately make my eyes blank and stupid and let my jaw drop slightly. 'No,' I say, feigning astonishment, 'I don't think so.' 'But you and your mother are over there so much. Think a little. Haven't you ever seen any gentlemen in her apartment? Not even in the evenings?' 'No,' I lie, terrified. I'm afraid of this woman who wants to harm Ketty in some way. My mother has forbidden me to visit Ketty anymore, and she only goes over there herself when my father is not around. Mrs Poulsen gets nothing else out of me and lets me go with a certain coolness. Several days later a petition goes around in the building and because of it, my parents have a fight when they come to bed and think I'm asleep. 'I'm going to sign it,' says my father, 'for the children's sake. You can at least protect them from witnessing the worst filth.' 'It's those old bitches,' says my mother hotly. 'They're jealous because she's young and pretty and happy. They can't stand me, either.' 'Stop comparing yourself to a whore,' snarls my father. 'Even though I don't have a steady job, you've never had to earn your own living – don't forget that!' It's awful to listen to, and it seems as though the fight is about something totally different, something they don't have words for. Soon the day arrives when Ketty and her mother are sitting out on the street on top of all their plush furniture, which a policeman, pacing back and forth, is guarding. Ketty looks right through all the people, full of contempt, holding her delicate umbrella up against the rain. She smiles at me, though, and says, 'Goodbye, Tove. Take care of yourself.' A little later they drive away in the moving van and I never see them again.

9

Something terrible has happened in my family. Landmands Bank has gone under and my Granny has lost all of her money. Five hundred kroner saved over an entire lifetime. It's a nasty business that only strikes the small investors. 'The rich pigs,' my father says, 'will see that they get their money.' Granny cries pitifully and dries her red eyes with a snow-white handkerchief. Everything about her is clean and neat and proper, and she always smells like the cleaners. The money was supposed to be used for her funeral, which she always seems to be thinking about. She pays money into a funeral coffer – she never can forget that I once thought this was the same as a coffin. It still makes her laugh whenever she thinks of it. I'm very fond of Granny, not at all in the same terrified way as I am of my mother. I'm allowed to visit her by myself, because that's what she wants and my mother doesn't dare go against her will. She told me Granny was very angry with her when she was expecting me because, since they'd had a boy, there was no reason to have any more children. Now Granny doesn't know how she's going to get a decent burial, since we don't have any money and Aunt

Rosalia with her drunken husband doesn't, either. Uncle Peter is certainly very rich, but with his proverbial stinginess, no one dreams of him contributing anything for his mother-in-law's funeral. Granny is seventy-three years old and she herself doesn't think she has long to live. She's even smaller than my mother, slight as a child and always dressed in black from head to toe. Her white, silky-soft hair is pinned up on her head, and she moves as nimbly as a young girl. She lives in a one-room apartment and she only has her old-age pension to live on. Whenever I visit her for coffee, I have rye bread with real butter, which I scrape back with my teeth until it's all on the last mouthful; it tastes better than anything I ever get at home. Since Edvin started his apprenticeship, he visits her every Sunday. Then she gives him a whole krone because he's the only boy in the family. My three cousins and I don't get anything. Every time I'm at Granny's, she asks me to sing in order to see whether I sing a little less off-key than last time. 'That's almost right,' she says encouragingly, even though I can hear that the tones coming from me don't sound like the ones I want to produce at all. You can't speak to her without being addressed first, but she herself likes to talk and I like to listen to her. She talks about her childhood, which was awful because she had a stepmother who practically beat her to death every other minute for the smallest trifles. Then she became a maid and was engaged to my grandfather, who was named Mundus and was a coach builder before he began to drink heavily. 'The Bellowing Drunk' they called him in the building, and when he hanged himself, Granny had to go out as a washerwoman in order to keep the wolf from the door. 'But my three little girls got a start in life,' she says with understandable pride. Once I let slip that I would have liked to have known my grandfather, and she says, 'Yes, he was handsome right up to the end, but a heartless scoundrel! If I wanted to, I could tell you things . . .' Then she presses her lips tightly together over her toothless gums and won't say any more. I think about the word 'heartless' and am afraid that I'm like my dreadful grandfather. I often have a nagging suspicion that I'm not capable of really feeling anything for anyone, with the exception of Ruth, of course. One day when I'm at Granny's and have to sing for her, I say, 'I've learned a new song in school.' And with a false and quavering voice, I sit on her bed and sing a poem I've written. It's very long and – like 'Hjalmar and Hilda', 'Jørgen and Hansigne', and all of my mother's ballads – it's about two people who can't have each other. But in my version, it ends less tragically with the following verse:

Love, rich and young,
bound them with a thousand chains.
Does it matter that the bridal bed
is found on country lanes?

When I've gotten this far, Granny wrinkles her forehead, stands up, and smooths down her dress as if defending herself from an unpleasant impression. 'That's not a nice song, Tove,' she says sternly. 'Did you really learn it in school?' I answer affirmatively, heavy-hearted because I thought she would say, 'That was very beautiful – who wrote it?' 'One must get married in a church,' says Granny mildly, 'before having anything to do with each other. But you couldn't know that, of course.' Oh, Granny! I know more than you think, but I'll keep quiet about it in the future. I think about a few years ago when I discovered with astonishment that my parents were married in February the same year that Edvin was born in April. I asked my mother how that could be possible, and she answered briskly, 'Well, you see, you never carry the first one more than two months.' Then she laughed, and Edvin and my father frowned. That's the worst thing about grownups, I think – they can never admit that just once in their lives they've acted wrongly or irresponsibly. They're so quick to judge others, but they never hold Judgement Day for themselves.

I only see the rest of my family together with my parents, or at least with my mother. Aunt Rosalia lives on Amager like Granny. I've only visited her a couple of times, because Uncle Carl, whom they call The Hollow Leg, is always sitting in the living room, drinking beer and grumbling, which isn't good for children to see. The living room is like everyone else's, with a buffet along one wall, a sofa against the other, and between them a table with four high-backed chairs. On the buffet, as in our apartment, there's a brass tray with a coffee pot, sugar bowl and cream pitcher that are never used, just polished bright and shiny for all special occasions. Aunt Rosalia sews for the department store Magasin and often visits us on her way home. Over her arm, in a big alpaca wrap, she carries the clothes that she's going to sew, and she never puts it down while she's visiting us. She's only going to stay 'a minute', and always keeps her hat on as if to deny she's been here several hours when she finally leaves. She and my mother always talk about events from their youth, and in that way I find out a lot that I shouldn't know. Once, for example, my mother hid a barber in the wardrobe in her room because my father unexpectedly came to visit. If my mother hadn't gotten him to leave again, the barber would have suffocated. There are lots of stories like that, and they laugh heartily at them all. Aunt Rosalia is only two years older than my mother, while

Aunt Agnete is eight years older and wasn't really young with them. She and Uncle Peter often come to play cards with my parents. Aunt Agnete is pious and suffers from it whenever someone swears in her presence, which her husband does frequently just to annoy her. She is tall and wide and has a Dagmar cross resting on her bosom, which Uncle Peter calls the balcony. If I were to believe my parents, he is evil and cunning incarnate, but he's always friendly to me, so I don't really believe them. He's a carpenter and never out of work. They live in a three-room apartment in Østerbro and have an ice-cold parlor with a piano, and they only set foot in it on Christmas Eve. It's said that Uncle Peter inherited an enormous sum of money that he keeps in various bank accounts in order to fool the tax authorities. Sometimes the employees at the shop where he works are invited to visit other companies, where they are hosted free-of-charge. When he went with them to Tuborg, he drank so much that he had to be taken to the hospital and have his stomach pumped out the following day. And when he visited the Enighed Dairy, he downed so much milk he was sick for the next week. Otherwise he never drinks anything but water. My three cousins are all older than me and rather ugly. Every evening they sit around the dinner table, knitting furiously. 'But they're not too bright,' says my father, and there's not so much as a single book in that whole big apartment. My parents make no bones about saying we've turned out better than those girls. Uncle Peter was married once before, and from that marriage he has a daughter who's only seven or eight years younger than my mother. Her name is Ester, and she's a great hulk with a wriggling, bent-over walk. Her eyes look like they're about to pop out of her head, and whenever she visits us she talks baby-talk to me and kisses me right on the mouth, which I despise more than anything else. 'Sweetie pie' she calls my mother, whom she goes out with in the evening, much to my father's dismay. One time they're going to a masquerade at Folkets Hus and I hold the mirror while they put on their make-up, and I think my mother is fantastically beautiful as 'The Night Queen'. Ester is a 'coachman from the eighteenth century', and her arms stick out of the puff sleeves like heavy clubs. They have to hurry because my father will be arriving soon. My mother stands there in all of the black tulle, which is covered with hundreds of shiny sequins. They fall off as easily as her own frail happiness. Just as they're going out the door, my father comes home from work. He stares my mother in the face and says, 'Ha, you old scarecrow.' She doesn't answer, just slips past him without a word, on Ester's heels. My father knows that I heard him, and he sits down across from me with an uncertain expression in his kind, melancholy eyes. 'What do you want to be when you grow up?' he asks awkwardly. 'The Night Queen,' I say cruelly, because here is that 'Ditlev' who always has to spoil my mother's fun.

10

I've started middle school and with that the world has begun to widen. I was allowed to continue because my parents have figured out I still won't be much more than fourteen when I finish school, and since they're giving Edvin training, I shouldn't be left out. At the same time, I've finally gotten permission to use the public library on Valdemarsgade, which has a section with children's books. My mother thinks that I'll get even stranger from reading books that are written for adults; and my father, who doesn't agree, doesn't say anything since I come under my mother's authority and in crucial matters he doesn't dare go against the world order. So for the first time I set foot in a library, and I'm speechless with confusion at seeing so many books collected in one place. The children's librarian is named Helga Mollerup, and she's known and loved by many children in the neighborhood because whenever there's no heat or light at home, they're allowed to sit in the reading room right up until the library closes at five o'clock in the evening. They do their homework there or leaf through books, and Miss Mollerup throws them out only if they start getting noisy, because it's supposed to be completely quiet, like in a church. She asks me how old I am and finds books she thinks are right for a ten-year-old. She is tall and slim and pretty, with dark, lively eyes. Her hands are big and beautiful and I regard them with a certain respect, because it's said that she can slap harder than any man. She's dressed like my teacher, Miss Klausen, in a rather long, smooth skirt and a blouse with a low white collar at the neck. But, unlike Miss Klausen, she doesn't seem to suffer from an insurmountable aversion to children – on the contrary. I'm placed at a table with a children's book in front of me, the title and author of which I've fortunately forgotten. I read, '"Father, Diana has had puppies." With these words, a slender young girl fifteen years old came storming into the room, where, in addition to the councilman, there were . . .' etc. Page after page. I don't have it in me to read it. It fills me with sadness and unbearable boredom. I can't understand how language – that delicate and sensitive instrument – can be so terribly mistreated, or how such monstrous sentences can find their way into a book that gets into the library where a clever and attractive woman like Miss Mollerup actually recommends it to defenseless children to read. For now, however, I can't express these thoughts, so I have to be content with saying that the books are boring and that I would rather have something by Zacharias Nielsen or Vilhelm Bergsøe. But Miss Mollerup says that children's books are exciting if you just have patience enough to keep reading until the plot gets going. Only when I stubbornly insist on having access to the shelves with the adult books does she give in, astonished, and offer to get some books for me if I'll tell her which ones, since I can't go in there myself. 'One by Victor Hugo,' I say. 'It's pronounced Ügó,' she says, smiling, and pats me on the head. It doesn't embarrass me that she corrects my pronunciation, but when I come home with *Les Misérables* and my father says approvingly, 'Victor Hugo – yes, he's good!' I say didactically and self-importantly, 'It's pronounced Ügó.' 'I don't give a damn how it's pronounced,' he says calmly. 'All those kinds of names should be said the way they're spelled. Anything else is just showing off.' It's never any use to come home and tell my parents anything people said who don't live on our street. Once when the school dentist requested that I ask my mother to buy me a toothbrush and I was dumb enough to mention it at home, my mother snapped, 'You can tell her that she can darn well buy you a toothbrush herself!' But whenever she has a toothache, she first goes around suffering for about a week, while the whole house echoes with her miserable moaning. Then, out on the landing, she asks the advice of another woman, who recommends that she pour schnapps on a wad of cotton and hold it against the infected tooth, which she spends several more days doing, with no results. Only then does she get all dressed up in her finest and venture out to Vesterbrogade, where our doctor lives. He takes his pincers and pulls out the tooth and then she has peace for a while. A dentist never comes into the picture.

In the middle school the girls are better dressed and less sniveling than in the primary school. None of them has lice or a harelip, either. My father says that now I'll be going to school with children of people who are 'better off', but that that's no reason for me to look down on my own home. That's true enough. The children's fathers are mostly skilled workers, and I make my father into a 'machinist', which I think sounds better than stoker. The richest girl in the class has a father who owns a barbershop on Gasværksvej. Her name is Edith Schnoor and she lisps from sheer self-importance. Our classroom teacher is named Miss Mathiassen, a small, lively woman who seems to enjoy teaching. Together with Miss Klausen, Miss Mollerup, and the principal at the old school (the one who resembled a witch), she gives me the distinct impression that women can only have influence in the working world if they're completely flat-chested. My mother is an exception; otherwise all the housewives at home on my street have enormous busts that they consciously thrust out as they walk. I wonder why that is. Miss Mathiassen is the only female teacher we have. She's discovered that I like poetry, and it doesn't work to play dumb with her. I save that for the subjects that don't interest me – but there are lots of those. I only like Danish and English. Our English teacher is named Damsgaard, and he can be terribly short-tempered. Then he pounds the table and says, 'Upon my word, I'll teach you!' He uses this mild oath so often that before long he's known exclusively as 'Upon my word'. One time he reads aloud a sentence that's supposed to be especially difficult, and he asks me to repeat it. It goes like this: 'In reply to your inquiry I can particularly recommend you the boarding house at eleven Woburn Place. Some of my friends stayed there last winter and spoke highly about it.' He praises my correct pronunciation, and that's the reason I can never forget that idiotic sentence.

All the girls in my class have poetry albums, and after I've nagged my mother long enough, I get one too. It's brown and it says 'Poetry' on the outside in gold letters. I let some of the girls write the usual verses in it, and in between I put in some of my own poems with the date and my name underneath so that posterity will have no doubt that I was a child genius. I hide it in one of the dresser drawers in the bedroom under a stack of towels and dishcloths, where I think it will be relatively safe from profane eyes. But one evening Edvin and I are home alone because my parents are out playing cards with my aunt and uncle. Otherwise Edvin is usually out in the evening, but he's been too tired for that since he started his apprenticeship. It's a bad workplace, he says, and he often begs my father to let him find a different one. When that does no good, he starts shouting and says that he'll run off to sea and leave home and much more. Then my father shouts, too, and then when my mother interferes in the fight and takes Edvin's side, there's an uproar in the living room that almost drowns out the racket downstairs at Rapunzel's. It's Edvin's fault that nearly every evening now all peace in the living room is destroyed, and sometimes I wish that he'd follow through with his threats and leave. Now he sits sulking and withdrawn, leafing through *Social-Demokraten*, while only the ticking clock on the wall breaks the silence. I'm doing my homework, but the silence between us oppresses me. He stares at me with his dark, thoughtful eyes that are suddenly just as melancholy as my father's. Then he says, 'Aren't you going to bed soon, damn it? You can never be alone in this damn house!' 'You can go into the bedroom, you know,' I answer, hurt. 'I bloody well will, too,' he mumbles, grabbing the newspaper and going out. He slams the door hard after him. A little while later, to my surprise and uneasiness, I hear a burst of laughter from in there. What can be so funny? I go inside and stiffen with horror. Edvin is sitting on my mother's bed with my poor album in his hand. He's completely doubled up with laughter. Bright red in the face with shame, I take a step toward him and put out my hand. 'Give me that book,' I say and stamp my foot. 'You have no right to take it!' 'Oh God,' he gasps and doubles up with laughter, 'this is hilarious. You're really full of lies. Listen to this!' Then, interrupted by fits of laughter, he reads:

Do you remember that time we sailed
along the still, clear stream?
The moon was mirrored in the sea.
Everything was like a lovely dream.

Suddenly you lay the oar to rest,
and let the boat go still.
You said nothing, but my dear –
the passion in your gaze did thrill.

You took me in your arms so strong.
Lovingly you kissed me.
Never, never will I forget
that hour spent with thee.

'Oh no! Ha ha ha!' He falls back and keeps on laughing, and the tears stream from my eyes. 'I hate you,' I yell, stamping my foot powerlessly. 'I hate you! I wish you'd drown in a marl pit!' With those last words, I'm just about to rush out the door, when Edvin's insane laughter takes on a new, disturbing sound. I turn around in the doorway and look at him lying on his stomach across my mother's striped comforter with his face hidden in the crook of one arm. My precious book has fallen to the floor. He sobs inconsolably and uncontrollably, and I am horrified. Hesitantly, I approach the bed, but I don't dare touch him. That's something we've never done. I dry my own tears with the sleeve of my dress and say, 'I didn't mean it, Edvin, the part about the marl pit. I . . . I don't even know what it is.' He keeps sobbing without answering and suddenly turns over and gives me a hopeless look. 'I hate them, the boss and the assistants,' he says. 'They . . . beat me . . . all day and I'll never learn to paint cars. I'm just sent out to get beer for all of them. I hate Father because I can't change workplaces. And when you come home, you can never be alone. There's not one damn corner where you can have anything for yourself.' I look down at my poetry album and say, 'I can't have anything for myself, either, you know – and neither can Father or Mother. They're not even alone when they . . . when they . . .' He looks at me, surprised, and finally stops crying. 'No,' he says sadly. 'Jesus, I've never thought about that.' He gets up, regretting, of course, that his sister has seen him in a moment of weakness. 'Well,' he says in a tough voice, 'it probably all gets better when you move away from home.' I agree with him about that. Then I go out and count the eggs in the pantry. I take two and move the rest around so it looks like there are more of them. 'I'm going to mix us an egg schnapps,' I yell toward the living room and start the preparations. At that moment, I like Edvin much better than in all the years when he was distant and wonderful, handsome and cheerful. It wasn't really human that he never seemed to feel bad about anything.

II

Gerda is going to have a baby and Tin Snout has vanished. Ruth says he had a wife and children, and that I should never have anything to do with a married man. I can't imagine I'll ever have anything to do with an unmarried man either, but I keep that to myself. My mother says I'll be thrown out if I ever come home with a child. Gerda isn't thrown out. She has just stopped working at the factory where she earned twenty-five kroner a week, and she stays home now with her big stomach, singing and humming all day long, so you can hear from far away that she hasn't lost her good spirits by any means. Her golden braid has long since been cut off, and in my heart I don't call her Rapunzel anymore, although, as a matter of fact, the fairytale girl had had twins by the time the blinded prince found her in the desert. It sounds so nice and remote that you can easily miss it, and when I was little, I never thought about how it might happen. Last year the landlady's Olga had a baby by a soldier, who also disappeared without a trace, but she was over eighteen and she later got married to a policeman who didn't worry about who the child's father was. Whenever I see women with a big stomach, I try my best to stare only at their faces, where I vainly search for a sign of transcendent happiness like in Johannes V. Jensen's poem: 'I carry in my swollen breast a sweet and anxious spring.' They don't have the kind of glorious expression in their eyes I myself will have when I'm someday expecting a child, I'm sure of that. I have to find poems in books of prose because my father doesn't approve of me lugging home poetry collections from the library. 'Castles in the air,' he says contemptuously, 'they have nothing to do with reality.' I've never cared for reality and I never write about it. When I'm reading Herman Bang's *Ved vejen*, my father takes the book between two fingers and says with every sign of disgust, 'You may not read anything by *him*. He wasn't normal!' I know it's terrible not to be normal, and I have my own troubles trying to pretend that I am. So it comforts me that Herman Bang wasn't either, and I finish reading the book in the reading room. I cry when I get to the end: 'Under the grave's turf sleeps poor Marianne. Come, girls, weep for poor Marianne.' I want to write poetry like that, that anyone and everyone can understand. My father doesn't want me to read anything by Agnes Henningsen, either, because she's a 'public female' – which he doesn't bother to explain any further. If he saw the book with my poems, he would probably burn it. After Edvin found it and laughed at it, I always keep it with me – in my school bag during the day, and otherwise in my underpants, where the elastic keeps it from falling out. At night it's under my mattress. Edvin said later, by the way, that he actually thought the poems were good, if only they had been written by someone other than me. 'When you know the whole thing is a lie,' he says, 'you just die laughing over it.' I'm pleased by his praise, because the part about it being a lie doesn't bother me. I know that you sometimes have to lie in order to bring out the truth.

We've gotten new neighbors since Ketty and her mother were thrown out. It's an older couple with a daughter named Jytte. She works in a chocolate store, and in the evening she often visits us when my father is working the graveyard shift. Then she and my mother have lots of fun because my mother gets along best with women who are younger than she is. Jytte gladly brings chocolate to Edvin and me, and we eat it happily, even though my father says that it's probably stolen. As a result of Jytte's generosity, something awful happens to me. One day when I come home from school, my mother says, 'Well, wasn't that a good lunch you had with you today?' I blush and stammer and don't know what she's talking about. I always throw my lunch away untouched because it's wrapped in newspaper. The others have wax paper around theirs, which my mother would never in her life give in to. 'Oh yes,' I say miserably, 'it was great.' 'I wonder whether she really steals it,' says my mother talkatively. 'You'd think the owner would keep an eye out for that.' Relieved, I understand then that there was some chocolate in my lunch packet, and I feel very happy, because that's a sign of love. It's so strange that my mother has never discovered when I'm lying. On the other hand, she almost never believes the truth. I think that much of my childhood is spent trying to figure out her personality, and yet she continues to be just as mysterious and disturbing. Practically the worst thing is that she can hold a grudge for days, consistently refusing to speak to you or listen to what you're saying, and you never find out how you've offended her. She's the same way with my father. Once, when she made fun of Edvin for playing with girls, my father said, 'Oh well, girls are a kind of human being, too.' 'Humph . . .' said my mother, pressed her lips tight, and didn't open them again until at least a week had passed. Actually I was on her side, because of course girls and boys shouldn't play together. They can't at school, either, unless they're sister and brother. But a boy wouldn't dare be seen with his little sister either, and whenever it's absolutely necessary for Edvin and me to go down the street together, I have to walk three paces behind him and under no circumstances reveal that I know him. I'm nothing to brag about. My mother doesn't think so either, because when we're going to the commemoration of Folkets Hus, she makes a serious effort to get me to look half-way decent. She singes my stiff, yellow hair with the curling iron, and tells me briskly to curl up my toes so that they'll fit into a pair of shoes we borrowed from Jytte. 'She's pretty enough, damn it,' consoles my father, who is having trouble himself with the collar on his white shirt that was bought for the occasion. Edvin is now so grown up that he's mad at having to go out with his family, so he omits his usual lovable remarks about how I'm so ugly that I'll never get married. It's a very special evening, because after making a speech to the workers, Stauning will personally present a gift to all of Vesterbro's recruiters, and among them is my father. Sunday after Sunday he trudges up and down stairs in our neighborhood to enlist members in the political club, and my mother brings him to despair by withdrawing him from it once a month whenever the membership fee of fifty øre is due. Then he mumbles a bunch of curses, grabs his old hat, and rushes after the man to sign up again. She harbors an inarticulate hatred for Stauning and the party, and now and then she hints that my father was once something almost as criminal as a Communist. She doesn't say the word out loud – she doesn't dare – but sometimes I think about the forbidden book he was always reading during my early childhood, the one with the red flag that the happy worker family is looking up at, so there's probably some truth to her insinuations.

My heart beats faster when Stauning goes up to the podium, and I'm sure that my father's does, too. Stauning speaks the way he usually does, and I understand at most half of it. But I enjoy his calm, dark voice that soothingly settles over my soul, assuring me that nothing really evil can happen to us, as long as Stauning exists. He talks about instituting the eight-hour day, even though that's a long time ago now. He talks about the unions and about the criminal scabs who should never be tolerated at any workplace. I quickly promise myself, Stauning, and our Lord that I will never be a scab. Only when he talks about the Communists, who damage and divide the party, does he raise his voice to an angry thunder, which quickly gives way, however, to a soft, almost gentle explanation of the unemployment, which my mother isn't alone in blaming him for. But no, it's due solely to the worldwide depression, he says, and I find the expression pleasant sounding and appealing. I imagine a deeply grieving world where everyone has pulled down their shades and turned off the lights, while the rain streams down from a gray and inconsolable heaven without a single star. 'And now,' says Stauning finally, 'I have the great pleasure of presenting a prize to each of our industrious recruiters as a reward for their work for our great cause!' I blush with pride that my father is among them and look sideways at where he's sitting. He twists his mustache nervously and smiles at me, as if he knows that I share his joy. The battle over the workplace is still creating a coldness between him and Edvin, who looks as though he's about to fall asleep. Then Stauning says each name loudly and clearly, grasps each man's hand in turn, and gives each a book. Everything swims before my eyes when it's my father's turn. The book he receives is called *Poetry and Tools*, and Stauning has written his name and some words of acknowledgement on the title page. On the way home, my father, who is still elated over the honor, says: 'I'll let you read it when you're grown up. I know you like poetry.' My mother and Edvin aren't with us. They're going to the dance afterwards, which doesn't interest my serious father, and I'm only a child. Later my mother puts the book so far back on the bookshelf that you can't see it when the glass door is closed. 'A lovely reward for wearing out the steps every blessed Sunday,' she says scornfully to my father. 'And then he talks about scabs and being underpaid. Good Lord!' My father isn't allowed to have his happiness in peace, either.

12

Time passed and my childhood grew thin and flat, paperlike. It was tired and threadbare, and in low moments it didn't look like it would last until I was grown up. Other people could see it too. Every time Aunt Agnete visited us, she said, 'Goodness gracious, how you're growing!' 'Yes,' said my mother and looked at me with pity, 'if only she'd fill out a bit.' She was right. I was as flat as a paper doll and clothes hung from my shoulders like from a hanger. My childhood was supposed to last until I was fourteen, but what was I going to do if it gave out beforehand? You never got answers to any of the important questions. Full of envy, I stared at Ruth's childhood, which was firm and smooth and without a single crack. It looked as if it would outlive her, so that someone else might inherit it and wear it out. Ruth herself wasn't aware of it. When the boys on the street yelled at me, 'How's the weather up there, sister?' she sent a series of oaths and curses after them so that they ran off in terror. She knew I was vulnerable and shy and she always defended me. But Ruth wasn't enough for me anymore. Miss Mollerup wasn't either, because she had so many children to look after, and I was only one of them. I always dreamed of finding a person, just one, to whom I could show my poems and who would praise them. I had started thinking a lot about death, and I thought of it as a friend. I told myself that I wanted to die, and once when my mother went into town, I took our bread knife and sawed at my wrist, hoping to find the artery – all the while bawling at the thought of my despairing mother who would soon throw herself sobbing over my corpse. All that happened was that I got some cuts; I still have faint marks from them. My only consolation in this uncertain, trembling world was writing poetry like this:

Once I was young and all aglow,
full of laughter and fun.
I was like a blushing rose.
Now I am old and forgotten.

I was twelve years old then. Otherwise all of my poems were still 'full of lies', as Edvin said. Most of them dealt with love, and if you were to believe them, I was living a wanton life filled with interesting conquests.

I was convinced that I would be sent to a reformatory if my parents ever saw a poem like this:

It was joy I felt, my friend,
when our lips met,
knowing this was the moment
we were born for – and yet . . .

My vague young dream vanished.
The door to life stands open.
Life is beautiful, my friend, thanks,
you christened me in passion.

I wrote love poems to the man in the moon, to Ruth, or to no one at all. I thought my poems covered the bare places in my childhood like the fine, new skin under a scab that hasn't yet fallen off completely. Would my adult form be shaped by my poems? I wondered. During that time I was almost always depressed. The wind in the street blew so cold through my tall, thin body that the world regarded with disapproving looks. In school I always sat and glared at the teachers, as I did at all grownup people. One day a substitute music teacher calmly came over to my seat, and said quietly but clearly, 'I don't like your face.' I went home and stared at it in the mirror over the dresser. It was pale, with round cheeks and frightened eyes. Across my top front teeth there were small dents in the enamel, which came from having had rickets as a child. I knew that from the school dentist, who said you got the disease from bad nutrition. I kept that to myself, of course, because it wasn't anything to talk about at home. When I couldn't explain my growing melancholy to myself, I thought that the worldwide depression had finally hit me. I also thought a lot about my early childhood, which would never return, and it seemed to me that everything was better then. In the evening, I sat up on the windowsill and wrote in my poetry album:

> Slender strings that break
> are ne'er tied together again,
> unless their tone does slake,
> unless a note does die then.

Then, unlike later on, there wasn't any Kai Friis Møller to whisper in my ear, 'Watch out for inverted word order, Miss Ditlevsen, and for the word ne'er!' My literary models at that time were hymns, ballads, and the poets of the 90s.

One morning I woke up and felt really terrible. My throat hurt and I was freezing as I stepped out onto the floor. I asked my mother whether I could stay home from school but she frowned and told me to spare her such nonsense. She couldn't stand unexpected events or visits that weren't announced ahead of time. Burning with fever, I went to school and was sent home already during first period. By then my mother had collected herself and accepted that I was sick. I fell asleep as soon as I got into bed again and when I woke up, my mother was in the midst of a massive house-cleaning of the whole apartment. She was hanging up clean curtains in the bedroom, and turned around when I called. 'It's good you woke up,' she said. 'The doctor will be here in a little while; if only I get done.' I was terribly afraid of the welfare doctor, and my mother was, too. When she had changed the bed linens and dug out my ears with a bobbypin, the doorbell rang and, flustered, she rushed out and opened the door. 'Hello,' she said respectfully, 'I apologize for the inconvenience . . .' She didn't get any further before she was interrupted by his violent fit of coughing. Hacking and sputtering into his handkerchief, the doctor swept her aside with his cane. 'Yes, yes,' he bellowed when he caught his breath. 'All those stairs – they'll be the death of me. And there's no room to breathe. It's no way to run a practice. I remember you well – you're the one with the teeth. But who in heaven's name is sick? Oh, it's your daughter – where the hell is she?' 'In here.' My mother led the way and the doctor pulled in his stomach with great difficulty as he went past the marriage bed over to me. 'Well,' he shouted and bent his face over me, 'what's the matter with you? You're not playing hooky, are you?' He looked loathsome, and I pulled the comforter all the way up to my chin. He fixed his bulging black eyes on me and I felt like saying that even though we were poor, we were not in the least deaf. His hands were densely covered with hair and a thick black tuft stuck out of each ear. He roared for a spoon, and my mother just about fell over her own feet as she ran off to the kitchen to get one. He shone a little light down my throat and felt the sides of my neck and then said ominously, 'Is there diphtheria in your school? Well? Any of your classmates?' I nodded. Then he grimaced as if he tasted something sour and shouted, 'She's got diphtheria! She has to go to the hospital at once! God damn it!' My mother stared at me reproachfully, as if she'd never expected me to present a busy doctor with anything so impudent. The doctor grabbed his cane furiously and stomped into the living room to write up an admission form. I was horrified. The hospital! My poems! Where should I hide them now? Sleep overpowered me again, and when I woke up, my mother was sitting on the edge of the bed. She asked very gently if there was anything I wanted, and to please her, I asked for a piece of chocolate even though I knew that I couldn't swallow it. Thanks to Jytte, we always had chocolate in the house now. While we waited for the ambulance, I explained to her that I wanted to take my poetry album with me in case someone at the hospital would like to write in it. She had no objection. She sat next to me in the ambulance and stroked my forehead or my hands the whole time. I couldn't remember when she'd ever done that before, and it made me both embarrassed and glad. Whenever I walked down the street or stood in shops, I always looked with a mixture of joy and envy at mothers who held their small children in their arms or caressed them. Maybe my mother had done that once, but I couldn't remember it. At the hospital, I was put in a big ward where there were children of all ages. We all had diphtheria, and most of them were just as sick as I was. I put my poetry album in a drawer, and no one thought it strange that I had it there. Although I lay there for three months, I remember almost nothing about my stay. During visiting hours, my mother stood outside the window and shouted in to me. Shortly before I went home, she talked to the head doctor, who said that I was anemic and didn't weigh enough. Both things hurt my mother's feelings. During the first days after I came home, she made me rye porridge and other fattening foods, even though my father was unemployed again. During my long absence, Ruth had attached herself to the landlady's fat, white-haired Minna, who would soon be thirteen, and with whom she was now always hanging around the trash-can corner, even though she wasn't nearly old enough for that kind of promotion. I felt abandoned and alone. Only the night and the rain and my silent evening star – and my poetry album – gave me some slight comfort during that time. I wrote poetry exclusively like this:

Wistful raven-black night,
kindly you wrap me in darkness,
so calm and mild, my soul you bless,
making me drowsy and light.

The rain quiet and fine
drums so softly at the window.
I lay my head on the pillow
on the cool linen's incline.

Quietly I sleep,
blessed night, my best friend.
Tomorrow I'll wake to life again
my soul in sorrow deep.

One day my brother said to me that I should try to sell one of my poems to a magazine, but I didn't think anyone would pay money for them. I didn't really care, either, as long as someone would print them, but I would never come face to face with that 'someone'. Someday when I was grown up, my poems would of course be in a real book, but I didn't know how that would come about. My father probably knew, but he had said that a girl can't be a poet, so I wouldn't tell him anything about it. It was enough for me anyway to write the poems; there was no hurry to show them to a world that so far had only laughed and scorned them.

13

Uncle Peter has killed Granny. At least that's what my parents and Aunt Rosalia say. He and Aunt Agnete picked her up on Christmas Eve and there was a violent snowstorm. All three of them waited at least fifteen minutes for the streetcar, and in spite of his fabulous wealth, it didn't occur to Uncle Peter to pay for a taxi home. By evening Granny had pneumonia, and they put her to bed on a sofa made up in the parlor, which of course is heated every Christmas, 'But you know,' says my mother, 'how damp it is in a room that's only heated three days a year.' There Granny lay all through the Christmas holidays and received visits from all of us, and she was completely convinced that she was going to die. The rest of us didn't believe it. She lay in a white, high-necked nightgown, and her slender hands that looked like my mother's constantly crept restlessly over the comforter, as if searching in vain for something very important. Now that she didn't have her glasses on, you saw that her nose was long and sharp, her eyes deep blue and very clear, and her sunken mouth had a stern, inflexible expression whenever she wasn't smiling. She talked nonstop about her funeral and the five hundred kroner that she lost when Landmands Bank scandalously folded. My mother and my aunts laughed heartily and said, 'You'll have a fine funeral, Mama, when it comes time for that.' I think I was the only one who took her seriously. She was seventy-six years old, after all, so it couldn't be much longer, I thought. We agreed on the hymns to be sung: 'Church bell, not for the big cities but for the little town were you cast', and 'If you've put your hand to the Lord's plough, then don't look back'. The latter was not, of course, a funeral hymn, but Granny and I were both so fond of it, and we sang it together so often whenever I visited her. On my part, there was also a little spite involved in the choice. My father hated that hymn more than any other because the line 'If sobs strangle the voice, then think of the golden harvest' was proof, in his opinion, of the church's animosity toward the working class.

I wanted so much to write a hymn for Granny myself, but I couldn't. I'd tried so many times, but they always sounded like one of the old hymns, so sadly I had to give up. On the second day after Christmas, something terrible happened. The three sisters were sitting by Granny's bed and Uncle Peter was in the room, when suddenly the doorbell rang and one of my cousins opened the door to The Hollow Leg who, in an awful state, pushed his way in to the sickbed. Aunt Rosalia threw her hands over her face and burst into tears. The Hollow Leg swung at her and shouted that she damn well better come home now, or he'd break every bone in her body. Uncle Peter stepped forward and grabbed hold of the drunken man, and we children were shooed out of the room. There was a terrible uproar, women's screams, and, in the midst of it all, Granny's calm and authoritative voice, trying to appeal to any possible remaining decent side of his character. Then suddenly there was silence and we later learned that Uncle Peter had thrown him out bodily. He had never been allowed into their house before. It was the same thing at home on our street. Either the men drank – and most of them did – or else they harbored a violent hatred toward those who did. When Granny grew worse and the doctor said that she most likely wouldn't make it through the crisis, I wasn't allowed to visit her anymore. My mother was over there day and night, and came home with red eyes and discouraging news. When Granny died, I wasn't permitted to see her, either, but Edvin was. He said she looked just like when she was alive. But I did go to the funeral. I sat in Sunday church next to my mother and Aunt Rosalia, and already during the sermon, I was gripped by an attack of hysterical laughter. It was so terrible that I held my handkerchief over my nose and mouth, hoping they would think I was crying like the others. Fortunately, tears ran down my cheeks too. I was horrified that I couldn't feel anything at her death. I had really loved Granny, and the hymns that we'd chosen together were sung. Why then couldn't I grieve? Long after the funeral, my comforter was replaced by Granny's – my mother's only inheritance. In the evening when I pulled it up over me, Granny's special smell of clean linen flooded over me, and then I cried for the first time and understood what had happened. Oh, Granny, you'll never hear me sing again. You'll never spread real butter on my bread again, and what you've forgotten to tell me about your life will now never be revealed. Every evening, for a long time, I cried myself to sleep, for the smell continued to cling to the comforter.

14

'God help you if you don't deliver that wringer in a hurry,' says my mother, tossing the heavy machine over to me; I have to jump so it won't land on my toes. She's standing in the laundry room, bending over a steaming tub, and I know that she's half-insane on that one day of the month. But I'm in a terrible situation. She's given me ten øre to pay for renting the machine, and it costs fifteen øre an hour. It went up five øre last time, and then I had to promise to pay the remaining five øre next time. So they were supposed to get twenty øre today, and I had only ten. 'Mother,' I say timidly, 'I can't help it if it's gone up.' She raises her head and pushes the damp hair from her face. 'Get going,' she says threateningly, and I go out of the steaming room and up to the courtyard, where I look up at the gray sky, as if expecting help from it. It's late in the afternoon, and near the trash cans the usual gang is standing with their heads together. I wish I were one of them. I wish I were like Ruth, who is so little that she disappears in the middle of the crowd. 'Hi, Tove,' she yells happily, because she has no sense of having abandoned me. 'Hi,' I say and suddenly feel hope. I go over and signal Ruth to come over to me. Then I explain my errand to her and she says, 'I'll go along – I'll get it delivered all right. Give me the ten øre – it's better than nothing.' Everything is straightforward for Ruth, who never wonders at the grownups' behavior. I don't much, either, when it concerns my mother, whose unpredictable personality I've accepted. Over on Sundevedsgade, I wait on the corner, ready to flee, while Ruth barges into the shop, throws the machine on the counter with the ten øre, and races over to me. We run all the way to Amerikavej and stand there, out of breath, laughing like in the old days when we'd pulled off something daring. 'The bitch yelled after me,' gasps Ruth. "It costs fifteen øre," she shouted, but she couldn't get past the machine fast enough with that fat stomach. Oh God, that was fun.' The clear tears leave streaks on the pretty little face, and I feel happy and grateful. As we go home, Ruth asks me why I don't want to join in at the trash-can corner. 'They're such fun, the big girls,' she says. 'They have such a great time.' If Ruth is old enough to be there, then I certainly am, too. When we reach the courtyard at home again, only Minna and Grete are in the trash-can corner. What Ruth sees in Minna, I don't know. Grete lives in the front building, and she's the daughter of a divorced mother who is a seamstress like my aunt. She's in the seventh grade, and I don't know her very well at all. She has on a knitted blouse that reveals two tiny little bulges in the front, what I'm so sadly lacking. When she laughs you can see that her mouth is crooked. It's almost dark in the corner, and it stinks terribly from the garbage cans. The two big girls are sitting on top of them, and Minna hospitably makes room for Ruth beside her. So I stand there, bolt upright like a milepost, and can't think of anything to say. This is a promotion that I've looked forward to for years, but now I don't know if there's much to it. 'Gerda is going to have her baby soon,' says Grete, banging her heels against the trash can. 'It'll be retarded like Pretty Ludvig,' says Minna hopefully. 'That's what happens to children who are conceived during a drunken binge.' 'The hell it does,' says Ruth. 'Most of us would be retarded then.' They always talk like that, and they have something nasty and dirty to say about everyone. I wonder whether they talk about us the same way when my back is turned. Giggling, they talk about drinking and sex and secret, unmentionable liaisons. Grete and Minna won't keep their virginity more than an hour after they're confirmed, they say, and they'll be careful not to have kids before they turn eighteen. I've heard it all before from Ruth, and the conversation in the trash-can corner seems to me deadly dull and boring. It oppresses me and makes me long to be away from the courtyard and the street and the tall buildings. I don't know whether there are other streets, other courtyards, other buildings and people. As yet I've only been out to Vesterbrogade whenever I had to buy three pounds of ordinary potatoes at the grocer's, who always gave me a piece of candy, and who later turned out to be 'The Drilling X'. In the daytime, he quietly minded his little store, and at night he fooled the police by breaking into the city's post offices. It took years to catch him. I'm far away in my thoughts when Ruth suddenly says, 'Tove has a boyfriend!' The two big girls crack up with laughter. 'That's a damn lie,' says Minna, 'she's too holy for that!' 'I'll be damned if it's a lie,' maintains Ruth, giving me a big smile, completely without malice. 'I know who it is, too. It's Curly Charles!' 'Oh, ha ha!' They double over with laughter, and I laugh the loudest. I do it because Ruth just wanted to amuse us, but I don't think there's anything funny about it. Gerda goes across the courtyard, sway-backed and weighted down, and the laughter ceases. In her hand she has a net bag with beer bottles that clink against each other. Her short hair has gotten darker than before and she has brown spots on her face. I quickly wish that she'll have a beautiful little baby with a normal mind. A girl, I wish for her, with golden hair in a long thick braid down her back. Maybe Gerda was in love with Tin Snout, for no one can see into a woman's heart. Maybe she cries herself to sleep every night, no matter how much she sings and laughs during the day. Once she stood in the trash-can corner and shouted about what would happen when she turned fourteen. I don't want to follow tradition in that way. I don't want to do it before I meet a man that I love; but no man or boy has looked in my direction yet. I don't want to have a 'stable skilled worker who comes right home with his weekly paycheck and doesn't drink'. I'd rather be an old maid, which I guess my parents have also gradually resigned themselves to. My father is always talking about 'a steady job with a pension' when I've finished school, but that seems to me just as horrible as the skilled worker. Whenever I think about the future, I run up against a wall everywhere, and that's why I want to prolong my childhood so badly. I can't see any way out of it, and when my mother calls me from up in the window, I leave the precious trash-can corner with relief and go upstairs. 'Well,' she says, very kindly, 'did you get the wringer delivered?' 'Yes,' I say, and she smiles at me as if I've successfully completed a difficult task she had given me.

15

Miss Mathiassen has told me to ask at home for permission to go to high school, in spite of the fact that at the exams I couldn't say how long the Thirty Years' War lasted. I'll never learn to understand those kinds of jokes. Miss Mathiassen says I'm intelligent and ought to continue studying. That's what I'd like to do, too, but I know that we can't afford it. Without much hope, I ask my father anyway and he gets strangely agitated and talks contemptuously about bluestockings and female graduates who are both ugly and stuck-up. Once he was going to help me write a composition about Florence Nightingale, but all that he could say about her was that she had big feet and bad breath – so I consulted Miss Mollerup instead. Otherwise my father has written a lot of my papers and gotten good grades from Miss Mathiassen. It didn't misfire until he wrote an essay on America and ended it like this: 'America has been called the land of freedom. Earlier it meant freedom to be yourself, to work, and to own land. Now it practically means freedom to starve to death if you don't have money to buy food.' 'What in the world,' said my classroom teacher, 'do you mean by that nonsense?' I couldn't explain it, and we only got a 'B' for the effort. No, I can't continue my studies, and I can only remain a child for a short time yet. I have to finish school and be confirmed and get a job somewhere in a house where there's a lot to be done. The future is a monstrous, powerful colossus that will soon fall on me and crush me. My tattered childhood flaps around me, and no sooner have I patched one hole than another breaks through somewhere else. It makes me vulnerable and irritable. I talk back to my mother and she says, gloating, 'All right, all right, just wait until you get out among strangers . . .' Their great sorrow is Edvin, who I've gotten so close to since he clashed with our parents. I don't have any deep or painful feelings about him, so he can confide in me whatever he likes without fear. But my father has always believed that he would be something great, because he had so many talents as a child. He could sing and play guitar and he was always the prince in the school play. All the girls in school and in the courtyard had a crush on him, and since we went to the same school, the teachers always said to me with amazement, 'Are you the one who has such a smart, handsome brother?' It pleased my father, too, that he was a member of the working-class Danish Youth group and put body and soul into the party. My father always said that he didn't respect government ministers who had never had a shovel in their hands, so who knows what future he once envisioned for Edvin? Now all of these dreams are crushed. Edvin is just waiting for the golden day when he becomes a journeyman and can bully the poor apprentices himself. He's also waiting to turn eighteen, because then he's going to move away from home and rent a room where he can have his things in peace. He wants to live somewhere where he can have girls visit him, because on that point my mother is completely intransigent. In her eyes, all young girls are enemy agents who are only out to get married and be supported by a skilled worker, whose training his parents have scrimped and saved to pay for. 'And now when he's going to be earning money,' she says bitterly to my father, 'and could pay some of it back, he runs away from home, of course. It's some girl who's put that into his head.' She says things like that when they've come to bed and think I'm asleep. I understand Edvin completely because this isn't a home you can stay in, and when I turn eighteen, I'm going to move out, too. But I also understand that my father is disappointed. Recently, when he and Edvin were fighting, Edvin said that Stauning drank and had mistresses. My father turned bright red in the face with anger and gave him a terrible slap, so that he tumbled over onto the floor. I'd never seen my father hit Edvin before, and he's never hit me, either. One evening when my parents were lying in bed discussing the problem, my father said that they should give Edvin permission to invite his girlfriend home. 'He doesn't have one – no one steady,' said my mother curtly. 'Yes he does,' said my father, 'otherwise he wouldn't be out every evening. You're chasing him away from home yourself this way.' As always, when my father on a rare occasion insisted on something, my mother had to give in, and Edvin was asked to invite Solvejg to coffee the next evening. I know a lot about Solvejg, but I've never met her. I know that she and my brother love each other, and that they're going to get married when he becomes a journeyman. I also know that he visits her home and that her parents like him very much. He met her at a dance at Folkets Hus. She lives on Enghavevej and is seventeen just like him. Her father repairs bicycles and has a workshop on Vesterbrogade. She herself is a trained beautician and earns a lot of money.

The evening arrived and we all watched anxiously over

my mother's movements. I helped her place our only white tablecloth on the table, and Edvin tried in vain to catch her eye in order to smile at her. He had on his confirmation suit that was too short at the wrists and ankles. My father had on his Sunday best and was sitting on the edge of the sofa, fumbling nervously with the knot in his tie, as if he were the guest. I got the platter with the cream puffs and placed it in the middle of the tablecloth. Then the doorbell rang and my brother almost fell over his own feet as he ran out to open the door. Bright laughter sounded from out in the hallway, and my mother pressed her lips tightly together and grabbed her knitting, which she started working on furiously. 'Hello,' she said shortly and gave her hand to Solvejg without looking up. 'Please sit down.' She could just as well have said, 'Go to hell', but it didn't look like Solvejg was aware of the tense atmosphere. She sat down, smiling, and I thought she was very pretty. Her blond hair was in a wreath on her head, she had pink cheeks with deep dimples, and her dark blue eyes had an expression like they were always laughing. She didn't notice how silent we were, but she talked in a cheerful and self-confident manner, as if she were used to giving orders. She talked about her work, about her parents, about Edvin, and about how happy she was to visit him at home. My mother looked more and more unyielding, and knitted as if she were doing piecework. Finally Solvejg noticed it after all, because she said, 'It's really so strange! Since Edvin and I are going to get married, you'll be my mother-in-law, you know.' She laughed heartily over this, but completely alone, and suddenly my mother burst into tears. It was excruciatingly embarrassing, and none of us knew what to do. She cried as she continued to knit, and there was nothing moving or touching about her tears. 'Alfrida!' said my father admonishingly; he never called her by her first name. I desperately grabbed the coffee pot. 'Won't you have another cup?' I asked Solvejg, and poured her a full cup without waiting for an answer. I thought that maybe she might think this was something quite normal for us. 'Thank you,' she said and smiled at me. For a minute everyone was silent. My brother looked down at the tablecloth with a dark expression. Solvejg made much of putting cream and sugar in her coffee. Tears slid like rain out of my mother's fiercely downcast eyes, and suddenly Edvin pushed back his chair so it crashed against the buffet. 'Come on, Solvejg,' he said, 'we're going. I knew she'd ruin everything. Stop blubbering, Mother. I'm going to marry Solvejg whether you like it or not. Goodbye.' With Solvejg in hand, he rushed out to the hall without giving her time to say goodbye. The door banged hard after them. Only then did my mother take off her glasses and dry her eyes. 'There, you see,' she said reproachfully to my father, 'what comes from his insisting on being an apprentice? That girl will never let go of such a goldmine!' Wearily he lay down on the sofa again and loosened his tie and opened the top button of his shirt. 'That's not it,' he said without anger, 'but you're driving your children away like this.'

Edvin never brought any girlfriend home again, and later when he got married, we first saw his wife after the wedding. It wasn't Solvejg.

16

My childhood's last spring is cold and windy. It tastes of dust and smells of painful departures and change. In school everyone is involved with preparations for exams and confirmation, but I see no meaning in any of it. You don't need a middle school diploma to clean house or wash dishes for strangers, and confirmation is the tombstone over a childhood that now seems to me bright, secure, and happy. Everything during this time makes a deep, indelible impression on me, and it's as if I'll remember even completely trivial remarks my whole life. When I'm out buying confirmation shoes with my mother, she says, as the sales-clerk listens, 'Yes, these will be the last shoes we give you.' It opens a terrifying perspective on the future and I don't know how I'll go about supporting myself. The shoes are brocade and cost nine kroner. They have high heels and, partly because I can't walk in them without spraining my ankles, and partly because – in my mother's opinion – I'll be as tall as a skyscraper when I wear them, my father chops off a piece of the heels with an axe. That makes the toes turn up, but after all, I'll only wear them on that one day, my mother consoles me. On his eighteenth birthday, Edvin moved to a room on Bagerstræde, and now I sleep on a bed made up on the sofa in the living room, which I perceive as still another unhappy sign that my childhood is over. Here I can't sit in the window-sill because it's full of geraniums, and there's only a view of the square with the green gypsy wagon and the gas pump with the big round lamp, which once made me exclaim, 'Mother, the moon has fallen down.' I don't remember it myself, and in general the grownups have completely different memories about you than you yourself have. I've known that for a long time. Edvin's memories are different than mine, too, and whenever I ask him whether he can remember some event or other I thought we experienced together, he always says no. My brother and I are fond of each other, but we can't talk to each other very well. When I visit him at his room, his land-lady opens the door. She has a black mustache and seems to suffer from the same suspicions as my mother. 'His sister,' she says, 'that's a good one. I've never known a lodger who has so many sisters and cousins as he has.' Things are not good with Edvin even though he now has a whole room to him-self. He smokes cigarettes and drinks beer and often goes out to dances in the evening with a friend named Thorvald. They were apprentices together and want to have their own work-shop someday. I've never met Thorvald, because neither of us can bring anyone home, no matter what sex they are. Edvin is unhappy because Solvejg has left him. One day she came up to his room where they could finally be alone together, and said that she didn't want to marry him after all. Edvin blames my mother, but I think Solvejg has found someone else. I've read somewhere, you see, that real love only grows greater with opposition, but I keep quiet about that because it's prob-ably better for Edvin to believe that my mother has scared her away. His room is very small and the furniture looks like it's ready for the dump. I never stay very long at Edvin's because there are long pauses between our words, and he looks just as relieved when I leave as he looks happy when I arrive. I talk about little things from home. For example, I wear a pair of oiled leather boots that, as usual, I've inherited from him. My father varnished the soles of them so that they'll last longer and he also gave the toes a couple of swipes, so that they turned up and are completely black while the rest of the boots are brown. One day my mother threw some rags over to me, 'Rub your boots with them and then throw them into the stove,' she said. 'My boots?' I asked happily, and she laughed long and hard at me. 'No, you goof, the rags!' she said. Things like that make Edvin laugh too, and that's why I tell him about it now, when he's no longer part of our daily life. Nothing is like it was before. Only Istedgade is the same, and now I'm allowed to go there in the evening, too. I go there with Ruth and Minna, and Ruth doesn't seem to notice that there is something like hatred between Minna and me. Sometimes we go over to Saxogade to visit Olga, Minna's big sister who married a policeman and has it made. Olga minds the baby and I'm allowed to hold it in my arms. It feels unbelievably nice. Minna wants to marry a man in uniform too, 'because they're so handsome', she says. Then they'll live near Hedebygade, because that's what everyone does when they get married. Ruth nods approvingly and prepares herself for the same fate, which seems desirable to both of them. I smile in agreement as if I'm also looking forward to such a future, and as usual, I'm afraid of being found out. I feel like I'm a foreigner in this world and I can't talk to anyone about the overwhelming problems that fill me at the thought of the future.

Gerda has had a lovely little boy, and she strolls proudly up and down the street with him while her parents are at work.

She's only seventeen, and you're first supposed to have children when you're eighteen. She's disliked because she won't admit by her attitude and bearing that things have gone awry for her and consequently politely accept the pity that the street offers her. Everyone is outraged that she refused to accept the basket full of baby clothes that Olga's mother had collected for her. There she goes, just like that, allowing her parents to support her beyond a reasonable age. 'If that were you,' says my mother, 'you'd have been kicked out long ago.' Oh, how I'd like to hold my own little baby in my arms! I would support it and figure out everything some way or other. If only I'd gotten that far. At night when I'm in bed, I imagine meeting an attractive and friendly young man whom I ask with polite phrases to do me a great favor. I explain to him that I'd very much like to have a child and ask him to see that I get one. He agrees, and I clench my teeth and close my eyes and pretend that it's someone else this is happening to, someone who's of no concern to me. Afterwards, I don't want to ever see him again. But such a young man is not to be found in the courtyard or on our street, and I write a poem in my poetry album, which now lies in the bottom of the buffet drawer:

A little butterfly flew
high in the blue-tinged sky.
All common sense, morality
and duties did it defy.

Drunk with the spring day's charm
with trembling wings unfurled,
it was borne by the sungold rays
down to the beautiful world.

And into a pale pink apple blossom
which had just opened wide,
flew the little butterfly
and found a lovely bride.

And the apple blossom closed,
over was the wild flight.
Oh, thank you, little ones. You've taught me
how to love with delight.

17

My granny was hardly cold in her grave before my father took us out of the state church. The expression was my mother's. Granny doesn't have a grave. Her ashes are in an urn at Bispebjerg Crematorium, and I feel nothing standing there looking at that stupid vase. But I go there often because my mother wants me to. She cries steadily every time we're there, and I have a guilty conscience when she says, 'Why aren't you crying? You did at the funeral.' Now that Edvin's gone, I'm always with my mother whenever I'm not in school or down on the street. I've also been to a dance at Folkets Hus with her, but it wasn't fun dancing with her because I'm a head taller than she is and I feel very big and clumsy compared to her. While she was dancing with a gentleman, a young man came and asked me to dance. That had never happened before, and I was about to say no, because I don't know any dance steps other than those my mother taught me at home in the living room when she was in one of her light-hearted moods. But the young man already had his arm around my waist and since he danced well, so did I. He was completely silent, and just to say something, I asked him what he did.

'I'm in the courier corps,' he said briefly. I thought it had something to do with 'curing' and decided he was a doctor. That was certainly something different from a 'stable skilled worker'. Maybe he would dance with me the whole evening, and maybe he was already falling a little in love with me. My heart beat faster and I leaned against him just a little. 'It's night, now the thieves are at work,' he sang in my ear with the music. Suddenly it stopped and he set me next to my mother, bowed stiffly, and disappeared forever. 'He was good-looking,' said my mother. 'If only he comes back.' 'He's a doctor,' I bragged and told her that he was in the courier corps. 'Oh, good God,' laughed my mother, 'that's just a messenger service!'

We're not members of the state church, and for that reason I'm going to have a civil confirmation. That separates me from all the girls in my class who go to a pastor, but it doesn't matter much since I've given up on being like them. They take turns visiting each other on Saturdays when Victor Cornelius plays for the radio's Saturday dances. Boys are invited then too and many of my classmates already have someone they're going steady with. We don't have a radio at home, and it's no fun anymore to put on the headphones and listen to the crackling of the crystal set my brother made at school. And even if we had a radio, my parents wouldn't have been inclined to give a Saturday dance in my honor. I'm taking exams now and I don't care whether I get good or bad grades. Maybe I'm disappointed after all that I can't go to high school. Only one of the girls in my class is allowed to. Her name is Inger Nørgård and she's just as tall and lanky as I am. She never does anything except study and gets A's in every subject. The others say that she'll be an old maid – that's why she's going to continue in school. I've never really talked to her, no more than with anyone else in school. I have to keep everything to myself, and sometimes I think I'm about to suffocate. I've stopped going around on Istedgade in the evening with Ruth and Minna because more and more their conversations consist of nothing but giggling references and coarse, obscene things that can't always be transformed into gentle, rhythmic lines in my increasingly sensitive soul. I only talk to my mother about very trivial things, about what we eat, or about the people who live downstairs. My father has grown very quiet since Edvin moved away, and for him I'm just someone who should 'make a good start', with all the terrible events he imagines with that expression. One day when I'm visiting my brother, he says to my astonishment that his friend Thorvald would like to meet me. He's told Thorvald that I write poems, and he asks if Thorvald may read them. Horrified, I say no, but then my brother says that Thorvald knows an editor at *Social-Demokraten* who might possibly print my poems if they're good. He says this in between fits of coughing because he can't tolerate the cellulose lacquer he works with. Finally I give in and promise to come over with my poetry book the next evening, then Thorvald will look at my poems. Thorvald is also a journeyman painter, eighteen years old, and not engaged. The latter I verify since I've already started dreaming about him as the kind young man who, almost without a word, will understand everything.

With my poetry album in my school bag, I walk over to Bagerstræde the next evening. I look firmly at the people I meet because soon I'll be famous, and then they'll be proud that they met me on my way to the stars. I'm terribly afraid that Thorvald will laugh at my poetry as Edvin did long ago. I imagine that he looks like my brother, except he has a thin black mustache. When I enter Edvin's room, Thorvald is sitting on the bed next to my brother. He stands up and puts out his hand. He is little and solid. His hair is blond and coarse and his face is covered with pimples in all states of ripeness. He is visibly shy and the whole time he runs his hand through his hair so that it stands straight up in the air. I stare at him horrified because I think that I can't possibly show him my poems. 'This is my sister,' says Edvin completely superfluously. 'She's damn pretty,' says Thorvald, twisting his hair in his fingers. I think it's very kind of him to say that, and I smile at him as I sit down on the room's only chair. You shouldn't be swayed by people's appearance, I think, and maybe he really thinks I'm pretty. At any rate, he's the first person who's ever said that. I take the book out of my bag and hold it in my hands for a while. I'm so afraid that this influential person will think the poems are bad. I don't know whether they're any good at all. 'Give it to him now,' says my brother impatiently, and I hand it to him reluctantly. As he pages through it and reads with a serious, furrowed brow, I feel as if I'm in a completely different state of existence. I'm excited and moved and scared and it's as if the book is a trembling, living part of myself that can be destroyed with a single harsh or insulting word. Thorvald reads in silence and there's not a smile on his face. Finally he shuts the book, gives me an admiring look with his pale blue eyes and says emphatically, 'They're damn good!' Thorvald's language reminds me of Ruth's. She can hardly form a sentence, either, without embellishing it with some seldom-varying swear word. But you shouldn't judge a person by that, and at the moment I think Thorvald looks both wise and handsome. 'Do you really think so?' I ask happily. 'God damn, yes,' he avows. 'You can easily sell them.' His father is a printer, Edvin explains, and he knows all the editors. 'Yes,' says Thorvald with pride, 'I'll take care of it, by beard. 'I only edit the children's page, you know, and we can't use these. Come back in a couple of years.' He snaps shut my poor book and hands it to me, smiling. 'Goodbye, my dear,' he says. Somehow or other I edge myself out the door with all my crushed hopes. Slowly, numbed, I walk through the city's spring, the others' spring, the others' joyous transformation, the others' happiness. I'll never be famous, my poems are worthless. I'll marry a stable skilled worker who doesn't drink, or get a steady job with a pension. After that deadly disappointment, a long time passes before I write in my poetry album again. Even though no one else cares for my poems, I have to write them because it dulls the sorrow and longing in my heart.

God. Just let me take the book home and I'll show it to the old man.' 'No,' I say quickly, and grab for the book. 'I . . . I want to go there myself and show it to this editor. You just need to tell me where he lives.' 'All right,' says Thorvald amenably. 'I'll tell Edvin and then he can explain it to you.' I pack the book away in my school bag again and am in a hurry to get home. I want to be alone to dream about my happiness. Now it doesn't matter about confirmation, it doesn't matter about growing up and going out among strangers, it doesn't matter about anything except the wonderful prospect of having just one poem printed in the newspaper.

Thorvald and Edvin keep their word, and a couple of days later I have a note in my hand on which it says: 'Editor Brochmann, Sunday Magazine, *Social-Demokraten*, Nørre Farimagsgade 49, Tuesday, two o'clock.' I put on my Sunday clothes, rub my mother's pink tissue paper across my cheeks, make her think that I'm going to take care of Olga's baby, and stroll out to Nørre Farimagsgade. I find the door in the big building with the editor's name on a sign and knock cautiously. 'Come in,' sounds from the other side. I step into an office where an old man with a white beard is sitting at a big, cluttered desk. 'Sit down,' he says very kindly and motions toward a chair. I sit down and am gripped by an intense shyness. 'Well,' he says, taking off his glasses, 'what do you want?' Since I'm unable to utter a word, I can't think of what else to do except hand him the by now rather grubby little book. 'What's this?' He leafs through it and reads a couple of the poems half-aloud. Then he looks at me over his glasses: 'They're very sensual, aren't they?' he says, astonished. I turn bright red in the face and say quickly, 'Not all of them.' He reads on and then says: 'No, but the sensual ones are the best, by God. How old are you?' 'Fourteen,' I say. 'Hmm . . .' Irresolutely he strokes his

18

During the preparations for my confirmation, the big question is whether The Hollow Leg will be invited. He has never visited us before, but now all of a sudden he's stopped drinking. He sits the whole day drinking just as many bottles of soda pop as he used to drink beers. My mother and father say it's a great joy for Aunt Rosalia. But she doesn't look happy, because the man is completely yellow in the face from a bad liver and apparently doesn't have long to live. The family thinks that's to her advantage, too. Now I'm allowed to visit them and it's no longer necessary to protect me from seeing and hearing anything that's not good for me. But Uncle Carl hasn't changed at all. He still mumbles gruffly and inarticulately down at the table about the rotten society and the incompetent government ministers. At intervals he issues short, telegraphic orders to Aunt Rosalia, who obeys his slightest gesture as she always has. The soda pop bottles are lined up in front of him and it's incomprehensible that any person is capable of consuming so much liquid. I wonder at my parents. When you go down into the basement for coal, you usually fall over some drunk who's sleeping it off wrapped up in the ruins of an overcoat, and on the street, drunken men are such an everyday sight that no one bothers to turn around to look at them. Almost every evening, a bunch of men stand in the doorway drinking beer and schnapps, and it's only the very young children who are afraid of them. But throughout our whole childhood, we weren't allowed to see Uncle Carl, even though it would have pleased Aunt Rosalia beyond words. After long discussions between my mother and father and between my mother and Aunt Agnete, it's decided that he will be invited to my confirmation. So the whole family will be there except for my four cousins, since there's just not room for them in the living room. My mother is in a good mood because of the big event, and she says I'm ungrateful and odd because I can't hide that I think all of the preparations have nothing to do with me.

The exams are over and we've had the graduation party at school. Everyone cheered now that they were leaving the 'red prison', and I cheered loudest of all. It bothers me a lot that I don't seem to own any real feelings anymore, but always have to pretend that I do by copying other people's reactions. It's as if I'm only moved by things that come to me indirectly. I can cry when I see a picture in the newspaper of an unfortunate family that's been evicted, but when I see the same ordinary sight in reality, it doesn't touch me. I'm moved by poetry and lyrical prose, now as always – but the things that are described leave me completely cold. I don't think very much of reality. When I said goodbye to Miss Mathiassen, she asked me whether I'd found a position. I said yes, and chattered on with false cheerfulness about how I was going to home economics school in a year and until then I had an au pair job at a woman's home where I would take care of her child. All of the others were going to work in offices or stores and I was ashamed that I was only going to be a mother's helper. Miss Mathiassen looked at me searchingly with her wise, kind eyes. 'Well, well,' she sighed, 'it's a shame though that you couldn't go to high school.' As soon as my confirmation is over, I'm going to start my job. I went there with my mother to apply for it. The woman was divorced and treated us with cool condescension. She didn't look as if she would be interested in discovering I wrote poetry and just had to pass the time until I could go back to Editor Brochmann at *Social-Demokraten* in a couple of years. It wasn't very elegant in the apartment, either, even though there was of course a grand piano and carpets on the floor. She's at work during the day and in the meantime I'm supposed to clean, cook, and take care of the boy. I haven't done any of these things before, and I don't know how I'm going to be worth the twenty-five kroner I'm supposed to earn every month. Behind me is my childhood and school, and before me an unknown and dreaded life among strangers. I'm closed in and caught between these two poles, the way my feet are squeezed down into the long, pointed brocade shoes. I sit in the Odd Fellows Hall between my parents and listen to a speech about youth as the future all of Denmark is counting on, and about how we must never disappoint our parents who have done so much for us. All of the girls are sitting with a bouquet of carnations in their laps just like me, and they look as though they're just as bored. My father is tugging at his stiff collar and Edvin is suffering from fits of coughing. The doctor said he should change jobs, but that's impossible, of course, after he's been through four years of training to become a journeyman painter. My mother is wearing a new black silk dress with three cloth roses at the neck, and her newly permed hair frizzes around her head. She had to fight to have it done, partly because my father didn't think they could afford it, and partly because he thinks it's 'new-fangled' and 'loose'. I liked her hair better when it was long and smooth. Now and then she puts her handkerchief up to her eyes, but I don't know whether she's really crying. I can't see any reason for it. I think about the fact that once the most important thing in the world was whether my mother liked me; but the child who yearned so deeply for that love and always had to search for any sign of it doesn't exist anymore. Now I think that my mother cares for me, but it doesn't make me happy.

We have pork roast and lemon mousse for dinner, and my mother, who gets angry and irritable at any domestic effort, doesn't relax until it's time for dessert. Uncle Carl is seated next to the stove and he sweats so much he has to constantly wipe his bald, round head with his handkerchief. At the other end of the table sits Uncle Peter, who is a carpenter and represents the cultured branch of the family along with Aunt Agnete, who sang in the church choir as a child. She has written a song for me because she has a 'vein' that flows on all such occasions. It deals with various uninteresting events of my childhood and each verse ends like this: 'God be with you on your way, fa-la-la, then luck and happiness will always follow you, fa-la-la.' When we sing the refrain, Edvin looks at me with laughter in his eyes, and I hurriedly look at the printed words of the song in order not to smile. Then Uncle Peter taps his glass and stands up. He's going to make a speech. It's like the one at the Odd Fellows Hall, and I only listen with half an ear. It's something about stepping into the adult ranks and being hard-working and clever like my parents. It's a little too long. Uncle Carl says, 'Hear, hear!' every second, as if he'd been drinking wine, and Edvin coughs. My mother has shining eyes and I cringe with discomfort and boredom. When he's done and everyone has said 'Hurrah', Aunt Rosalia says softly as she envelops me with her warm glance, 'The adult ranks – Good Lord! She's neither fish nor fowl.' I can feel my lips quiver and quickly look down at my plate. That's the most loving and maybe also the truest thing that is said at my confirmation. After dinner everyone can finally stretch their legs, and they all seem to be in a better mood than when they arrived, maybe also because of the wine. They admire the little wristwatch that I got from my parents. I like it too, and think that it makes my thin wrist look a little more substantial. I got money from the others, more than fifty kroner, but it's to be put in the bank for my old age, so that doesn't excite me much.

After the guests have left and I've helped my mother clean up, we sit together at the table and talk for a while. Even though it's past midnight, I'm wide awake and very relieved that my party is over. 'God, how he stuffed himself,' says my mother, meaning Uncle Peter. 'Did you see that?' 'Yes,' says my father indignantly, 'and drank! When it's free he can really put it away.' 'And he pretended that Carl wasn't even there,' continues my mother. 'I felt bad for Rosalia.' Suddenly she smiles at me and says, 'Wasn't it a lovely day, Tove?' I think about how much trouble and expense this has cost them. 'Oh yes,' I lie, 'it was a good confirmation.' My mother nods in agreement and yawns. Then she's struck by an idea. 'Ditlev,' she says with a happy voice, 'since Tove is going to be earning money now, can't we afford to buy a radio?' The blood rushes to my head with fright and rage. 'You're not going to buy a radio with my money,' I say hotly. 'I have plenty of use for it myself.' 'I see,' says my mother, cold as ice, getting up and stomping out the door, which she slams after her so that the plaster clatters down from the wall. My father looks at me, embarrassed. 'Don't take it so literally,' he explains. 'We have a little in the bank – we can use that to buy a radio. You just have to pay for your room and board here at home.' 'Yes,' I say, regretting my temper. Now my mother won't speak to me for days, I know. My father says good night kindly and goes into the bedroom, where I'll never again sit on the windowsill and dream about all the happiness that's only attainable by grown-up people.

I'm alone in my childhood's living room where my brother once sat and pounded nails into a board while my mother sang and my father read the forbidden book I haven't seen for years. It's all centuries ago and I think that I was very happy then, in spite of my painful feeling of childhood's endlessness. On the wall hangs the sailor's wife staring out to sea. Stauning's serious face looks down at me, and it's a long time since my God was created in his image. Although I'm going to be sleeping at home, I feel like I'm saying goodbye to the room tonight. I have no desire to go to bed, and I'm not sleepy, either. I'm seized by a vast sadness. I move the geraniums on the windowsill and look up at the sky where an infant star shines in the bottom of the new moon's cradle, which rocks gently and quietly between the shifting clouds. I repeat to myself some lines from Johannes V. Jensen's *Bræen*, which I've read so often that I know long passages by heart. 'And now like the evening star, then like the morning star shines the little girl who was killed at her mother's breast; white and self-absorbed like a child's soul that wanders alone and plays so well by itself on endless roads.' Tears run down my cheeks because the words always make me think of Ruth, whom I've lost for good. Ruth with the fine, heart-shaped mouth and the strong, clear eyes. My little lost friend with the sharp tongue and the loving heart. Our friendship is over just as my childhood is. Now the last remnants fall away from me like flakes of sun-scorched skin, and beneath looms an awkward, an impossible adult. I read in my poetry album while the night wanders past the window – and, unawares, my childhood falls silently to the bottom of my memory, that library of the soul from which I will draw knowledge and experience for the rest of my life.

Youth

I

I was at my first job for only one day. I left home at seven-thirty in order to be there in plenty of time, 'because you should try especially hard in the beginning', said my mother, who had never made it past the beginning at the places where she'd worked in her youth. I was wearing the dress from the day after my confirmation that Aunt Rosalia had made. It was of light blue wool and there were little pleats in the front so that I didn't look quite as flat-chested as usual. I walked down Vesterbrogade in the thin, sharp sunshine, and I thought that everyone looked free and happy. When they'd passed the street door near Pile Allé, which would soon swallow me up, their step became as light as dancers', and happiness resided somewhere on the other side of Valby Bakke. The dark hallway smelled of fear, so I was afraid that Mrs Olfertsen would notice it, as if I'd brought the smell with me. My body and my movements became stiff and awkward as I stood listening to her fluttering voice explaining many things and, in between the explanations, running on like an empty spool that babbled about nothing in an uninterrupted stream – about the weather, about the boy, about how tall I was for my age. She asked whether I had an apron with me, and I took my mother's out of the emptied school bag. There was a hole near the seam because there was something or other wrong with everything that my mother was responsible for, and I was touched by the sight of it. My mother was far away and I wouldn't see her for eight hours. I was among strangers – I was someone whose physical strength they'd bought for a certain number of hours each day for a certain payment. They didn't care about the rest of me. When we went out to the kitchen, Toni, the little boy, came running up in his pajamas. 'Good morning, Mummy,' he said sweetly, leaning against his mother's legs and giving me a hostile look. The woman gently pulled herself free from him and said, 'This is Tove, say hello to the nice lady.' Reluctantly he put out his hand and when I took it, he said threateningly, 'You have to do everything I say or else I'll shoot you.' His mother laughed loudly and showed me a tray with cups and a teapot, and asked me to fix the tea and come into the living room with it. Then she took the boy by the hand and went into the living room her high heels clacking. I boiled the water and poured it into the pot, which had tea leaves in the bottom. I wasn't sure if that was correct because I'd never had or made tea before. I thought to myself that rich people drank tea and poor people drank coffee. I pushed the door handle down with my elbow and stepped into the room, where I stopped, horrified. Mrs Olfertsen was sitting on Uncle William's lap, and on the floor Toni lay playing with a train. The woman jumped up and began pacing back and forth on the floor so that her wide sleeves kept cutting the sunshine up into little fiery flashes. 'Be so good as to knock,' she hissed, 'before you come into a room here. I don't know what you're accustomed to, but that's what we do here, and you'd better get used to it. Go out again!' She pointed toward the door and, confused, I set the tray down and went out. For some reason or other it stung me that she addressed me formally, like a grownup. That had never happened to me before. When I reached the hallway, she yelled, 'Now knock!' I did. 'Come in!' I heard, and this time she and the silent Uncle William were each sitting on their own chair. I was bright red in the face from humiliation and I quickly decided that I couldn't stand either of them. That helped a little. When they had drunk the tea, they both went into the bedroom and got dressed. Then Uncle William left, after giving his hand to the mother and the boy. I was apparently not anyone you said goodbye to. The woman gave me a long typewritten list of what kind of work I should do at various times during the day. Then she disappeared into the bedroom again and returned with a hard, sharp expression on her face. I discovered that she was heavily made up and radiated an unnatural, lifeless freshness. I thought her prettier before. She knelt down and kissed the boy who was still playing, then stood up, nodded slightly toward me, and vanished. At once the child got up, grabbed hold of my dress, and stared up at me winsomely. 'Toni wants anchovies,' he said. Anchovies? I was dumbfounded and completely ignorant of children's eating habits. 'You can't have that. Here it says . . .' I studied the schedule, 'ten o'clock, rye porridge for Toni; eleven o'clock, soft-boiled egg and a vitamin pill; one o'clock . . .' He didn't feel like listening to the rest. 'Hanne always gave me anchovies,' he said impatiently. 'She ate everything else herself – you can too.' Hanne was apparently my predecessor; and besides, I wasn't prepared to force a lot of things into a child who only wanted anchovies. 'OK, OK,' I said, in a better mood now that the adults had gone. 'Where are the anchovies?' He crawled up onto a kitchen chair and took down a couple of cans, then he found a can opener in a drawer. 'Open it,' he said eagerly, handing it to me. I opened the can and put him up on the kitchen counter as he demanded. Then I let one anchovy after another disappear into his mouth, and when there weren't any more, he asked to go down to the courtyard to play. I helped him get dressed and sent him down the kitchen stairs. From the window I could keep an eye on him playing. Then I was supposed to clean house. One of the items said: 'Carpet sweeper over the rugs.' I took hold of the heavy monstrosity and navigated it onto the big red carpet in the living room. To try it out, I drove it over some threads which, however, did not disappear. Then I shook it a little and fiddled with the mechanism so that the lid opened and a whole pile of dirt fell out onto the carpet. I couldn't put it back together again; since I didn't know what to do with the dirt, I kicked it under the rug, which I stamped on a bit to even out the pile. During these exertions, it had gotten to be ten o'clock and I was hungry. I ate the first of Toni's meals and fortified myself with a couple of vitamins. Then came the next item: 'Brush all of the furniture with water.' I stared astonished at the note and then around at the furniture. It was strange, but that must be what was done here. I found a good stiff brush, poured cold water into a basin and again started in the living room. I scrubbed steadily and conscientiously until I'd done half of the grand piano. Then it dawned on me that something was terribly wrong. On the fine, shiny surface, the brush had left hundreds of thin scratches and I didn't know how I was going to remove them before the woman came home. Terror crept like cold snakes over my skin. I took the note and again read: 'Brush *all* of the furniture with water.' Whatever way I interpreted the order, it was clear enough and didn't exempt the grand piano. Was it possible that it wasn't a piece of furniture? It was one o'clock and the woman came home at five. I felt such a burning longing for my mother that I didn't think there was any time to waste. Quickly I took off my apron, called Toni from the window, explaining to him that we were going to look at toy stores. He came upstairs and got dressed and, with him in hand, I raced through Vesterbrogade so he could hardly keep up. 'We're going home to my mother,' I said, out of breath, 'to have anchovies.' My mother was very surprised to see me at that time of day, but when we came inside and I told her about the scratched grand piano, she burst out laughing. 'Oh God,' she gasped, 'did you really brush the piano with water? Oh no, how could anybody be so dumb!' Suddenly she grew serious. 'Look here,' she said, 'it's no use you going back there. We can certainly find you another job.' I was grateful but not especially surprised. She was like that, and if it had been up to her, Edvin could have changed apprenticeships. 'Yes,' I said, 'but what about Father?' 'Oh,' she said, 'we'll just tell him the story about Uncle William – Father can't stand that kind of thing.' A light-hearted mood possessed us both, like in the old days, and when Toni cried for anchovies, we took him with us down to Istedgade and bought two cans for him. A little before four o'clock, my mother and the boy went back to Mrs Olfertsen's, where my mother got back the apron and the school bag. I never found out what was said about the damaged grand piano.

2

I'm working in a boarding house on Vesterbrogade near Frihedsstøtten. It would be just as unthinkable for my mother to send me to another part of the city as to America. I start at eight o'clock every morning and work twelve hours in a sooty, greasy kitchen where there's never any peace or rest. When I get home in the evening, I'm much too tired to do anything except go to bed. 'This time,' says my father, 'you have to stay at your job.' My mother also thinks that it's good for me to be working, and besides, the trick with Uncle William can't be repeated. The only thing I think about is how I can get out of this dreary existence. I don't write poetry anymore since nothing in my daily life inspires me to do so. I don't go to the library either. I'm off every Wednesday afternoon after two o'clock, but then I go straight home to bed too. The boarding house is owned by Mrs Petersen and Miss Petersen. They are mother and daughter, but I think they look like they're about the same age. Besides me there's a sixteen-year-old girl whose name is Yrsa. She's way above me, because when the boarders eat, she puts on a black dress, a white apron, and a white cap and bustles back and forth with the heavy platters. She's the serving girl and waits on the guests. In two years, the ladies promise me, I'll also be allowed to serve and get forty kroner a month like Yrsa. Now I get thirty. It's my job to see that there's always a fire in the stove, to clean the rooms of the three lodgers, the bathroom, and the kitchen. Even though I rush through everything, I'm always behind with it all. Miss Petersen scolds, 'Didn't your mother ever teach you to wring out a rag? Haven't you ever cleaned a bathroom before? Why are you making faces? For your sake I hope you never encounter anything more difficult than this!' Yrsa is little and thin, and she has a narrow, pale face with a snub nose. When the ladies take a nap before dinner, we drink a cup of coffee at the kitchen counter and she says, 'If you didn't always have black fingernails, you'd be allowed to serve. That's what I heard Mrs Petersen say.' Or, 'If you washed your hair once in a while, the guests would be allowed to see you, I'm sure of that.' For Yrsa there's nothing in the world outside of the boarding house and no higher goal than to rush around the table at every mealtime. I don't reply to either her or the ladies' remarks, which come like pellets from a slingshot and never really hit the mark. While Yrsa and I do the dishes and the ladies cook in the big pots on the stove behind us, they talk about their illnesses that drive them from doctor to doctor, because they're not satisfied with any of them. They have gallstones, hardening of the arteries, high blood pressure, aches everywhere, mysterious internal pains, and gloomy warnings from their stomachs every time they've eaten. On Sundays they march past the Home for the Disabled on Grønningen in order to get into a better mood by looking at the invalids; and in general they put everything and everyone down with nasty pleasure. They have something in particular against each boarder and they know everything about their private lives, the intimate details of which they discuss while they dish out the food on to Yrsa's platters, complaining about how much those people can eat. Sometimes I think that their low, mean thoughts penetrate my skin so I can hardly breathe. But most of the time I find this life intolerably boring and recall with sorrow my variable and eventful childhood. In that narrow strip of the day when I'm awake enough to talk with my mother a little, I ask her about what's happening in the building and in the family and greedily devour every refreshing bit of news. Gerda is working at Carlsberg now, and her mother stays home to take care of the baby. Ruth has begun to go around with boys. 'You could have expected that,' says my mother. 'You should never adopt other people's children.' Edvin has lost his job and has started to come by the apartment again. 'But you shouldn't feel bad about it,' says my mother, 'because now he doesn't cough so much.' It still shakes me a little, because my father always said that skilled workers could never be unemployed. 'My God,' says my mother excitedly, 'I almost forgot to tell you that Uncle Carl is in the hospital. He's terribly sick, and it's no wonder, considering how he's lived. Aunt Rosalia is over there every day, but it really will be best for her if he dies. And margarine has gone up two øre in Irma – isn't that steep?' 'So it costs forty-nine øre,' I say because I've always kept up on the prices, since I've either gone shopping with my mother or by myself. 'If only Father can stay at the Ørsted Works,' she says. 'Now he's been there three months – even though it's no fun working at night.' Her chattering voice spins softly around me in the growing darkness until I fall asleep with my arms on the table.

One evening I wake up as usual from this position at the sound of the clinking cups and the smell of coffee. As I sleepily raise my head, my eye is caught by a name in the newspaper: Editor Brochmann. I stare at it wide awake, and slowly I realize that it's an obituary. It hits me like the lash of a whip. It never occurred to me that he could die before the two years were up. I feel like he's deserted me and left me behind in the world without the slightest hope for the future. My mother pours the coffee and puts the pot down over his name. 'Drink now,' she says and settles herself on the other side of the table. She says, 'Pretty Ludvig has been put in an institution. His mother died, you know, and then they just came and took him away.' 'Yes,' I say and again feel that we're infinitely far from each other. She says, 'It'll be nice for you when you can get that bicycle. There's only two months left.' 'Yes,' I say. I pay ten kroner a month at home, ten are put in the bank for my old age, and the remaining ten are my own. At the moment I couldn't care less about that bicycle – about anything. I drink my coffee and my mother says, 'You're so quiet, there's nothing the matter, is there?' She says it sharply, because she only likes me if my soul is resting completely in hers and I don't keep any secret part of it to myself. 'If you don't stop being so strange,' she says, 'you'll never get married.' 'I don't want to anyway,' I say, even though I'm sitting there considering that desperate alternative. I think about my childhood ghost: the stable skilled worker. I don't have anything against a skilled worker; it's the word 'stable' that blocks out all bright future dreams. It's as gray as a rainy sky when no bright ray of sun trickles through. My mother gets up. 'Well,' she says, 'we've got to go to bed. We have to get up early, you know. Good night,' she says from the door, looking suspicious and offended. When she's gone, I move the coffee-pot and read the obituary again. There's a black cross over the name. I see his kind face before me and hear his voice, 'Come back in a couple of years, my dear.' My tears fall on the words and I think this is the hardest day of my life.

3

I sank into a long-lasting stupor that robbed me of all initiative. 'You're going around asleep,' said the ladies, whose reproaches made less of an impression on me than ever. I lost the desire to talk with my mother, and one evening when Edvin came with an invitation from Thorvald, I said no. I had no desire to go out dancing with that young man who had liked my poems. Maybe his father knew another editor who would also die before I was old enough to write real, grown-up poems. I'd gotten cold feet and didn't dare expose myself to any more disappointments. Summer had come. When I went home in the evening, the fresh breeze cooled my stove-flushed cheeks like a silk handkerchief, and young girls in light dresses walked hand in hand with their sweethearts. I felt very alone. Of the girls in the trash-can corner, Ruth was the only one I knew now, and she always yelled 'Hi' to me when I went through the courtyard. I looked up at the front building's wall, flooded with life and memories, my childhood's wailing wall, behind which people ate and slept and argued and fought. Then I went up the stairs in my red dress with blue polka dots and puff sleeves – the only summer dress I had. Sometimes Jytte was sitting in the living room, smoking cigarettes, which she also offered to my mother. My mother smoked awkwardly and ineptly and always got smoke in her eyes. Now Jytte was working in a tobacco factory. My father said that she stole the cigarettes, but my mother didn't care. She always had to have a girlfriend who was much younger than her, because she was so youthful. But there were gray streaks in her black hair and she had put on weight around her hips. That's why she often went to the steambaths at the public bathhouse on Lyrskovgade, and when she came home, she gleefully told us about how terribly fat all the other women were.

One evening the boarding house's kitchen doorbell rang, and when I opened the door, Ruth was standing outside. 'Hi,' she said, smiling, 'are you going home now? There's something I want to tell you.' 'Yes,' I said, 'just wait outside.' I poured out the last of the dishwater, took off my apron, and slipped out to her, as if she were a secret contact that no one must discover. What did she want with me? It was a long time since anyone had wanted me for anything. She had on a white muslin dress with a wide, black patent leather belt around her waist and short sleeves. She was wearing lipstick and her eyebrows were plucked like my mother's. Even though she was still slightly built, she seemed to me very grown-up in appearance. We didn't speak until we reached the street, but then Ruth began to chatter on as if there'd never been any question of a separation between us. She told me that Minna had finished school and now had a live-in job in Østerbro. 'In Østerbro?' I repeated, dumbfounded. 'Yes,' said Ruth, 'but she's always had a screw loose.' It didn't fill me with the joy you would have expected. I just thought that Ruth never missed anyone. She had written Minna off with a shrug of her shoulders, just as she presumably had written me off a year ago. There was no room for deep or lasting feelings in her heart. When we reached Sundevedsgade, where I usually turned off, we stopped. 'But you know,' said Ruth, 'you haven't even heard what I wanted to tell you.' Reluctantly I continued on with her, because now my mother would have to wait for me in vain, and if too much time passed, she'd go over to the boarding house and ask for me. Then when she found out that I'd left, she would be sure that some accident had occurred. But Ruth radiated faintly some of the old magic and power to get me to do things that I never would think of myself. Ruth said that she had a sweetheart, a boy sixteen years old, whose name was Ejvind and who lived on Amerikavej. He was an apprentice mechanic and someday they would get married. He had taken her virginity, and it was 'damned great'. And then she'd gotten to know a very rich man who was an antiquarian bookseller and lived on Gammel Kongevej. It was him that she wanted me to visit with her. She had visited him alone but he'd tried to seduce her, and that, she said, she wouldn't do to Ejvind. The rich man was named Mr Krogh, and his best friend was Holger Bjerre, whom he was going to persuade to make Ruth a chorus girl. 'You too,' she said, 'he's promised me.' 'Me?' A gleam of hope streaks through my soul. A chorus girl is on stage dancing every evening, and in the daytime she can do whatever she wants. I know, of course, that they'd never permit it at home, but the world is never totally real when I'm with Ruth. 'And you know what,' she says eagerly, 'he's very old and he's sick, too. When I was over there, I thought he was going to die of a heart attack, he coughed and puffed and gasped so much. He lives all alone and if we're really nice to him, maybe he'll will us everything he owns, and then Ejvind can get his own workshop.'

She looks up at me delightedly, with her clear, strong eyes, and the crazy plan puts me in a good mood. I know very well what it is Ruth wants of me, and I say, 'I won't do it, but I'd like to meet him.' Ruth laughs and holds her hand in front of her mouth while wiping her nose with her thumb at the same time. She says that he looks horrid, but I should think about the money and our future as chorus girls. Mr Krogh lives on the top floor of a building that doesn't at all look like it houses millionaires. When we've rung the bell, we hear a violent coughing on the other side of the door. 'There, you can hear he's not long for this world, by God,' whispers Ruth. After a lengthy rattling with security chains and keys, the door is opened a crack and Mr Krogh's face appears. He looks at us suspiciously for a moment, then he loosens the chain and lets us come in. 'Oh,' I exclaim, 'what a lot of books!' The living room is practically wallpapered with books and large paintings like I've otherwise only seen in museums. Mr Krogh doesn't say anything until we sit down. He looks at me intently and asks kindly, 'Do you like books?' 'Yes,' I say and look at him more closely. He's not as old as Ruth said, but not young either. He's completely bald and has plump, red cheeks, as if he were out in the fresh air a lot. His eyes are brown and a little melancholy like my father's. I like him very much and sense that he likes me too. He makes coffee for us and Ruth asks whether he has spoken to Holger Bjerre. 'No . . . I'm afraid he's on vacation right now.' When he looks at Ruth, his glance slides searchingly up and down her body, but luckily he doesn't seem to be interested in mine. He offers us cakes and talks about the fine weather and about the city's young girls who spring up from the cobblestones like flowers. 'It is,' he says, 'a refreshing sight.' Ruth is bored and kicks my legs under the table. I say, 'Do you think I could be a chorus girl too, Mr Krogh?' 'You!' he says astonished. 'No, you're not suited for that at all.' 'Yes, she is,' protests Ruth, 'if she gets a permanent and make-up and things like that. She's pretty without clothes on.' I blush and for the first time in my life I feel irritated with Ruth. Mr Krogh looks from her to me and says, 'How in the world did you two ever find each other?' I ask if I can take a look at his books, and when he hears that I prefer reading poems, he shows me where they are. I take out a volume at random and open it. Delighted and happy, I read:

– the pitchers are filled with wine,
the twilight-veiled earth.

Baudelaire: *Les fleurs du mal* I read on the title page, and I go over to Mr Krogh and ask him how it's pronounced. He tells me and says that I can borrow the book if I promise to return it. I promise and sit down again at the table. Only now do I notice that Mr Krogh is in his dressing gown. He has a coughing fit again, during which he turns bright red in the face and, wheezing for air, he asks Ruth to thump him on the back. While she does this, she laughs soundlessly at me, but I don't laugh back. Between Mr Krogh and me there's a silent understanding that I don't remember having experienced with anyone else before. I wish fiercely that he were my father or my uncle. Ruth notices this and frowns, annoyed. 'I have to go home,' she says sulkily, 'I'm going to meet Ejvind.' When we're about to leave, Mr Krogh tries to kiss Ruth but she turns her sweet face away, and I feel sorry for him. I wouldn't have anything against kissing him but he just gives me his hand and says, 'You can borrow all the books from me that you like, just as long as I get them back. I'm always home this time of the evening.' When I get home, my mother is sitting at the table with a swollen face and red eyes. She asks me where in heaven's name I've been and where I got that book from. I say that I've been over at Edvin's and that his cough really has gotten better. The book I borrowed from one of the lodgers. When I get into bed, the thought strikes me with terror that Mr Krogh could die like my editor. I desire with all my heart to make contact with a world that seems to consist entirely of sick old men who might keel over at any moment, before I myself have grown old enough to be taken seriously.

4

Uncle Carl is dead. 'He died quietly in his sleep,' says Aunt Rosalia, and he died with his hand in hers. She is sitting on the edge of a chair, with her hat on and her sewing over her arm like always, even though she doesn't have anything to go home to now. Her eyes are completely swollen from crying and my mother can't really find any way to comfort her. My mother has always thought it would be best for Aunt Rosalia if Uncle Carl died, but it doesn't look like Aunt Rosalia thinks so. At the funeral we're all present, including Uncle Peter and Aunt Agnete, who didn't want to have anything to do with Uncle Carl when he was alive. My three cousins are there too. They're little and fat and pasty-white in the face, and my mother says gloatingly that they'll never get married, and so what do their parents have to be so stuck-up about? She and my father have always put down Aunt Agnete and Uncle Peter, and yet they still play cards with them a couple of times a week. It irritates me when I get home from work, because then I can't go to bed until they've left. While the minister preaches over Uncle Carl, I don't laugh like at my Granny's funeral, but I think about the fact that no one except

Aunt Rosalia has known him or knew what he was really like. First he was a hussar, then he was a blacksmith, then he drank beer, and finally soda pop. That's all that the rest of us know. We have coffee in a restaurant near the cemetery, and there's an oppressive mood because Aunt Rosalia refuses to be cheered up by anything whatsoever. Her tears fall into her coffee cup and she has to keep lifting the black veil of her funeral hat to dry them away. 'He was handsome as a young man,' she says to my mother, 'wasn't he, Alfrida?' 'Yes, he was,' says my mother. 'He was handsome back then.' Aunt Rosalia says, 'I know that none of you liked him because he drank. He suffered a great deal because of that. His own family didn't like him either.' It's embarrassing, and no one answers, because she's right, of course. 'Well,' says Edvin, getting up, 'I have to go now. I have to meet a friend.' After he's gone, I look around at my family, at these faces that have surrounded me my whole childhood, and I find them tired and aged, as if the years that I've used to grow up in have exhausted them completely. Even my cousins, who are not much older than me, look worn out and used up. My father is very quiet and serious, as always when he's wearing his Sunday suit. It's as if it's lined with dark and depressing thoughts that he puts on along with the suit. He's talking with Uncle Peter in a low voice, mumbling. Even at the funeral they discuss politics, but they don't get excited about it like they usually do. My father is still working at the H. C. Ørsted Works, and my mother has finally gotten the radio that she wanted me to pay for. She has it on all day long and only turns it off when there's someone in the living room she wants to talk to. When my father's home, he's always lying on the sofa, sleeping. Then when my mother turns off the radio, he wakes up with a start and says, 'It's damn near impossible to sleep with that God-awful noise.' We think that's really funny. But I'm not really involved with all that goes on at home anymore – not like before. I'm really only alive when I'm at Mr Krogh's. I visit him as often as I dare, without provoking my mother. I say that I'm visiting Yrsa, but my mother can't understand why we're suddenly friends, since I've always said that I didn't like her. I borrow books from Mr Krogh and return them again after I've read them. He always greets me in his silk dressing gown, with red slippers on his feet; he pours us coffee from a silver coffeepot. If he doesn't have any pastry, he gives me fifty øre to go down and buy some. We drink coffee at a low table with an etched brass surface. Mr Krogh has long, white hands that always tremble slightly, and he has a low, pleasant voice that I love to listen to. He does most of the talking when I'm there, because he doesn't like me to show my curiosity. One evening when I asked him why he wasn't married, he said, 'You're not supposed to know everything about a person – remember that. Then it stops being exciting.' I don't know, either, whether Ruth still comes there, whether she's going to be a chorus girl, or whether Mr Krogh even knows Holger Bjerre at all. Ruth doesn't think so. Whenever I meet her in the courtyard or on the street, she says, 'That Krogh is full of lies, and he's a dirty old man. Hasn't he made a pass at you yet?' 'No,' I say and think she's talking about someone completely different than the Mr Krogh I know. 'Well, I don't dare go there alone,' she says. Another day she says that he's stingy since he never gives me any presents. 'Why should he?' I ask. She gives me a look bursting with impatience. 'Because,' she says, 'he's old and you're young. He's completely crazy about young girls, and he has to pay for that – what else?' One evening when Mr Krogh has lit the candles in a tall silver candleholder that's standing on the table between us, I gather my courage and say, 'Mr Krogh, when I was little, I wrote poems.' He smiles. 'Yes,' he says, 'and you want to show them to me?' I blush because he's guessed what I want from him, and I ask him how he knows. 'Oh,' he says, 'either that or something else. People always want something from each other, and I've known all along that you wanted to use me for something.' When I make a protesting gesture, he says, 'There's nothing wrong with that – it's completely natural. I want something from you, too.' 'What?' I ask. 'Nothing in particular,' he says, taking his long thin pipe out of his mouth. 'I just collect eccentrics – people who are different, special cases. I'd like to see your poems. Thump me on the back.' The last comes out in gasps, and he gets quite blue in the face. He coughs at each thump I give him and he doubles up so that his arms hang down to the floor. I wonder what kind of illness he suffers from. I don't dare ask whether it's fatal, but already the next evening I rush over to his apartment with my poetry album, half-convinced that he's no longer among the living. But he is, and as soon as we're sitting at the coffee table, I hand him the book, very afraid of disappointing him, accustomed as he is to reading the greatest poetry. He puts his pipe down and pages through the book, while I tensely watch his face. 'Yes,' he says, nodding, 'children's poems!' He reads aloud:

> Sleeping girl, I'll sing a hymn for you.
> No sight has ever brought me joy so true
> as you lying motionless and sweet,
> smiling in your dreams, the white sheet
> barely covering your young breast,
> oh, how that sight to me was blest,
> but you were unaware.

There are four or five verses, and he mumbles them all to himself. Then he looks at me kindly and gravely and says, 'That's interesting. Who were you thinking of when you wrote that poem?' 'No one,' I say, 'well, yes, maybe Ruth.' He laughs heartily. 'Life is funny,' he says then. 'You realize it first when you're about to lose it.' 'But Mr Krogh,' I say terrified, 'you're not that old – not any older than my father.' 'Oh no,' he says, 'but even so, I've lived a long time.' He shuts the book and puts it on the table. 'These poems,' he says, 'can't be used for anything, but it looks like you're going to be a poet someday.' A wave of happiness floods through me at these words. I tell him about Editor Brochmann, who said that I should come back in a couple of years, and he says that he knew him well. He also says that someday when I write something good, something that other people will take pleasure in reading, I should show it to him and then he'll see that it's published. The candles flicker in the holder and the dark evening sky is full of stars. I'm terribly fond of Mr Krogh, but I don't dare tell him so. We're silent for a long time. From the bookshelves there issues a pleasant smell of leather, paper, and dust, and Mr Krogh looks at me with a sorrowful glance, as if what he wants to tell me will never be said, exactly like my father has always looked at me. Then he gets up. 'Well,' he says, 'you'd better go. I have some work to do before I go to bed.' Out in the hallway he puts his hand under my chin and says, 'Will you give an old man a kiss on the cheek?' I kiss him carefully, as if my kiss could bring about his feared death. It's a soft, old man's cheek that reminds me of my Granny's.

5

Hitler has come to power in Germany. My father says that it's the reactionaries who've won and that the Germans don't deserve any better since they voted for him themselves. Mr Krogh calls it a catastrophe for the whole world and is gloomy and depressed as if from some personal sorrow. The ladies at the boarding house cheer and say that if Stauning were like Hitler, we wouldn't have unemployment, but he's weak and corrupt and drunken and everything he does in the government is wrong. They listen to the news on the radio instead of taking a nap before dinner, and they come back with shining eyes and say that the Reichstag fire was set by the Communists and now it will certainly be proved at the trial. My father and Mr Krogh say that the Nazis started it themselves, and if I have any opinion at all, it's to agree with them. But most of all, I'm terrified – as if the swells from the great ocean of the world could capsize my fragile little ship at any moment. I don't like reading the newspapers anymore, but I can't avoid them entirely. My father shows me Anton Hansen's dark, satirical drawings in *Social-Demokraten*, and they increase my fear. There is an old Jew with a large sign on his back, surrounded by laughing SS-men. On the sign it says in German: 'I am a Jew, but I don't want to complain about the Nazis.' I have to tell my father what it means. Mr Krogh subscribes to *Politiken*. He shows me a drawing of Van der Lubbe and the caption underneath:

> Tell us what you know
> about Torgler and the fire.
> –
> You know, we want to know, damn it.
> Say that Dimitroff
> and Popoff were waiting by the stairs,
> then you'll save your neck.

'Oh yes,' he says, 'now the German intelligentsia is in for it.' I ask him what 'German intelligentsia' means and he explains it to me. Among other things, it means the artists. A poet is an artist, and Mr Krogh has said that I'll be a poet someday. The ladies read *Berlingske Tidende,* and there, they say, the truth is written about Hitler, who may save all of Europe and create a kind of paradise for us all. More than ever I want to get away from the boarding house's close, filthy kitchen and the people I'm with there every day. My father is always sleeping when I come home and a couple of hours later he leaves for work. One evening when he wakes up, I ask him whether I can look for another job. I say that I hate washing dishes and cleaning and doing any kind of domestic work at all. I would rather work in an office and learn to type. 'Not yet,' he says, 'first you have to learn to take care of a house properly and cook for your husband when he comes home from work.' 'She'll learn that soon enough,' my mother comes to my aid, 'when she has use for it one day.' She also says, 'You talk like she's going to get married tomorrow. She's only just turned fifteen.' My father presses his lips together and frowns. 'Is it you or me who decides?' he says. Then my mother keeps quiet, but she's insulted too, and the atmosphere in the living room is tense. When my father has left, she puts down her knitting and smiles. 'We'll pretend,' she says, 'that one of the lodgers has made a pass at you. Then you can look for another job.' 'OK,' I say relieved, astonished that I never thought of that before. A couple of days later, my father is sitting on the sofa when I come home. 'Well,' he says, 'Mother told me what happened. Now you've reached the age when you need to watch out for yourself. You're not to go back there. Mother can go and pick up your paycheck, and then you'll have to start looking for another job.' Then I stay home for a while. We buy *Berlingske Tidende* and I send in replies for many office jobs but get no response. I also go around Vesterbro and apply for those jobs where you're supposed to appear in person. I talk to fine gentlemen in big, light offices and they all ask me what my father does. When I tell them, they figure that I'll have to live on my salary and it's never intended for that. But finally I succeed in getting a job where the director just asks me whether I'm a member of the union. When he hears that I'm not, he hires me immediately for forty kroner a month. It's in a nursing supply company on Valdemarsgade and I'm to be stock clerk. 'Scab company,' says my father when he hears the part about the union, but he gives in anyway, because even for a girl it's not easy to find a job.

While all of this was going on, I didn't have a chance to visit Mr Krogh. He had never asked me where I lived and was not inquisitive in general, just as he didn't like others to be, either. One evening I go out to see him again. It's winter and I have on Edvin's made-over coat, which is more warm than beautiful. I'm looking forward to seeing my friend again and to telling him about my new job, which for now I'm happy with. I cut through the usual passageway from Vesterbrogade, and when I reach Gammel Kongevej, I stop as if paralyzed, completely uncomprehending. The yellow building isn't there anymore. Where it had stood, there is just a space with rubble, plaster, and rusty, twisted water pipes. I go over and brace my hand against the low remains of a wall, because I don't think my legs will support me any longer. People go past me with closed faces, wrapped up in their own evening errands. I feel like grabbing one of them by the arm and saying, 'There was a building here yesterday – can you tell me where it is? Where is Mr Krogh?' He must be living somewhere else now, of course, but how do you find someone who has disappeared? I don't understand how he could do this to me. But maybe he knew so many young girls and I was just one of them. He'd said that he collected eccentrics, but maybe I wasn't eccentric enough. As I walk slowly home, still half-numbed by this misfortune, I think that this wouldn't have happened if I'd written good poems. I don't think it would have happened, either, if he'd desired my body, as he obviously desired Ruth's, but no one has yet shown any interest whatsoever in me in that way; my father's warning is completely unnecessary. At home on my street, Ruth is standing with her apprentice mechanic in front of the stairwell to the front building. I stop and button my coat at the neck because the wind is icy cold, which I first notice now. 'Mr Krogh's building was torn down,' I say. 'Do you know where he's living?' 'Nope,' she says over the young man's shoulder, 'and I don't give a damn, either.' They disappear into each other's embrace again and I walk past, across the courtyard. As I go up the stairs to the back building, I'm gripped by the fear that I'll never get away from this place where I was born. Suddenly I can't stand it and find every memory of it dark and sad. As long as I live here I'm condemned to loneliness and anonymity. The world doesn't count me as anything and every time I get hold of a corner of it, it slips out of my hands again. People die and buildings are torn down over them. The world is constantly changing – it's only my childhood's world that endures. Up in the living room it looks like it has always looked. My father is sleeping and my mother is sitting at the table knitting. Her gray hair is gone because, in the greatest secrecy, she has it dyed – wherever she gets the money from for that . . . Once in a while my father says, 'It's strange that your hair is still black. Mine is completely gray now.' He's naive and believes everything we say, because he himself never lies. 'Where have you been?' asks my mother, looking at me suspiciously. 'At Yrsa's,' I say, not caring whether she believes me. She says, 'It's cold in here; put some more coals in the stove.' Then she puts the water on for coffee and I decide that, like Edvin, I'm going to move out when I'm eighteen. I won't be allowed to until then. When I live somewhere else – away from Vesterbro – it'll be easier for me to make contact with people like Mr Krogh. While we're drinking coffee, I glance through the newspaper a bit. It says that Van der Lubbe has been executed and that Dimitroff made a complete fool of Göring at the trial. I turn to the obituaries, but don't find Mr Krogh's name among the dead. It strikes me that it was as if he lost interest in me when Hitler came to power; again my little ship trembles with a vague fear of capsizing.

6

I have to be at work at seven o'clock in the morning and, with Mr Jensen, I clean the rooms and put them in order before the office personnel and the director arrive. Mr Jensen is sixteen years old, tall and thin and silly. He blows up condoms and lets them fly around over my head while I'm washing the floor, and he tries to kiss me so that, laughing, I have to defend myself with the rag in one hand. He's just a boy, and I'm not offended by his coarseness. In the director's office, he sits in the chair with his feet up on the desk and a cigarette between his lips. 'Don't I look like him?' he asks, twisting his long bangs around his fingers. He says that I'm prudish because I'm a virgin and because I won't kiss him. 'If you were in love with me,' I say, 'then I would.' He insists that he is, but I don't believe him. One morning when I'm in the process of washing the floor in the director's office, the director suddenly comes through the door and, as I feverishly gather up the scrub brushes and bucket, he takes hold of me from behind and grabs my breasts with both hands. He does it rather like the way my mother touches the meat at the butcher's, and I turn red with shame and outrage and slip past him with the bucket and scrub brushes without saying a word. I tell Mr Jensen about it and he says I should have slapped his fingers because he always goes to bed with the female employees, and I shouldn't put up with that. He's married and has lots of children because he's a Catholic. But afterwards I don't feel very bad about it. He is the first man who has shown interest in my body, and I've gotten it into my head that without that, I will never get ahead in the world. When the two office secretaries and the stock room supervisor arrive, the orders have to be taken care of. It's my job to pack the goods at the long counter in the stock room. Thermometers, absorbent cotton, vaginal syringes, hot-water bottles, condoms, trusses. Mr Jensen has carefully explained what everything is used for, and sex seems to me extremely complicated and not very appealing. One thing is for before and one thing is for afterwards; during Mr Jensen's explanations, which certainly don't present it very simply, I feel quite inadequate. The stock room supervisor is named Mr Ottosen, and the pretty secretaries are openly in love with him. When they stand at the counter with their papers, explaining something to him, he slips his arm around their waists, and they lean toward him, starry-eyed. Two pretty, chic young girls with tiny curls all over their heads, high heels, and wide patent leather belts around their waists. Someday when I work in an office, I want to try to look just like them. I'll try to pay attention to what dresses I wear and how my hair looks. But I put off these exertions because they bore me. I'm wearing a brown smock that the company issued me. When I'm looking for a job, I rub my cheeks with my mother's tissue paper, and that's all I've ever done for my appearance. My hair is long, blond and straight, and I wash it with brown soap whenever I think it needs it. Mr Krogh said that I had beautiful hair, but maybe he couldn't find anything else to praise me for. In any case, I very often stand next to Mr Ottosen, and I've also tried leaning ever so slightly against him, but he never puts his arm around my waist or seems to notice my weak overture at all. I think about that a lot and reach the conclusion that most women exert an irresistible attraction over men – but I don't. It's both sad and strange, but it does protect me from having children too soon, like most of the girls on my street. One day Mr Jensen asks me if I'd like to go to the movies in the evening. I say yes, because ever since I was a child I've wanted to be allowed to see a movie. My parents wouldn't let me. For once I tell the truth at home, and my mother looks very excited. She wants to know everything about Mr Jensen, and in her mind she has me married to him at once. But I don't know what his father does or what plans he himself has for the future, so I can't satisfy her curiosity. My father is very happy that he's a member of Danish Socialist Youth (DSU) which, to his regret, Edvin won't join. 'Without a doubt,' he says, twisting the ends of his mustache, 'a very sensible young man.' So for the first time I'm sitting in a movie house next to a very scrubbed Mr Jensen, who is wearing his confirmation suit that ends just short of his not completely clean wrists. We've hung our coats over the backs of the seats. First there's someone who plays the piano. Then the lights go out and flashing commercials flicker across the screen. When they're over and the lights go on again, I'm about to get up because I think that's all there is, but Mr Jensen pulls me down in the seat again. 'It's just starting now,' he says patiently. The film is called *The Cabin Boy*, and the boy is the handsome and touching Jackie Coogan. I'm completely enchanted and forget where I am and who I'm with. I cry as if I were being beaten and mechanically accept the handkerchief Mr Jensen puts into my hand. When he puts his hand on my knee, I push it away as if it were a dead object. With the captain, the cabin boy goes down with the ship, sacrificing his life for a beautiful, violently sobbing woman and her little girl. I bawl loudly and can't stop when the lights go on. 'Shh . . . ,' says Mr Jensen embarrassed, taking me by the arm as we go out. 'Why aren't you crying?' I ask. 'Don't you think it was sad?' 'Yes, I do,' says Mr Jensen, 'but to come right out and cry at the movies!' We walk down Søndre Boulevard and Mr Jensen laces his fingers through mine. I give him a sidelong glance and discover that he has long eyelashes. Maybe he really is in love with me. The snow creaks under our feet and the sky is bright with stars. His arm shakes a little, but that could be from the cold. Home in the dark doorway, he embraces me and kisses me. I don't resist, but it doesn't make me feel anything. His lips are cold and hard as leather. 'Why don't we use our first names?' he asks in a hoarse voice. 'OK,' I say, 'what's your name?' His name is Erling, and we agree to still use our last names at work.

Whenever there's nothing to do in the stock room in the afternoon, I'm sent up to the attic to put metal boxes in order in long rows. I like the work because I'm all alone in the dark and dusty room. I lie on the floor and place the boxes in even rows according to what it says on them: zinc salve, lanolin. I sink into a sweet melancholy and rhythmic waves of words stream through me again. I write them down on brown wrapping paper and conclude sorrowfully that the poems are still not good enough. 'Children's poems,' said Mr Krogh. He also said, 'In order to write a good poem, you have to have experienced an awful lot.' I think that I have, but maybe I'll experience even more. Then one day I write something that is different from anything I've written before, only I don't know what the difference is. I write the following:

There burns a candle in the night,
it burns for me alone,
and if I blow at it,
it flames up,
and flames for me alone.
But if you breathe softly
and if you breathe quietly,
the candle is suddenly more than bright
and burns deep in my own breast,
for you alone.

I think it's a real poem, and the pain at Mr Krogh's disappearance springs up again, because I want so much to show it to him. I want so much to tell him that now I understand what he meant. But for me he's just as dead as the old editor, and I can't find any new wedge into the world that is moved by poems and, I hope, by people who write them. 'You were gone a long time,' says Erling when I come downstairs. He acts the whole time as if we are going steady. He's standing there packing a douche bag (it's used afterwards, he has explained to me), and says, as he bends the red tubes under the monstrosity, 'Why don't we sleep together at a hotel on Saturday? I've saved up for it.' 'No,' I say, because if I can write real poems now, it doesn't matter that I'm a virgin. On the contrary, I may have use for it when I meet the right man. 'God Almighty,' says Erling irritated, 'are you saving it for the coroner?' 'Yes,' I say, laughing so I can hardly stop. I don't really know myself what virginity and poems have to do with each other, so how could I explain the strange connection to Erling?

7

Every Saturday evening, Erling and I go to the movies. He waits for me, leaning against the wall of the front building, his hands buried in the pockets of his father's coat, which he inherited just like I've inherited my brother's. If I keep him waiting too long, he chews on matches and twists his hair in his fingers. As we go out through the doorway, my mother opens the window and yells, 'Goodbye, Tove.' That means she approves of the relationship, and Erling takes it to mean that too. He asks me whether he's going to meet my parents soon. 'No,' I say, 'not yet.' My mother asks whether Erling has a clubfoot or a harelip, since they aren't allowed to meet him. I don't want to visit Erling's parents, either, because then they'll think that we're engaged. It would be both easier and more fun for me if I had a girlfriend, but I don't anymore; so Erling is better than nothing. I like him a lot because he's also a little strange, and he's like me in many ways. His father is a laborer and often unemployed. He has a grown-up sister who is married. He himself wants to be a schoolteacher, but he can't get into the teachers' college until he's eighteen. He's saving money for it. He says that it's outrageous that they use unorganized labor in the company, but if he joins the union, he'll be thrown out. He earns twenty-five kroner a week. I pay for myself when we go to the movies, both because he can't really afford to pay for the two of us, and because I think it makes me more independent. All of these evenings proceed in the same way. When the movie is over, he walks me home, and inside the dark doorway, he embraces and kisses me. I observe him with a certain cold curiosity, wanting to see how excited I can make him. If I were in love with him, I would be passionate too, but I'm not, and he knows it. At a certain moment I loosen his cold hands from around my neck and say, 'No, don't do that.' 'Oh yes,' he whispers breathlessly, 'it doesn't hurt at all.' 'No,' I say, 'but I don't want to.' I feel sorry for him and kiss his leathery lips before I go. He asks me when I will want to, and just for something to say, I promise to do it when I turn eighteen, because that's still such a terribly long way off. I also feel a little sorry for myself because his embraces don't make the slightest chord in me sing. I wonder whether I'm abnormal in that way too. 'Damned great,' Ruth had said, and she was only thirteen. All of the girls in the trash-can corner said the same thing, but maybe they were lying. Maybe it was just something that they said. 'When do we get to meet your sweetheart?' says my mother upstairs in the living room. 'When I met your father, I invited him home right away.' She also says that he's obviously only out after one thing, and if I let him have his way, he won't want anything more to do with me. 'And you can't come back here with a kid,' she says. One evening I say that she wasn't nearly so eager for Edvin to bring his girlfriend home, and she says sharply that it's totally different with a boy. There's no rush, and a man can always get married, but a girl has to be supported and she always has to think of that. My father says that she should stop pestering me. He says that it's smart of Erling to want to be a schoolteacher because they make good money and are never unemployed. 'White-collar workers,' says my brother, who fortunately has found work again, 'and they're the worst kind.' My brother is annoyed that I've got a boyfriend because he's always teased me that I'd never get married. He is listening to the news on the radio about Crown Prince Frederik's wedding, which greatly interests my mother. 'Turn off all that royalty junk,' says my father from deep in the sofa. 'Now we have one more mouth to feed, that's all.' At work, the office secretaries are completely ecstatic over the enchanting Crown Princess Ingrid. They take up one of their usual collections and walk through the stock room with a long list on which they write down what everyone donates for a bouquet for the royal house. I've given a krone, and a few days ago I gave a krone for the director's daughter's confirmation. He has so many children that there are constantly collections for their christenings or birthdays. 'Before you know it,' says Erling, 'your whole salary is used up for that nonsense.' Erling is a Social Democrat like my father and my brother, and he dreams of a revolution that will lift the masses. I like to hear him develop this plan, because it would further my own personal interests if the poor came to power. Erling wants to change the social democracy and make it more red. 'Actually,' he says, 'I'm a syndicalist.' I don't ask him what that is because then I'll get a long, incomprehensible speech about politics. Once he takes me along to a meeting at Blågårds Plads, but things get violent and the police take out their nightsticks and break up the brawling factions. 'Down with the cops,' yells Erling, who is in his DSU uniform, and immediately he gets a bop on the head that makes him give out a howl. Terrified, I grab him by the arm, and hand in hand we run down the street that echoes with the fleeing steps of the crowd. That's not for me and I never do it again. At work, besides us, there are two laborers and a driver. We all eat lunch together in a little room behind the stock room. It's not heated and that too, says Erling, is outrageous. As a rule, we all sit with our coats on. We sit on upside-down beer crates, and I get along well with this little group of people. I'm not shy with them – not even when they ask me, for example, if I really know what a truss or a vaginal syringe is used for. But I tell them that they should join the union, and one day when I'm in a light-hearted mood, I climb up on one of the beer crates and imitate Stauning when he speaks: 'Comrades!' I stroke my invisible beard and drop my voice to a low pitch, and my audience is very appreciative. They laugh and clap, and then I forget all about it. A little later, Mr Ottosen comes in and says that the director wants to speak to me. I haven't been alone with him since that day he grabbed my breasts, and I'm afraid that he wants something like that from me. 'Sit down,' he says curtly, pointing to a chair. I sit down on the very edge and, to my horror, I see that his face is dark with anger. 'We can't use you here,' he says hotly. 'I won't have Bolsheviks in my company.' 'No,' I say, not knowing what Bolsheviks are. He pounds the desk, so I jump. Then he gets up and comes over to my chair and sticks his red face right down into mine. I turn my head away a little because he has bad breath. 'You've urged my people to join the union,' he yells, 'but do you have any idea what would happen then?' 'No,' I whisper, even though I really do know. 'They'd be fired,' he roars and again pounds his hand on the desk, 'just like I'm firing you now – without a reference! You can pick up your check at the front office.' He straightens up and goes back to his place. I feel like I ought to burst into tears, but instead I'm filled with a dark joy that I can't define. This man regards me as dangerous, as significant in an area I know nothing about. 'There's nothing to laugh about,' he yells, so I must have been sitting there smiling. 'Get out!' He points to the door and I hurry to get out. 'I never want to see you again,' he screams after me and slams the door. Over in the stock room Mr Ottosen and Erling are looking astonished. They ask me what in the world is the matter and I tell them proudly. Mr Ottosen shrugs his shoulders. 'You're young,' he says, 'and badly paid, so you can easily find some other work to do. And you just have yourself, of course. I have a wife and four children, so I'll keep my mouth shut.' Erling says that I should have kept my opinions to myself, and I get furious with him. 'There'll never be a revolution here in Denmark,' I say hotly, 'as long as there are people like you that won't risk their own neck.' Then, indignantly, I go in to the secretaries and ask for my check, which is already waiting for me. The snow is piled high in the streets as I go home and an ice-cold wind whistles right through my coat. I've suffered for what I believe in, and I'm eager to tell my father about it. I feel like a Joan of Arc, a Charlotte Corday, a young woman who will inscribe her name in the history of the world. The poetry writing is going too slowly anyway. With straight back and head held high, I go up the stairs, and full of wounded dignity I step into the living room, where my father lies sleeping with his backside to the world. My mother asks me why I'm home already and when I tell her, she says that I shouldn't get involved in things that don't concern me. She says furiously that it was a good position and that no man will marry a girl who is constantly changing jobs. This time she doesn't back me up, and I clear my throat loudly and make a bit of racket at the table so my father will wake up.

And he does. When he sits up, rubbing his eyes, my mother says, 'Tove was thrown out. It's because of all your blabber about unions that she's gotten into her head.' When my father hears the details, his face takes on a furious expression. 'Who the hell do you think you are?' he yells, pounding his fist on the table so that the light fixture dances on its hooks. 'Here you've finally gotten a decent job and then you're thrown out for such foolishness. You don't know anything about politics. These are bad times and there are so many scabs that you could feed the pigs with them. But the next job you get you'll have to keep or else you'll be just like your mother.' They glare angrily at each other like they always do when there's trouble with Edvin or me. I keep quiet and really don't know what I had expected. But in the space of a few minutes, I've lost my suddenly awakened interest in politics, in red banners and revolutions. Erling and I go to the movies a few more Saturdays – then he stops leaning against the wall waiting for me. I miss him a little, because he made me less lonely, and I especially miss the attic with the metal boxes, where I wrote my first real poem. 'What's become of your young man?' asks my mother, who had dreamed of being mother-in-law to a schoolteacher. 'He found someone else,' I say. My mother has to have very concrete reasons for everything. She says, 'You should take more trouble with your appearance. You should buy a spring suit instead of that bicycle. When you're not naturally pretty,' she says, 'you have to help things out a bit.' My mother doesn't say such things to hurt me; she's just completely ignorant of what goes on inside other people.

8

'Can you tell who I look like?' Miss Løngren is staring at me with her bulging eyes, and I really can't see who she resembles. She smiles, raising and lowering her eyebrows. Maybe she looks a little like Chaplin, but I don't dare say that, since she's easily insulted. Now she's already frowning impatiently. 'Don't you ever go to the movies, young lady?' she says. 'Yes, I do,' I say miserably and wrack my brain in vain. 'In profile, then,' she says, turning her head. 'Now you can see it. Everyone says so.' Her profile doesn't tell me anything either other than that she has a crooked nose and a weak chin. In the middle of my ordeal, the phone rings. She takes it and says, 'I. P. Jensen.' She always says it in a high, threatening tone, so I don't understand how the person on the other end dares state their business. It's an order, and she writes it down, holding the receiver at her right ear with her left hand. After she has hung up, she says, 'Greta Garbo – now you can see, can't you?' 'Oh yes,' I say, wishing I had someone to laugh with. But I don't. In a strange way, I'm all alone here. I'm employed in the office of a lithographer's shop. In the innermost room resides the owner, who is called Master. Whenever he's in, his door is always closed. In the front office there are two desks. Carl Jensen, one of the sons, sits at one of them with his back to Miss Løngren's chair. She sits across from me by the telephone and the switchboard, and at the end of our desk there's a little table with a typewriter, which I'm supposed to learn to use. But all day long I have practically nothing to do, and no one seems to know why I was hired. There is an apartment upstairs above the offices, and this is where the other son, Sven Åge, lives. He is a lithographer and works across the courtyard in the print shop. Carl Jensen is thin and quick in his movements like a squirrel. He has brown, close-set eyes that are slightly crossed, which gives him a shifty appearance. He never speaks to me, and when he and Miss Løngren are both there, they act as if I were invisible. They flirt a lot with each other, and sometimes Carl Jensen turns in his chair, which can spin all the way around, and tries to kiss Miss Løngren. She swats at him and laughs loudly, flattered; I think it looks ridiculous because they're so old. Whenever Master goes through the office, they bend low over their work, and I quickly write down some figures or words that I afterwards slowly and carefully erase. Carl Jensen is not there very often, and I feel Miss Løngren's peering and attentive glance constantly resting on me. She comments on every move I make. 'Why are you always looking at the clock?' she says. 'It won't make the time go any faster.' She says, 'Don't you have a handkerchief? That sniffing is getting on my nerves.' Or, 'Why is it always me who has to get up to close the door? You're young, too.' The word 'too' astonishes me. One day she asks me how old I think she is. 'Forty,' I say cautiously, because I'm certain that she's at least fifty. 'I'm thirty-five,' she says, insulted, 'and people even say that I look younger than that.' Whenever I make an effort to be completely still and rest my gaze on a neutral spot, she says, 'Are you falling asleep? You've got to do *some* work for those fifty kroner that you get a month.' I happen to yawn, and she asks me with her manly voice whether I ever sleep at night. All day long I have to listen to these remarks and when I get home in the evening, I'm just as tired as when I was working at the boarding house. But I was the one who wanted to work in an office and I have to stay until I'm eighteen, even though it's a shocking thought. I enter the work orders in a book and I'm finished with that in an hour. Miss Løngren doesn't like me to practice on the typewriter because it makes such a racket. One day Master asks her timidly whether I could take care of the switchboard, and she says angrily that she doesn't want to sit with her back to the customers. Behind me there's a counter where the walk-in business takes place. Master seems to be just as afraid of her as I am. He's a heavy little man with a blue, spongy nose, which Miss Løngren says he didn't get for nothing. Whenever she has to find him, she always calls Grøften restaurant in Tivoli, which seems to be his permanent abode when he's not in his office. Once in a while he calls me in and gives me some slips of paper that I have to type up for him. They're letters and they all start with 'Dear brother' and are signed 'With fraternal greetings'. Sometimes they're about a brother who's passed away, and as I write about all of his magnificent qualities, especially in relation to the brothers, I can be quite moved, and I think there's a rare and beautiful closeness in that family. But one day when I venture to ask Miss Løngren how many brothers Master has, she breaks into loud laughter and says, 'They're his lodge brothers, all of them. He's a member of the Order of Saint George.' Afterwards, she tells the son about it and he turns his chair all the way around to see what such an idiot looks like. Every Friday evening I go around the print shop and hand out the pay envelopes. It's something of an ordeal because the workers make witty or fresh remarks to me, and I can't find a response right off the top of my head. I'm not one of them like in the nursing supply company. This job, my father says, is the best one I've had and I have no excuse for not staying there. Everyone is in the union – I am too. Master pays the dues, and I'm supposed to go to shorthand class, which Master will pay for too. I don't know why I'm supposed to learn shorthand since I'm only allowed to write to the brothers. Miss Løngren writes the invoices and the business letters. I get the impression that she was against hiring me and now is keeping me from learning anything at all. I sit and stare at her from eight in the morning until five in the evening, and it's hard and exhausting work. I've never met such a person before. Sometimes she's friendly and asks me, for example, whether I'd like an apple. She gives it to me, but when I crunch it in my mouth, she wrinkles her brow and says, 'Can't you even eat an apple without making a racket?' And if I visit the bathroom too often, she asks me whether I have indigestion. One day she says that her niece is going to be confirmed and she asks me whether I know anyone who could write a confirmation song. Just to surprise her, I say that I can, and she looks at me doubtfully. 'It has to be good,' she says, 'like the ones you read in the kiosk display windows.' I promise that it'll be good, and reluctantly she lets me try. I write the song to the required tune, 'The Happy Coppersmith', and Miss Løngren is impressed. 'It really is,' she says, 'just as good as the ones you pay money for.' She shows it to the son and he says to her, 'Well, I'll be damned', and 'you wouldn't have thought that of Miss Ditlevsen.' He turns his chair around and stares curiously at me with his shifty eyes. To me he doesn't say anything, as usual. 'Yes,' says Miss Løngren, 'something like that is a gift.' I find them both very stupid. Miss Løngren can't even speak correct Danish. For example, she says 'anyways' and she says it often. Whenever she wants to give her words emphasis, she says, 'I say, and I'll keep on saying, that . . .', etc. But naturally she doesn't keep on saying it. I have to spend two more years in this pointless way, and I find the thought almost unbearable. When I get home in the evening, Jytte is almost always there, and it wears me out listening to her and my mother talking. Jytte is big and blonde and pretty, and she herself says that she'll never get married because she so quickly tires of men. She's had a long series of lovers and is always entertaining my mother with stories about the latest one. They laugh a lot about it, and here too I feel myself left out. My father snores loudly and I can't go to bed until he leaves for work and Jytte has gone over to her own apartment. But I can't understand why I can barely tolerate people or how they ought to talk so that I'll listen willingly. They should talk the way Mr Krogh talked; when I'm walking in the street I always think that it's him turning the corner or cutting across the street. I run to catch up, but it's never him. They're in the process of putting up a new building where his once stood, and I never look in that direction when I go through the passage on my way home. I know that I could look him up in the telephone book, but my pride stops me. I didn't mean anything to him. I just amused him for a moment – then he shrugged his shoulders and turned his back. But I'm withering in this existence, and I've got to figure out something. I remember a column in the *Politiken* classified section headed 'Help Wanted: Theater and Music'. That would be something to do in the evening, and now I'm allowed to stay out until ten o'clock. Music is a closed realm for me, but I'd like to be an actress. In great secrecy I send in a reply to an ad looking for actors for an amateur theater. I get a letter from 'Succès Theater Company', which meets in a café on Amager, where I'm told to appear on a certain evening. I dress in my brown suit which, at my mother's insistence, I bought instead of the bicycle, and take the streetcar out to the restaurant. There I say hello to three serious young men and a young girl, who, like me, is there for the first time. We sit at a table and the leader says that he is thinking of putting on an amateur comedy called *Aunt Agnes*. He has the scripts with him, and after a short, appraising look, he decides that I'm to play Aunt Agnes. It is, he explains, a comic role that I'm wonderfully suited for. The woman is about seventy years old, but that can easily be taken care of with a little make-up. In the play, there's a young couple – the man will be played by himself and the girl by Miss Karstensen. I look over at the young girl and find her very beautiful. Her hair is platinum blond, her eyes deep blue, and her teeth white and perfect. I can easily see that I couldn't play her part. Still, I hadn't imagined my debut as a comic woman of seventy. When the roles are handed out and we've been ordered to meet again after we've learned our lines, we drink a cup of coffee and part. Miss Karstensen and I walk together to the streetcar. She asks if she may call me by my first name. Her name is Nina and she lives in Nørrebro. I ask her why she answered the ad. 'Because I was dying of boredom,' she says. She sways her hips a little as she walks, and I already feel happy in her company. Nina is eighteen and I'm sure that we're going to be friends.

9

The leader of our theater company is called Gammeltorv. He is twenty-two and has a wife and child. We rehearse at his house, and his wife is mad because the noise wakes up the baby. 'She doesn't have any feeling for art,' says Gammeltorv apologetically. But *he* does. When he directs us, he uses his head and arms and legs like famous conductors. He rages and yells at us and begs us, practically in tears, to put more soul into the lines and to throw ourselves totally into the roles. Aunt Agnes is a very silly and gullible person, constantly being made a fool of by the young couple; that's the comic part of the play, because the lines themselves are not funny. They are few and brief. The climax occurs when the woman comes into the living room with a tea tray in her hands. When she sees that the couple is sitting in a tight embrace on a love seat, she drops the tray, claps her hands, and says, 'God save us all!' When she says that, the hall is supposed to roar with laughter, says Gammeltorv, and I'm saying the words as if I were reading them out of a book! 'Again!' he roars, 'Again!' At last I succeed in putting enough astonishment into the lines, and he says that it will work when there are real cups on the tray. These his wife refuses to supply for me. At home in our living room, I act out Aunt Agnes for my mother, who is very enthusiastic. 'Maybe,' she says, 'you'll be a real actress. It's a shame that you can't sing.' Nina can – she has to trill a love-song duet with Gammeltorv, and in my opinion she does it very beautifully. The play is going to be performed in Stjernekroen on Amager, and Gammeltorv thinks there will be a full house because there's a dance afterwards. Nina and I are really looking forward to it. Nina is from Korsør, and her fiancé, who is a forester, lives there. He's coming to the opening. Nina works at *Berlingske Tidende* in the classified ad department, and she lives in a rented room in Nørrebro. It's a depressing and unheated room, where we sit on the edge of the bed with our coats on and confide our future plans to each other while we can hear the fire roaring in the family's stove on the other side of the thin wall. Some day Nina will marry her forester, because she wants to live her life in the country, but until that time she wants to have fun and enjoy her youth in Copenhagen. She says that when we're not so busy with the play anymore, we'll go to taverns and find someone to dance with. A girl can't sit in a pub alone, but when there are two, it's OK. I remember Mr Krogh's remark that people always want to use each other for something, and I'm glad that Nina has some use for me. Since I've met her, I don't think about Ruth as often. For that matter, she and her parents have moved away, so I never see her anymore when I come home in the evening. Nina grew up with her grandmother, who owns a hotel in Korsør. Her mother lives in Copenhagen with a man she's not married to. She is poor and cleans house for people; Nina says that some evening I should come home with her to meet her. My mother has no desire to meet Nina. 'Why does she live in Copenhagen,' she says, 'when her fiancé is in Korsør? Your girlfriends are always a bad influence.' At the office, Miss Løngren says sternly, 'You've been looking so happy lately. Has something nice happened at home?' I deny it, terrified, and try to look less glad. I'm taking a course in shorthand on Vester Voldgade, and it's lots of fun. Sometimes I think exclusively in shorthand symbols. One evening when I leave the office for home, Edvin is standing outside, looking very happy. As we walk home together, he tells me that soon he's going to marry a young girl whose name is Grete and who is from Vordingborg. They're going to be married in secret, and they've already found an apartment in Sydhavnen. I'm filled with a dark jealousy and have trouble sharing his enthusiasm. My mother and father are not to know until the wedding is over. 'They'll be furious,' I say, and feel a little sorry for them. 'You know Mother,' he just says, 'she freezes my girls out.' I tell him that on that point I'll have it easier, because my mother was delighted with Erling, even though she never got to meet him. He says that's the way it is most places, and there's nothing very strange about it. He asks how it's going with my poems and whether I will try another editor. 'They can't all die, you know.' I say that I've gradually begun to write better poems, but until I can do it well enough, I don't want to try again. But Edvin thinks that my children's poems are just as good as the ones you read in schoolbooks and newspapers, and I can't explain the indefinable difference between a good and a bad poem, because I've just recently found out myself. We stand there talking in front of the doorway at home for a little while as we stamp our feet to keep warm. Edvin doesn't want to come up with me because then my mother will suspect that we walked home together and she doesn't like us to have anything together that she's not part of. He hasn't gotten over his old grudge against my father for the four hard apprentice years, either. 'He's the one I can thank for my cough,' he says bitterly and a little unjustly. Edvin is twenty years old now, and around his jaw the skin is dark after shaving. His black curls fall over his forehead, and his brown eyes resemble my father's and Mr Krogh's. Some day I'll marry a man with brown eyes. Then maybe my children will have them too; I think I'll have the first one when I'm eighteen. Nina is completely horrified that I still have my virginity, and she thinks it's a defect that should be remedied as soon as possible. She says she was afraid too, because you hear so many things, but in reality it was wonderful. Nina has bought a long, slinky silk dress for the dance at Stjernekroen. It's cut low in the back, and she bought it on credit. It cost two hundred kroner, and I can't understand how she's ever going to pay for it. She laughs and says that of course she wasn't crazy enough to give her real name. I'm impressed – as always when someone dares to do something I don't. Over at Stjernekroen we're busy getting dressed and putting on make-up. I'm wearing Gammeltorv's grandmother's black dress. It reaches to the floor and underneath I have a pillow bound around my stomach. On my head I have a wig made of gray yarn, and Gammeltorv has drawn black lines on my face. They're supposed to be wrinkles. I have to walk bent over like a jackknife because I'm plagued by rheumatism in various places. We peek out through a hole in the curtain. We look down at our families and count to see if they're all there yet. They fill only the first three or four rows, and the rest of the hall is almost empty except for a few young people who are sitting, yawning, totally uninterested because they've only come for the sake of the dance. Nina shows me her forester, who is sitting right behind Aunt Rosalia. He looks like he's aloof from it all, but then Nina has told me that he's very much against her living in Copenhagen. 'What's he mad about?' asks Gammeltorv, who's looking with us. Then the band strikes up and the curtain lifts. My heart pounds violently from excitement, and I'm not sure that my Aunt Agnes will make anyone laugh. But it's an unusually receptive audience. They clap and enjoy themselves, and after every act Gammeltorv says that it can't help but be a success; have we seen that man writing on a notepad? That's a reporter from *Amagerbladet* and he's obviously been sent over because it's a big event. Finally the moment comes when, with the tray in my hands, I surprise the young folks on the love seat. I drop the tray, clap my hands, and cry out, 'God save us all!' At the same moment, a door is opened behind the stage entrance and the wig blows off my head. Horrified, I want to pick it up, but Gammeltorv shakes his head from the sofa because a hearty laughter swells up toward me from the hall. Laughter and clapping and stamping on the floor. Only Nina sends me an offended look because isn't *she* the star? When the curtain falls, Gammeltorv takes both my hands. 'You've saved the whole show,' he says, 'you'll have the leading role in the next play.' My family praises me too, and Edvin says that I have talent. He thinks he does too, but he's never had a chance. He dances with me a lot, and I'm grateful to him for that. He dances well, and Nina gives him a sidelong glance as she dances past with her forester. He's shorter than her and in general doesn't look like much. Edvin also dances with my mother and with both aunts, and at twelve o'clock my mother says that we have to go home, so I have to leave my friends. The next time we meet at the café on Strandlodsvej, Gammeltorv shows me a clipping from *Amagerbladet*, where, among other things, it says, 'A quite young girl, Tove Ditlefsen, was a great success as Aunt Agnes.' Even though my name is misspelled, it's a strange feeling to see it in print for the first time. 'And here,' says the enterprising Gammeltorv, 'are the scripts for the new play, *Trilby*. Trilby is a poor little girl who's in a magician's power. He forces her to sing and she sings beautifully.' 'And who,' says Nina coolly, 'is going to play Trilby?' 'Tove is,' he says, 'and since she can't sing, she just has to open and close her mouth. Then you stand in the wings and sing.' Nina gets red in the face with anger. She takes her purse and gets up. 'I won't have any part of it,' she says. 'You can sing yourself while she opens and shuts her mouth. I've had enough.' I stare at her, horror-stricken. 'I don't want any part of it, either,' I say. 'Nina is prettier than I am. So why should I play Trilby?' Suddenly we're all standing up. Gammeltorv pounds the table. 'Is it your theater company or mine?' he yells. 'Ha,' snorts Nina, 'Succès Theater Company! Any idiot can put an ad in a newspaper and pretend that he's somebody. I'm leaving!' 'Me too,' I yell, and rush out on her heels. I have to run to catch up with her. Suddenly we stand still, as if by mutual agreement. We're standing between two lampposts and the road is completely empty of people. There's a touch of spring in the air. Nina's narrow face wreathed with the fine halo of hair is still dark with anger, but suddenly she breaks into laughter and I do the same. 'So you were supposed to be the star,' she laughs. 'Oh, how funny.' We imagine how I was supposed to stand, opening and shutting my mouth without a sound coming over my lips while Nina sang with full voice, hidden from the audience. We laugh so we can hardly stop, and we agree that neither of us has talent for the theater. We'll have fun ourselves instead of entertaining others. We'll cut loose in the big, exciting city and find some young men we can fall in love with. Some young men who are nice to look at and who have money in their pockets. Now that we're not going to spend any more evenings with the idiotic rehearsals for *Aunt Agnes*, we have lots of time. The only tiresome thing about it is that I have to be home at ten o'clock, but for the time being there's nothing to be done about that.

10

Aunt Rosalia is in the hospital. One day when my mother went out to visit her, Aunt Rosalia said, laughing, 'I'm young again, Alfrida.' My mother said that she should go to the doctor, but my aunt wouldn't. Like my mother, she only goes to the doctor under dire circumstances. My mother told me about it in the evening when I came home from the office. I didn't understand what the mysterious remark meant, but my mother explained that my aunt had started to bleed after it had stopped many years ago. Although my mother has never informed me about anything regarding those matters, she always assumes that I know all about it. But there were obviously gaps in the trash-can corner's sex education. It took my mother a long time to persuade my aunt to go to a doctor, and when she finally did, he put her in the hospital at once. Now she's going to have an operation, and she talks about it as if it were a picnic. 'It's cancer,' says my mother gloomily. 'First her husband – now her. And just when she was going to have some good years, now that she's gotten rid of that beast.' My mother is sincerely worried and unhappy about it, because she's much more fond of Aunt Rosalia than of Aunt Agnete. I visit her with my mother the day before the operation. She's lying there eating oranges and talking cheerfully with the other patients in the ward. I can't believe that my mother is right, because she doesn't look sick and she's not in pain. But when we've said goodbye and come out into the hallway, a nurse comes over and asks my mother who my aunt's nearest relatives are. When she hears that we are, she asks my mother to come in and talk to the doctor. In the meantime, I wait outside on a bench. My mother comes back with red eyes. She blows her nose loudly and leans on my arm as we leave. 'I thought so,' she sniffs. 'I was right. They don't know whether she'll survive the operation.' On the way to the office, I call Nina and say that I can't come over to her house that evening. I don't feel that I can leave my mother, and Jytte is no help when you're feeling bad about something. At the office, Miss Løngren says suspiciously, 'Well, so how was your aunt?' 'She has cancer,' I say solemnly, 'and she might die.' 'Well, well,' says Miss Løngren callously, 'we're all going to die, you know. Get to work now. Here are some letters.' I type letters to the brothers, and I've taken them in shorthand myself from Master's dictation. Carl Jensen comes in from the print shop and sits down in his revolving chair. He's wearing a gray smock and has a yellow pencil behind his ear. As far as I can see, he never does any work, but with Miss Løngren he doesn't have to pretend to do any, either. I can see that there's something he wants to say to her and that my presence is embarrassing him, but I calmly keep tapping at the typewriter, and I'm beginning to get faster at it. 'Løngren,' he says, leaning back so his face is close to hers, 'Sven Åge has his silver wedding anniversary in two weeks. Do you think it'd be possible to get someone to write a song for him?' His shifty eyes pass over me for a moment, but I don't look up. 'Oh God, yes,' says Miss Løngren, 'Miss Ditlevsen could, couldn't you?' The last words come loudly and shrilly and I don't dare pretend that I didn't hear them. 'Yes,' I say, addressing myself to Miss Løngren, 'sure I can.' 'Sure she can,' she says to Carl Jensen. 'She just needs some information, you know. What's happened through the years, things like that.' 'She'll have it,' says Carl Jensen, relieved. 'I'll bring it tomorrow.' I look at him sideways and suddenly I realize that it's a strange form of shyness that makes him unable to speak to me directly. That makes it less uncomfortable and puts the problem on his shoulders. The next day, I write the song while people walk past outside in the sunshine – independent people who can move about freely in the world between nine and five and who all have some personal goal that they've determined themselves. I write the ridiculous song while my aunt is being operated on and no one knows whether she'll survive. The telephone rings and Miss Løngren hands the receiver to me looking as if it's burning her fingers. 'It's for you,' she says sternly. 'It's a young woman.' Bright red in the face, I go around the desk and take the telephone as I stand close to Carl Jensen and Miss Løngren, who are completely silent. It's Nina, and I've forbidden her to call me. 'Hi,' she says. 'Just listen – I met a really sweet guy yesterday in the Heidelberg. He has a friend who's cute too. Tall, dark, and everything. You'll like him. I promised that we'd be there tonight. Then they'll both be there.' 'No,' I say in a low voice, 'I can't tonight. I have to be home.' 'Why?' she asks and, embarrassed, I whisper that I'll tell her some other time. I'm busy now. Nina is insulted and says that I'm strange. When she's finally found a young man for me, and I don't want to meet him. 'I've got to go,' I say. 'I'm busy. Goodbye.' Fumbling, I put down the receiver. 'Thank you,' I mumble, and go back to my place. 'Was that your girlfriend?' asks Miss Løngren after a long and oppressive silence. When I answer affirmatively, she says, 'She sounded rather frivolous. At your age, you have to be careful about the kind of girlfriends you have.' 'That's true,' says Carl Jensen, adding philosophically, 'In some ways, it's better to have a boyfriend – at least you know what's going on.' I keep working on the song, annoyed that there's nothing that rhymes with Sven Åge. Boa, Noah, protozoa, Balboa. Sven Åge is just as silent as his brother is talkative. He's fat like his father and his head is always tilted slightly, as if one neck muscle were too short. It gives him an endearing look. The brothers practically don't talk to each other at all because Sven Åge lives upstairs free of charge while Carl Jensen has to pay rent himself somewhere else. Furthermore, Sven Åge, as the oldest, is going to take over the press when Master dies. 'Sad,' says Miss Løngren sentimentally, 'that blood ties aren't stronger.' When I'm through with the song, I type it up on the typewriter, and when Master suddenly appears, I tear it out and stuff it away in the drawer because I'm not getting paid to write poetry for special occasions. When the product is done, I give it to Miss Løngren, and she's almost more enthusiastic than the time before. She stares at me as if I were a new Shakespeare and says, 'It's amazing – look here, Carl Jensen.' He takes the song and reads through it and agrees with her and stares at me for a long time without saying a word. Then he says to Miss Løngren, 'I wonder where she gets it from?' 'It's a gift,' determines Miss Løngren, 'a gift you're born with. I had an uncle who could do it, too. But it wore him out. It was as if all strength left him when he was done with a song. It's the same with mediums – they're completely exhausted by it, too. Aren't you tired, Miss Ditlevsen?' No, I'm not tired and my strength hasn't left me. But I want so badly to have a place where I can practice writing real poems. I'd like to have a room with four walls and a closed door. A room with a bed, a table and a chair, with a typewriter, or a pad of paper and a pencil, nothing more. Well, yes – a door I could lock. All of this I can't have until I'm eighteen and can move away from home. The attic with the metal boxes was the last place where I had peace. That and my childhood windowsill. I walk home, caressed by the soft May air. Now it stays light for a long time in the evening and I'm not cold in my brown suit. The jacket just reaches my waist and the skirt is pleated. I have a pleasant feeling of being well dressed when I wear it. Nina says I should have a bigger wardrobe, but I don't have any money. I pay twenty kroner a month at home now that I get all my meals there; ten kroner goes in the bank; and then there's twenty kroner left, a little less when medical insurance is paid for. Most of it I use for candy, because it's an inner battle to pass unscathed by a chocolate store. I also need money for the soda pop that I drink when I go to dance halls with Nina. The young men who might pay for it unfortunately don't show up until ten o'clock, when I have to say goodbye to the joys of nightlife. I think a little bit about what kind of young man Nina had chosen for me, and regret that I didn't get to meet him. But if my aunt is dead, I can't let my mother be alone. I always peek into baby buggies when I walk home, because I love to look at the little children who are lying asleep with upstretched hands on a ruffled pillowcase. I also like to look at people who in one way or another give expression to their feelings. I like to look at mothers caressing their children, and I willingly go a little out of my way in order to follow a young couple who are walking hand in hand and are openly in love. It gives me a wistful feeling of happiness and an indefinable hope for the future. Up in the living room my mother is sitting waiting for me. She's very pale and she has recently been crying. I'm fond of my mother, too, whenever she's prey to a simple and sincere emotion. 'She didn't die,' she says solemnly, 'but the doctor said that it's only a reprieve. The important thing now is that she doesn't find out what's wrong with her. Don't ever tell her.' 'I won't,' I say. My mother goes out to make coffee, and I look at my sleeping father's back. Suddenly I see that he is aged and tired. There's nothing definite to point to, it's just an impression that I get. My father is fifty-five years old, and I've never known him as young. My mother was first young, and then youthful, and she's still standing at that shaky stage. She lies without compunction that she's a couple of years younger, even to us, who know very well how old she is. She still gets her hair dyed and goes to the steambath once a week; these exertions fill me with a kind of compassion because they're an expression of a fear in her that I don't understand. I just observe it. When she puts the cups on the table, my father wakes up, rubs his eyes, and sits up. 'Have you told her?' he says grimly. 'No,' says my mother calmly, 'you can do it.' 'We've gotten a new apartment,' he says bitterly, 'over on Westend. It costs sixty kroner a month and I don't know where the money's going to come from when I'm unemployed again.' 'Nonsense,' says my mother harshly. 'Tove pays twenty, you know.' I'm horrified, because they shouldn't plan their future around my contribution. They shouldn't count on me in any way when they make plans behind my back. I ask them why they haven't told me before, and my mother says that they wanted to surprise me. There are three rooms and I'm to have one of them. And it looks out on the street so you can see what's going on. I feel a little happy after all, because I've always dreamed of having my own room. 'What the hell,' snaps my father, 'is she going to do in that room? Sit and bite her fingernails or pick her nose? Huh?' I get mad because he doesn't know anything about his own children. And whenever I get mad I always say something that I regret. 'I want to read,'

I say, 'and write.' He asks what in hell I want to write. 'Poems,' I yell. 'I've written lots of poems and once there was an editor who said they were excellent.' 'There, you see,' says my father, rubbing his face with his big hand, 'she's crazy, too. Did you know that she was fooling around with things like that?' 'No,' says my mother curtly, 'but that's her own business. If she wants to write, it's clear that she has to have her own room.' In offended silence, my father takes his lunchbox and puts on his jacket to go to work. When he puts on his cap, he stands there a little, looking uncomfortable. 'Tove,' he says with a tender voice, 'can I see your . . . uh . . . poems sometime? I know something about that kind of thing.' My anger disappears completely. 'Yes, you can,' I say and he nods at me awkwardly before he leaves. My father can regret and repent – an ability that my mother doesn't possess. When he's left, she tells me about the new apartment that we're going to move into on the first. 'Three enormous rooms,' she says, 'that are almost like ballrooms. It'll be nice to get away from this proletarian neighborhood.' When she's gone into the bedroom, I look around at our little living room. I look at the old dusty puppet theater that we were once so happy with when my father made it. It will probably not survive a move. I look at the wallpaper that bears various spots, many of whose origins I remember. I look at the sailor's wife on the wall, at the brass coffee service on the buffet, at the door handle that broke one time when my mother slammed the door after her and that has never been repaired. I look out the window over at the courtyard with the gas pump and the gypsy wagon. I look at all this, which has remained unchanged, and I realize that I detest changes. It's difficult to keep a grasp on yourself when things around you change.

II

Summer is over and fall has come. The wildly colored leaves blow through the streets, and it's cold for me to go out in the brown suit. Since Edvin's made-over coat doesn't fit me anymore, I buy a coat on credit. It's totally against my father's advice. He says that you should pay everyone their due and make sure that you don't owe anyone anything, because otherwise you'll end up in Sundholm. We live on Westend now, on the ground floor, in number 32. My room is called the parlor whenever I don't take outright possession of it, and it's only separated from the dining room by a flowered cotton curtain. There's a table with crooked legs, two leather armchairs, and a leather sofa – all bought used and quite worn. I sleep on the sofa at night and its curved back makes it impossible for me to stretch out completely. 'Then maybe you won't grow much more,' says my mother hopefully. I myself often wonder how tall a person can continue to grow, but with me it doesn't seem to have any end. I'll soon be seventeen and I'm earning sixty kroner a month. My salary is according to union scale. I don't get much pleasure from my room because if I go in there in the evening, my mother yells through the curtain, 'What are you doing now? It's so quiet.' Usually I'm not doing anything other than reading my father's books, which I've already read. 'You can read just as well in here,' yells my mother in a voice as if heavy steel doors separated us. When she's in a good mood, she sticks her head in around the curtain and says, 'Are you writing poetry, Tove?' But usually I'm not home in the evening anymore, I go to the Lodberg or the Olympia or the Heidelberg with Nina, and we sit with our soda pop and watch the dancing couples in the middle of the floor – as if we haven't come there to dance ourselves. As a rule it's Nina who is chosen first. I smile at the young man who wants to dance with her, as if I were her mother, certain that now she's in good hands. I continue to smile approvingly as they dance past me, and I also look at other people in the room with interest. I imagine that people will think I'm studying my surroundings with the intention of writing a book about them sometime. For my sake, people can think what they like, just not that I'm an overlooked girl who's only out to get engaged. Once when I get up to dance with a young man who has taken pity on me, a man at the neighboring table mumbles, 'Even an ugly duckling can find a mate.' It ruins the whole evening for me. Nina says that it first gets to be fun after ten, and can't I get permission to stay out until twelve? But my mother won't hear of it. Nina also wants to fix me up a bit. Together we go out and buy a bra with cotton padding and a black and red cossack dress on credit. I don't dare tell them that at home, so I say I got it from Nina. These items help a good deal, to my astonishment, since I'm still the same person, whether I have cotton padding or not. 'The world wants to be fooled,' says Nina, satisfied, because she really wants me to be just as big a success as she is. One evening a handsome and serious young man asks me to dance. He's badly dressed, and while we dance, he tells me that the next day he's leaving for Spain to take part in the civil war. He lays his cheek against mine as we dance and even though it scratches a little, I like his caress. I lean a little closer to him and I can feel the warmth of his hand on the skin on my back. I get a little weak in the knees and feel something that I've never felt before at anyone's touch. Maybe he feels the same, because he stays standing with his arm around my waist until the music starts again. His name is Kurt and he asks if he can walk me home. 'You'll be the last girl I'm with before I leave,' he says. Kurt has been unemployed for three years and he would rather sacrifice his life for a great cause than rot in Denmark. He lives on welfare. When he was working, he was a driver for a taxicab owner, and he's never learned anything other than how to drive a car. He sits down at our table, and Nina smiles happily because I've finally found a young man I may be able to hold on to. We've agreed to keep away from unemployed young men, but it's hard to find one who's not. At ten o'clock, Kurt walks me home. It's clear moonlight and my heart is rather moved. I'm walking through the streets with a man who soon will suffer a hero's death. That makes him different in my eyes than all the others. His eyes are dark blue and almond-shaped, his hair black, and his mouth red like a small child's. At home in the entryway, he takes my head in his hands and kisses me very tenderly. He asks me if I live alone and I say no. He himself lives in a room with a vile landlady who doesn't let him have girls visiting. While we're standing embracing each other, my mother opens the window and yells, 'Tove, get up here now!' We jump apart terrified, and Kurt says, 'Was that your mother?' I can't deny it, and now we have to part. And Kurt has to go down by Trommesalen in order to get food from a sandwich store where it's handed out at midnight, but you have to get in line a couple of hours ahead of time. I stand watching him as he walks down the almost empty street. He's not wearing an overcoat and he has stuck both hands in the pockets of his jacket. He's going to die soon, and I'll never see him again. When I get upstairs, I make a scene over my mother's interference, but she says that I can just invite the young men up so she can see that there's nothing unsavory about them. She doesn't want me to go around with people who can't bear the light of day. And for that matter, she has other things to think about, because soon Aunt Rosalia is coming home from the hospital, where she's now been several times. She's coming home to us to die. That's what the doctors have told my mother. There's nothing more they can do, and there's no room in the hospital for people that the doctors can't do anything else for. Aunt Rosalia will lie in my father's side of the bed next to my mother. So my father will sleep on the sofa in the dining room. 'All of this,' says my mother, 'wouldn't have been possible in the old apartment', so it was as if an inner voice spoke to her when she begged my father to move.

One evening when I come home without a cavalier, I meet my father in the entryway. He's on his way out, as I'm going in. He looks enraged and bitter. 'Edvin's sitting up there,' he says. 'He's gotten married without saying a word to any of us. He's got a wife and apartment, and there's probably a kid on the way, too. Ha! – and him we've sacrificed so much for. Goodbye.' Before I let myself in (for now I have a key), I put on an astonished expression. 'Oh,' I say, 'are you here?' They're sitting in my room because Edvin is a guest now, and that's what you use a parlor for. My mother is bawling and Edvin looks very ill at ease. Maybe he regrets his pig-headedness, which also seems to me a little extreme. 'It was to surprise you,' he says meekly, 'and so you wouldn't have the expense of the wedding.' That only makes matters worse. My mother asks, offended, whether he thinks they couldn't afford a little wedding present, 'but I suppose we're just not fine enough.' Then Edvin shows us a picture of his wife. Her name is Grete and she has a round face with dimples. My mother studies it with a frown. 'Can she cook?' she asks and stops crying. Edvin has no idea. 'She doesn't look like she can,' says my mother. My mother herself is no great shakes in the kitchen, and everything edible that she makes has a cementlike consistency because she digs too deeply into the flour bag. While we drink coffee and eat pastry, she asks how much Edvin's rent is and whether his wife is going to work as long as there aren't any children. She's not, and my mother wonders how she'll manage to pass the time. It's very clear that she's already formed an unfavorable opinion of Grete that won't change for the better through personal acquaintance. The clock strikes eleven in the dining room and Edvin gets up to go. 'We'll come on Sunday, then,' he says dejectedly. When he's left, my mother wants to talk, and I want to be alone. I want to be alone to think about Kurt, and I want to write down some lines that came to me as I watched him go down the street without once turning around. At the corner of Westend and Matthæusgade there's a tavern where a band by the name of 'Bing and Bang' blares until two in the morning. Because of that, we practically have to shout at each other; it was far quieter in the old apartment. My mother asks me what kind of a young man I was standing there kissing. 'One I danced with,' I say. 'Other than that I don't know.' She says that I should always make a date before the young men leave. She suffers from a nagging fear that I'll never get engaged, and is prepared to receive any young man royally if he's just the least bit interested in me. 'You're too critical,' she says point-blank. 'You can't afford to be that way.' Finally she leaves and I sit down at the table with the crooked legs and take out paper and pencil. I think about the handsome young man who's going to die in Spain and then I write a poem that is good. It's called 'To My Dead Child' and has no obvious connection with Kurt. Still, I wouldn't have written it if I hadn't met him. When it's done, I'm no longer sorry that I'll never see him again. I'm happy and relieved and yet melancholy. It's so sad that I can't show the poem to a living soul and that everything still has to wait until I meet a person like Mr Krogh. I've shown Nina my poems and she thinks they're all good. I've shown my father the poem I wrote in the attic with the metal boxes, and he said that it was an amateur poem and that things like that were a good hobby for me – like when he did crossword puzzles. 'You train your brain with things like that,' he said. I can't explain to myself, either, why I want so badly to have my poems published, so other people who have a feeling for poetry can enjoy them. But that's what I want. That's what I, by dark and twisting roads, am working toward. That's what gives me the strength to get up every day, to go to the printing office and sit across from Miss Løngren's Argus eyes for eight hours. That's why I want to move away from home the same day I turn eighteen. Bing and Bang roars through the night; drunk people are thrown out into our courtyard from the café's back door. There they yell, swear, and fight, and not until morning is there silence in the courtyard and on our street.

12

Rumors of my poetic abilities have reached the print shop, and now orders come in every day. Carl Jensen receives them and brings them to Miss Løngren, who is still the only one I stand in direct contact with. I write songs for all kinds of occasions and when I go over to hand out the pay envelopes, the workers thank me, embarrassed, and just as embarrassed, I say that there's nothing to thank me for. I write songs and in shorthand I take important messages to the brothers or obituaries of dead brothers. They're printed in the Order of Saint George newsletter. All of this doesn't have much to do with office work, but Miss Løngren won't train me; when she was on vacation, everything was on the verge of collapse because I didn't know the first thing about anything. When I turn eighteen, I'll apply for a real office job and no longer work as a trainee. Then I can get a much higher salary. When I turn eighteen the world will be different in every way, and Nina and I will have the whole night at our disposal. Then I'll also have to see about getting rid of my virtue – Nina is very set on that. She herself was only fifteen when the forester took hers. Whenever we go out in the evening, she takes off her engagement ring. She only goes to bed with those young men who are not unemployed, and I haven't told her about Kurt. That's an experience I want to keep for myself. If I had lived in a room, I would have taken him in. But I don't know whether I would have taken in other young men who have walked me home and kissed me in the entryway. One day when Nina is pressuring me again because of my scandalous virginity, I tell her that I want to be engaged first. That's not something that I've thought about before, but the decision relieves me. In reality there has only been one real prospective buyer for my virtue, and it's a little embarrassing, because Nina talks as if everyone is out after it. Now that Aunt Rosalia is lying at home sick, my mother is a lot less concerned with what I'm doing. All day she sits in there by my aunt's bed, talking and laughing, and in the evening she goes to bed early and lies there, talking on until one of them falls asleep. My father has become totally superfluous in her world, and I think she would be completely happy if my aunt wasn't going to die. My aunt is yellow in the face and her skin is so stretched over her bones that you're continually reminded of her skull's existence. Her skin is so tight that she can't even close her mouth all the way anymore. If she's awake in the evening when I come home, she calls me in and I sit down by her bed for a while. I try to hold my breath the whole time because there's a terrible smell around the bed, and I hope that my aunt doesn't notice it herself. When she's in pain, my mother phones from the café on the corner for a nurse, who comes and gives her an injection of morphine. It makes her hazy, and she often mistakes my mother and me for each other. 'I'm going to die, Alfrida,' she says to me one evening. 'I know it. You don't have to hide it from me.' 'No,' I say unhappily, 'you're just sick. The doctor says you'll be well soon.' 'It was the same with Carl,' she says. 'The doctor said that I shouldn't tell him.' I don't answer, just put her emaciated hands underneath the comforter, turn off the light, and go into my own room where I can hear my father's snoring through the cotton curtain. I would have liked to speak honestly with my aunt because I'm sure that it would have made her happy, but I don't dare because of my mother, who acts out her sad comedy while my aunt pretends that she doesn't know anything. I think that I would want to know the truth when I'm going to die someday. I also think that if I meet a young man I like, I can't invite him up, as my mother always requests, because the smell from my aunt fills the whole apartment. We've all been out to Sydhavnen to visit my brother and his wife. They have a two-room apartment with a few pieces of furniture that were bought on credit, which made my father put on a foreboding expression. Grete is tiny and plump and smiling, and she sat on Edvin's lap the whole time, while my mother looked at her as if she were a vampire who would suck all strength out of him before long. She hardly spoke to her, and conversation was difficult, too, since my mother carefully avoided addressing her directly. I'm so tired of my family because it's as if I run up against them every time I want to move freely. Maybe I can't be free of them until I get married myself and start my own family. One evening when we're sitting in the Lodberg over our soda pop, a young man asks Nina to dance and steps onto the dance floor with her, and I sit as usual with my maternal smile, watching youth amuse itself. Then a young man bows before me and we step out onto the crowded dance floor. He hums in my ear to the music, 'The young man from Rome, don't count him out.' 'That's Mussolini,' I say. I happen to know that because my brother was outraged by the song that Liva Weel often sings. 'Who's that?' asks the young man, and I say that I don't know. I only know that it's a man in Italy who's just like Hitler, and that you shouldn't write Danish songs that praise him. 'Your girlfriend is dancing with my friend,' he says. 'His name is Egon. And I'm Aksel. What's your name?' 'Tove,' I say. Aksel dances well and he's in no way fresh during the dance like most of them. 'You dance well,' he says, 'better than most of the girls.' I tell him that I've never learned to dance and he says that it doesn't matter. I have rhythm in my body. It's very rare that any of the young men say anything while you dance with them, and I like Aksel. We dance past Nina and Egon; I smile at Nina, and Egon and Aksel say hi to each other. When the music stops, Aksel asks if they can sit at our table and I say yes. Nina's beautiful eyes shine with happiness when we reach our table. She asks, 'Don't you think Egon is handsome?' and I say, 'Yes, I do.' 'He's a carpenter,' she says, 'and he lives in a house on Amager with his parents, and Aksel lives across the street with his parents. In a house too.' Then they come over and sit down and I look closer at Aksel. He has a round, friendly face and everything about him reminds you that he was once a child. The light curly hair is a little damp on his forehead, the blue eyes have a trusting expression, and he has a deep cleft in his chin, which is only erased when he laughs. There's a faint scent of milk about him. Egon is shorter than he is, dark, and apparently somewhat older. Nina asks him how many rooms there are in his house, and I can see that she's far away in a dream about two rich men's sons who will lift up two poor girls into their carefree world. Maybe she's even considering giving the forester the sack. I have the impression that he's heavy and serious, and that Nina has a much too romantic picture of the future he'll provide for her in the country. When she's being very silly she calls him The Shrub, but no one else is allowed to. She's with him every weekend and I'm not permitted to meet him. He's not allowed to meet me, either, because she thinks that he'll think I'm a bad influence, like my mother thinks Nina is a bad influence on me. 'And what do you do?' Nina asks Aksel as we drink the beers we ordered. 'I'm a collection agent,' he says, smiling charmingly at her. I don't know what that is, but Nina looks disappointed. 'Oh,' she says, 'you go around with bills and things like that?' 'Drive,' he corrects her with a certain conceitedness. 'I drive a van.' Her face brightens a little and suddenly she suggests that we all celebrate our meeting. We drink to that, and I would much rather have had a soda pop. I don't like beer. Since it's past ten, I admit dispiritedly that I'll have to leave. Aksel jumps up gallantly and buttons his jacket, which is very broad across the shoulders. He's tall and extraordinarily knock-kneed. He takes me easily by the arm as we walk across the room together, and out in the cloakroom he helps me with my coat. As we walk through the cool streets, where the city's lights outshine the stars, he tells me that he's an adopted child and that his parents are quite old, but very nice. And to my astonishment, he asks me whether I feel like coming over to meet them someday. 'Sure,' I say. 'I want so much to have a steady girlfriend,' he says childishly and forthrightly. 'And the old folks want me so badly to get engaged.' At home in the entryway he kisses me according to program, but I can tell that he doesn't feel anything special by it, not even when I press myself lovingly against him. He says, 'The four of us can have fun together.' 'Yes,' I say, and promise to come out to visit him next Sunday. He asks curiously if I'm a virgin and I admit that I am. He grabs my hand and shakes it heartily. 'I respect that,' he says warmly. Disappointed and confused, I go to bed. I think about whether you can get engaged to a collection agent. I have a suspicion that it's just a nicer expression for bicycle messenger, except that he drives a van.

13

Aksel and I are formally engaged after knowing each other for two weeks, and treating each other as chastely as if we were brother and sister. Nina told Egon that I wouldn't go to bed with Aksel until we were engaged, and Egon told Aksel, who suggested the engagement as his own spontaneous idea. Now I'm an engaged girl, and my mother is thrilled. She thinks Aksel looks stable; just as she could tell that Edvin's wife couldn't cook, she can tell that Aksel doesn't drink. He behaves very gallantly toward my mother. 'Anyone can see,' she says to my father, who doesn't contradict her, 'that he's an educated person.' After spending several evenings with him, my father says, 'You know, he's never learned anything except how to drive a car.' 'Well,' says my mother offended, 'isn't that good enough? Maybe you know how to drive a car?' Aksel has promised to take my mother out driving someday; I don't give it much thought, however. But one day, while I'm innocently sitting in the office, there is a loud honking outside and Miss Løngren stares out the window. 'Who on earth is that?' she says astonished. 'They're waving over here. Is it someone you know?' I deny it, blushing, because Aksel and my mother are waving like mad and leaning out the window while Aksel honks the horn, long and rhythmically. 'It must be for the people upstairs,' I say miserably. 'What nerve,' says Miss Løngren, drawing the curtains tighter together. When I get home, I say furiously that I don't want any part of that stupid waving, and my mother says that she and Aksel had so much fun all day. They went to a pastry shop and Aksel treated her. Her eyes shine, as if she were the one who was engaged to him. Aksel's parents are both tiny and old and tremendously nice. They live in a bungalow in Kastrup. The father is a foreman in a factory and there's an air of affluence over the house. Aksel has his room down in the basement. He has a radio and a phonograph and over three hundred records, arranged on tall shelves like books. The room next door is a billiard room where all four of us play billiards when Nina and Egon are there. Aksel's parents call him Assemand and treat him as if he were a little boy. He's very loving toward them just as he is toward me. He has a warmth in his being that makes you feel secure and comfortable. One day Nina says that we're going to have a little party out at Aksel's. We're going to drink his father's homemade wine and we've gotten permission for this from Aksel's parents. We're also going to dance and play billiards and afterwards I must give Aksel the great pleasure of going to bed with him. 'When you've been drinking,' says Nina encouragingly, 'it doesn't hurt a bit.' Egon also thinks it's about time, Nina tells me, and it's really as if Aksel and I aren't even consulted. We don't talk about it at all and he still respects me to a fault. Nina and I go out there together and Aksel is a conscientious host. He opens the bottles and puts on records and we all get giddy from the wine, which doesn't taste nearly as terrible as beer. Egon sits and kisses Nina in between dances. She laughs and says if only The Shrub could see this, because she's told her secret to Egon, who makes fun of The Shrub, whom he imagines sitting on the doorstep, tamping his evening pipe as he watches the sunset. We all laugh loudly at this stereotype. 'Nina comes out,' elaborates Egon, encouraged by his success, 'with three sniveling kids hanging onto her dress, dries her hands on her apron and says, "Papa, it's time for evening coffee." ' Aksel doesn't kiss me at all and as time goes on, he grows more and more serious. I almost feel sorry for him because in so many ways he seems like a child. I myself have gotten very animated from the wine and I'm really set on going through with it now. It surely won't be any worse for me than for so many others. Sometime after midnight, Nina and Egon sneak into the billiard room and close the door behind them. 'What are you doing in there?' Aksel yells unnecessarily. Then he looks at me, uncertain and afraid. 'Well,' he says, 'I'd better make the bed.' He does this with slow, careful movements. 'Take off your clothes,' he says miserably, 'at least some of them.' It's like being at the doctor's. 'Why don't we talk a little first?' I ask. 'Sure,' he says and we sit down in separate chairs. He fills our glasses to the top and we empty them greedily. 'You should see about getting your front teeth filled,' he says gently. 'Yes,' I say astonished. Unlike the other procedure, though, it costs money to go the dentist. 'I can't afford it,' I add. Then he offers to pay for it and since I don't feel that I can accept, he says that he's going to support me someday anyway. So I thank him and agree to let him pay for the fillings. 'It's a shame,' he explains, 'because otherwise you're so pretty.' Suddenly there's a strange howl from the billiard room, and both of us gasp. 'It's Egon,' explains Aksel. 'He's so passionate.' 'Are you too?' I ask cautiously, because I'd like to be prepared for it if he's actually going to roar. 'No,' he says honestly, 'I'm not very passionate.' 'I don't think I am either,' I admit. A glimmer of hope appears in his eyes. 'We could,' he says optimistically, 'wait until another time?' 'Then they'll think we're crazy,' I say, nodding toward the billiard room. 'No. Well, we could turn out the light.' Aksel turns out the light. I clench my teeth and lie listening to his warm, kind, reassuring words. The whole thing isn't so bad, and he doesn't utter any animal-like sounds. Afterwards he turns on the light again, and we both laugh with great relief that it's over and that it wasn't anything special. 'I want to tell you,' he confesses, 'I've never been to bed with a virgin before.' Nina and Egon appear in the door with flushed cheeks and shining eyes. They look from the bed to us and then at each other, as if it were all their doing, but nothing is said about it. We continue dancing, because when I'm with Aksel, I'm allowed to come home late. With him I can do anything, so this wouldn't upset my mother, either, if she found out. Later Nina asks me if it wasn't wonderful, and of course I say yes. She says that it gets better and better each time. I hadn't considered that the procedure would be repeated. In reality I think that it was a completely insignificant event in my life – not nearly as important as my brief meeting with Kurt and what that meeting could have developed into. But still, I write in my diary that I've kept since I got my own room, 'As Nina gave herself to Egon with all of her warm, passionate body in the billiard room, I answered Aksel's question about whether I was innocent with a pure and chaste "yes," etc.' In my diary everything is sheer romanticism. I store it in the top dresser drawer in the bedroom at home. I've had an extra key made for it. In the drawer are also my two 'real' poems, three thermometers, and five or six condoms. The latter items I stole from the nursing supply company because at one time I thought of opening a nursing supply store. But I was thrown out before my stock was large enough. To my great relief, Aksel continues to treat me exactly as before, and he never refers to the embarrassing interlude. I think that he does everything that Egon tells him to do, just as I tend to do whatever Nina wants me to. When I'm alone with Nina, I pretend that Aksel and I are frequently together and maybe he does the same when he's with Egon. During the day Aksel drives around with my mother, who sits in the delivery van and waits while he's with customers. He works for a furniture company, and he tells me that there are many whores among the customers. My suspicious mother has discovered that he stays an especially long time with them, but he just says that it's difficult to get the money from them. My mother says that I shouldn't trust him, but actually I couldn't care less whether he goes to bed with the whores. I don't think it's any concern of mine or my mother's. It's worse that I sense a certain coolness from his parents whenever I'm visiting. I can't figure out how I've offended them. Once in a while I catch his mother staring at me sharply when she doesn't think I'll notice. She's very tiny and always dressed in black like my grandmother. She has wise brown eyes and completely white hair. I've never seen her without an apron. 'Has Aksel promised to pay your dentist bill?' she says one evening. 'Yes,' I say, feeling uncomfortable. 'He doesn't make very much,' says his mother. 'I'm afraid that you may have to pay it yourself.' There's something that I don't understand at all. One evening when I'm invited to dinner, I get there a little before Aksel. His parents look very serious. His mother says that Aksel isn't the man for me. He'll never be able to support a wife, and I'm too good for him. 'Let me,' says his father, waving at her with his hand. 'The thing is,' he says, 'many times we've paid the company back when there've been funds missing. I mean, when Aksel has taken money that isn't his. When it comes to money, he's a child. We thought it would help when he got engaged to a nice girl, but it hasn't helped. He's our only son and our greatest sorrow. He's run away from eleven apprenticeships, and the only things he thinks about are cars and records.' 'He's a good boy,' his mother defends him, wiping her eyes, 'but reckless and irresponsible.' 'I like him a lot,' I say. 'And I don't need to be supported. I can make a living writing poetry.' The latter slips out of me involuntarily and I look at Aksel's parents, horrified. They don't look very surprised. 'I knew you weren't an ordinary young girl. You can see that,' says his mother. Then Aksel drives up and stops out in the gravel with screeching brakes. He often drives home in the company van. As he rings the bell, his mother says, 'Now you can't say that you weren't warned.' I think it over for a few days and am very glad that people can see I'm not ordinary. It wasn't so many years ago that I was unhappy about that. I think a lot about my fiancé and I reach the conclusion that he's not suited to be a lifelong mate to a girl who wants to break into high society someday. But I can't get myself to break the engagement. I feel sorry for Aksel, who is still gallant and kind and respects me. But my mother also starts to wonder why Aksel always has money in his pocket and why he stays so long with the whores. She stops accompanying him in his van and she advises me to see about finding someone else, someone like Erling who wanted to be a schoolteacher, whom I spurned as if there were a whole line of young men waiting at my door. Nina is in the midst of a serious crisis, because she's considering breaking off with The Shrub and marrying Egon. When I tell her what I know about Aksel, she advises me to end things with him as soon as my dental work is done. The fillings are almost invisible, and when they're finished, Nina thinks that I can get whoever I want. She says that I've finally gotten some 'class', and that's what men notice. But I'm so happy when I'm with Aksel because I'm really fond of him. I'm happy and secure in his company. I stop visiting his parents, and he stops visiting mine. My mother treats him coldly now and my father asks him questions that only serve to show his ignorance. 'What do you think about the Olympics? Huh? Isn't it scandalous?' my father says to him. He means the Olympics in Berlin where our girl swimmers are, but Aksel knows nothing about any Olympics. He only knows a little about Hitler and the world situation, and he hasn't read *The Last Civilian* by Ernst Glaeser. I have, and so I know a lot about the persecution of the Jews and the concentration camps, and all of it fills me with fear. It's so pleasant with Aksel because he knows nothing about all the things that could terrify a person these days. That doesn't mean that he's an idiot, but my father's interrogation is only aimed at showing that he is. He senses that and stops visiting. So we're homeless when we're together and only have the taverns and the streets. One day he picks me up outside the office and, silently, we walk down H. C. Ørstedsvej. It's clear that there's something he wants to tell me. Finally it comes. 'I've been thinking,' he says, 'that we ought to take off our rings. I've never really been in love with you.' 'And I haven't been in love with you, either,' I say. 'No,' he says, 'I know that.' He takes great strides, out of sheer embarrassment, and I have to jog to keep up with him. 'And I'll be eighteen soon,' I say, not knowing what that has to do with anything. 'Yes,' he says, 'then you won't be a minor anymore.' We walk for a while without saying anything. 'And my mother says you're too good for me,' he explains. 'You should marry someone who has a lot of money and reads books and things like that.' 'Yes,' I say, 'I think so too.' At home in the entryway, he kisses me tenderly as always and then twists the ring off his finger. He puts it in his pocket and mine goes there too. 'Maybe,' he says, 'we'll see each other again.' His short, stiff eyelashes scratch my cheek for the last time. Then he walks down Westend with his scissors-shaped legs and his supple boy's back. He turns around and waves at me. 'Bye,' he yells. 'Bye,' I yell back, waving. Then I go up, taking a deep breath before I put the key in the door, because the smell is getting worse and worse. I go in to my mother and Aunt Rosalia. 'Now I'm not engaged anymore,' I say. 'That's fine,' says my mother. 'He wasn't much good.' 'Yes, he was,' I say and then keep quiet. I can't explain to my mother what was good about Aksel. 'There's something good about everyone, Alfrida,' says my aunt gently from her bed. And we both know she's thinking about Uncle Carl.

14

One morning when I turn the corner onto the road in Frederiksberg where the printer's is located, I see that the flag is at half-mast in the little front yard of the office building. My first thought is that perhaps it's Miss Løngren who is dead, which fills me with perverse glee. Then I'll be allowed to mind the switchboard and talk on the telephone. And I can call Nina as often as I like. In a rather good mood, I go up the stairs, but when I step in the door, Miss Løngren is sitting at her usual place and blowing her nose with a great blast. It's all red, as if she's been sitting in the hot sun. 'Master is dead,' she says with a breaking voice, 'quite suddenly. He was with the brothers at the lodge. In the middle of a speech he fell over the table. A heart attack – there was nothing to be done.' I sit down at my place and say nothing. Master was a very taciturn man that everyone was afraid of, even his sons. He had difficulty expressing himself in writing, and I always embellished the language in the letters to the brothers and in the obituaries, because he couldn't remember what he had dictated. Aside from dictating letters, he'd never spoken to me. Miss Løngren stares at me reproachfully while I enter the work lists.

'You could at least offer your condolences,' she says. 'What's that?' I ask. She doesn't condescend to give an explanation, but continues her reading of the newspapers. 'Did you hear King Edward's abdication speech?' she asks. 'It was gripping. To give up a throne for the sake of a woman! And he's so handsome. Princess Ingrid didn't get her hands on him after all.' 'He looks like Leslie Howard,' I venture to say, and now it's her turn to ask who's that. She shows me a picture of Mrs Simpson and says, 'It's just so strange that he would fall in love with such a middle-aged woman. I could understand it better if it had been a young girl.' She runs her fingers through her old-maid hairdo, as if the thought crosses her mind that the world would have better understood it if it had been for her sake. 'He was handsome when he was young,' she says dreamily, meaning suddenly Master. 'Carl Jensen looks like him, don't you think? I'll buy a black suit for the funeral – I owe him that. What are you going to wear? Well, you can wear your suit, since it's spring.' The death and the abdication have made her talkative. She says that there will certainly be big changes now, and these changes will probably mean that I'll be let go. It was completely Master's idea that I was hired at all. These bright prospects fill me with joy and comfort. There's only half a year until I turn eighteen and it's about time that I move out. In every way the air is too thick to breathe.

Aunt Rosalia doesn't have long to live, and the light-hearted conversations with my mother have stopped completely. My aunt is unable to eat and she is in a lot of pain. My father tiptoes around like a criminal because my mother snaps at him as soon as she sets eyes on him. Edvin and Grete still haven't been to visit us because my mother doesn't have the energy for housekeeping chores in her sorrow-laden condition. She sleeps very little at night, so I've gotten myself an alarm clock and make coffee myself in the morning. Every evening I'm with Nina, who – after an inner battle – has broken off the relationship with Egon because she'd rather live in the country with The Shrub. And almost every night, when the taverns have closed, I stand downstairs in the entryway kissing some young man who's usually unemployed and who I never see again. After a while I can't tell one young man from the next. But I've begun to long for the intimate closeness with another human being that is called love. I long for love without knowing what it is. I think that I'll find it when I no longer live at home. And the man I love will be different from anyone else. When I think about Mr Krogh, I don't even think that he needs to be young. He doesn't have to be particularly handsome, either. But he has to like poems and he has to be able to advise me as to what I should do with mine. When I've said goodbye to the night's young man, I write love poems in my diary, which has taken the place of my childhood poetry album. Some of them are good and some of them are not so good. I've learned to tell the difference. But I don't read many poems anymore, because then I easily end up writing something that resembles them. Master's funeral is a terrible trial for me. Carl Jensen gives a speech out in the cemetery for both the workers and the family. The wind carries the words in the other direction and I don't hear any of them. I stand behind the youngest and most insignificant of the personnel, and next to me is a delicatessen worker who is very pregnant. It starts raining and I'm freezing in my suit. Suddenly the thought strikes me that I could be pregnant, and it's odd that I haven't thought of that before. Aksel apparently didn't think of it either. How do you know if you're pregnant? Suddenly I think that there are all kinds of signs that I am, and if it's true, I don't know what I'm going to do. Nina has confided to me that she can't have children; otherwise she would have gotten pregnant long ago. She says that the young men never use anything; they couldn't care less. I think about my mother, who always says that I can't come home with a kid, but I especially think about how it will hinder me in my vague wandering toward an equally vague goal. I would like very much to have a baby, but not yet. Things must come in the proper order. When the speech is over and everyone is going over to drink coffee or beer, I tell Miss Løngren that I have to go home because my aunt is about to die. She looks like she doesn't believe me, but I don't care. I rush home and look at myself in the mirror in the hallway. I think I look bad. I feel my breasts and imagine they're tender. I think about cream puffs and imagine I feel nauseous. I smooth my hand over my flat stomach and imagine it's gotten bigger. At five o'clock I'm standing in Pilestræde, outside *Berlingske Tidende,* waiting for Nina. I confide my fear to her and she says that I should go to the doctor. The next day I stay home from work and go up to old, mean Dr Bonnesen; with difficulty I manage to blurt out my errand. 'You knew very well what could happen,' he snaps in a harassed tone, 'before you started these highjinks.' He gives me a urine bottle and the next morning I deliver it full. The next few days Miss Løngren asks me where my thoughts are, since I'm not listening to what is said to me. Her own thoughts are still jumping from Master to the Duke of Windsor and back again. I feel her searching glance on me like a physical pain and fervently hope for the promised layoff. Several days later I finally find out that I'm not pregnant, and I'm filled with enormous relief. 'I'm very romantic,' confesses Miss Løngren as she pages through a magazine full of pictures of the world's most celebrated couple. 'That's why I can cry over something like this. Can't you? Aren't you at all romantic?' Such questions always contain a lurking reproach, and I hurry to assure her that I'm very romantic. The word makes me think of dark Bedouins with scimitars, of moonlit nights by the river, of dark blue, star-filled nights. I think of loneliness and the complete lack of family or relatives, of a garret room with a candlestick and a pen scratching across the paper, and of a man whose face and name are hidden from me for the time being. 'Yes,' says Miss Løngren thoughtfully, 'I think you are, too. Otherwise you wouldn't be able to write such beautiful songs.' She also says, 'Why don't you set yourself up as a freelance poet? You could earn a lot of money at it.' I think for a moment that I could have a sign in the window at home: 'Songs composed for all occasions.' And then my name underneath. But my mother probably wouldn't want a sign like that in the window.

One night shortly after Master's funeral, my mother wakes me up. 'Come,' she says, 'I think it's about to happen.' Her face is totally unrecognizable from crying. My aunt has tensed her body into an arc and cast her head back so the hard sinews of her neck look like thick ropes under the yellow skin. Her throat rattles eerily and my mother whispers that she's unconscious. But her eyes are open and roll around in their sockets as if they want to get out of them. My mother says that I should go and call the doctor. I dress quickly and borrow the telephone in the café on the corner where Bing and Bang play noisily in the background. The doctor is a kind man who stands for a long time, looking sadly at my aunt. 'Should she be given the last one?' he says as if to himself as he draws the syringe. 'Yes,' pleads my mother, 'it's terrible to see her suffer like this.' 'All right.' He injects her in her bony leg and a little later all of her muscles relax. Her eyes close and she lies back and starts to snore. 'Thank you,' says my mother to the doctor, following him out without thinking about her wrinkled nightgown. Then we sit together by the deathbed and neither one of us thinks of waking my father. Aunt Rosalia is ours and only a minor character in his life. Late into the night, my aunt stops snoring and my mother puts her ear to her mouth to see if she's breathing. 'It's over,' she says. 'Thank God she found peace.' She sits back on the chair again and gives me a helpless look. I feel very sorry for her and I feel that I ought to caress her or kiss her – something completely impossible. I can't even cry when she's looking at me, although I know that someday she'll say that I didn't even cry when my aunt died. She'll mention it as a sign of my heartlessness and maybe it will happen when I move away from home soon. I've never told her that I'm going to. We sit close to each other but there are miles between our hands. 'And now,' says my mother, 'just when she was going to enjoy life.' 'Yes,' I say, 'but she's not suffering anymore.' In spite of the late hour, my mother makes coffee and we sit in my room drinking it. 'Tomorrow,' says my mother, 'I'll have to go over to tell Aunt Agnete. She's only visited her three times in all the time she's been lying here.' When my mother begins to be outraged at other people's behavior, she's temporarily saved from the deepest despair. She talks about how Aunt Agnete has never come through when it mattered – even when they were children. Then she always told on the other two and she always had to be a little better than them. I let my mother talk and don't need to say very much myself. I'm sorry that Aunt Rosalia is dead, but not as much as I would have been as a child. That night I sleep with an open window in spite of the ruckus from Bing and Bang, and I look forward to having the rotten, suffocating stench seep out of the apartment. Death is not a gentle falling asleep as I once believed. It's brutal, hideous, and foul smelling. I wrap my arms around myself and rejoice in my youth and my health. Otherwise my youth is nothing more than a deficiency and a hindrance that I can't get rid of fast enough.

15

'It was all for your sake that we moved,' says my mother bitterly. 'So that you could have a room to write in. But you don't care. And now your father's unemployed again. We can't do without what you pay at home.' My father sits up and rubs his eyes. 'Yes,' he says fiercely, 'yes we can. Things are pretty bad if you can't get by without your children. You sacrifice everything for them and just when you're going to have a little pleasure from them, they disappear. It was the same with Edvin.' 'It was a different matter with Edvin,' says my mother. 'He's a boy.' She says it out of sheer contrariness, and I breathe a little easier, because now it's become a fight between the two of them. We're sitting in the dining room eating dinner. It's become a habit that, because of my father's varying work schedule, we eat a hot meal at noon, even though it doesn't make any difference now. Because I'm unemployed too. I was laid off from the office two weeks before my birthday. But I've found a new job that I'm to start the day after tomorrow, and I've also found a room. I'm moving there tomorrow, and I've told my parents. While I carry the plates out, they argue about it. 'She's heartless,' says my mother crying, 'like my father. The night Rosalia died, she sat stiff as a board without shedding a single tear. It was really spooky, Ditlev.' 'No,' snaps my father, 'she's good enough at heart. You've just brought these children up all wrong.' 'And you,' yells my mother, 'haven't you brought them up? To be socialists and dry their snot in Stauning's beard. No, since Rosalia died, and now that Tove is moving out, I have nothing more to live for. You're always lying around snoring, whether you've got work or not. It's deadly boring to look at.' 'And you,' says my father furiously, 'you have nothing but your family and royalty in your head. As long as you can run off to the beauty salon every other minute, you don't care whether your husband is starving.' Now, fortunately, my mother is sobbing with rage and not with sorrow over my moving. 'Husband,' she howls, 'it's a hell of a husband I have. You don't even want to touch me anymore, but I'm not a hundred years old, and there are other men in the world!' Bang! She slams the door to the bedroom and throws herself onto the bed, continuing to sob so that you can probably hear it all over the building. I take the tablecloth off the table and fold it. Since we've moved to a better neighborhood, we don't use *Social-Demokraten* as a tablecloth anymore, and I don't have to look at Anton Hansen's gloomy drawings from Nazi Germany. My father rubs his hand hard over his face, as if he wants to move all of his features around, and says tiredly, 'Mother's in a difficult age. Her nerves aren't good. You ought to consider that.' 'Yes,' I say uncomfortably, 'but I want to live my own life, Father. I just want to be myself.' 'That's what you have your own room for, you know,' he says. 'There you can be yourself and write all the poems you want.' I despise it when they mention my poems – I don't know why. 'It's not just that,' I say on my way behind the curtain. 'I want to have a place where I can invite my friends.' 'Well, yes,' he says, rubbing his face again, 'and Mother won't allow that. But at any rate, you take good care of yourself.' 'Yes,' I promise, slipping at last into my own room. There I pack up my few possessions, but I have to wait to empty the dresser drawer in the bedroom until my mother has gone into the dining room again. I've rented a room in Østerbro because I don't think moving would be complete if I stayed in Vesterbro. I don't like my landlady, but I took the room anyway because it cost only forty kroner a month. I'm paying off my winter coat and my dentist bill, but I'll have enough money to get by, because at the Currency Exchange I'll get a hundred kroner a month. My landlady is big and heavy. She has wild, bleached hair and a dramatic demeanor, as if something catastrophic were about to happen any minute. In the living room there hangs a big picture of Hitler. 'Look,' she said when I rented the room, 'isn't he handsome? Someday he'll rule the whole world.' She's a member of the Danish Nazi Party and asked me whether I wanted to be a member too, because they wanted to include the Danish youth. I said no, I didn't have any sense for politics. And it's none of my business what she's like. The main thing is that the room is cheap. I move out there the next day. I ride over in the streetcar with my suitcase and my alarm clock, which won't fit into the suitcase. It starts to ring between two stops and I smile foolishly as I turn it off. It's a very temperamental alarm clock that only I can operate. It's crabby and asthmatic like an old man, and when it gets too sluggish and creaky, I throw it onto the floor. Then it starts ticking, all gentle and friendly again. The landlady greets me in the same loose-fitting kimono that I saw her in the first time, and she looks just as dramatic too. 'You're not engaged, are you?' she asks, pressing her hand to her heart. 'No,' I say. 'Thank God,' she lets out her breath, relieved, as if she's avoided a dangerous situation. 'Men! I was married once, dear. He beat me black and blue whenever he'd been drinking, and I had to support him too. Things like that aren't allowed in Germany. Hitler won't stand for it. If people won't work, they get put in concentration camps. Does that alarm clock ring very loudly? I have such trouble sleeping and you can hear every sound in this house.' It rings so a whole county can hear it, but I swear that it's as good as soundless. At last she leaves me and I can calmly look over my new home. The room is quite small. There's a sofa with a flowered covering, an armchair in the same style, a table, and an old dresser with crooked, dangling handles on the drawers. There's a key in one of them, so I can really have something all to myself. In one corner there's a curtain with a rod behind it. It's supposed to serve as a wardrobe. There's also a chipped wash basin and pitcher. Furthermore, it's ice-cold here, like in Nina's room, and there's no stove. When I've put my clothes behind the curtain, I go out and buy a hundred sheets of typing paper. Then, with my last ten kroner, I rent a typewriter, which I place on the rickety table when I get back. I pull the armchair over to it, but when I sit down in it, the seat falls apart. All that I wanted for my forty kroner was a table and chair, but maybe you have to go up to a higher price category to get that. I go out and knock on the door to the living room where the landlady is sitting listening to the radio. 'Mrs Suhr,' I say, 'the chair broke. Could I borrow an ordinary chair?' She stares at me as if the news were a real misfortune. 'Broke?' she says. 'That was a perfectly good chair. It dates all the way back to my wedding.' She rushes in to inspect the damage. 'You'll have to give me five kroner for damages,' she says then,

Rhythmic shouts of 'Heil' constantly interrupt him, and there's nowhere in the room I can hide. When the speech is over, Mrs Suhr comes into my room with shining eyes and feverishly flushed cheeks. 'Did you hear him?' she shouts enraptured. 'Did you understand what he said? You don't need to understand it at all. It goes right through your skin like a steambath. I *drank* every word. Do you want a cup of coffee?' I say no thanks, although I haven't had a thing to eat or drink all day. I say no because I don't want to sit under Hitler's picture. It seems to me that then he'll notice me and find a means of crushing me. What I do would be considered 'decadent art' in Germany, and I remember what Mr Krogh said about the German intelligentsia. The next day I start my job at the Currency Exchange typing pool and Hitler invades Austria.

putting out her hand. I say that I don't have money until the first. Then she'll add it onto the rent, she says angrily. I follow her when she goes out again, begging her for an ordinary chair. 'It's highway robbery,' she huffs, massaging her heart again. 'It doesn't pay at all to rent out rooms. You'll probably wind up dragging men into my home, too.' She sends Hitler an imploring glance, as if he personally could throw out any men who might appear. Then she goes into the other room where there is a row of stiff, upright chairs along one wall. 'Here,' she says crossly, as she selects the most worn of them, 'take this one, then.' I thank her politely and carry it into my room. It's a good height for the table. Then I begin to type up my poems, and it's as if it makes them better. I'm filled with calm during this work, and the dream that this will someday be a book develops with stronger and clearer colors than before. Suddenly my landlady is standing in the doorway. 'That thing,' she says, pointing to the typewriter, 'makes a horrible racket. It sounds like machine guns.' 'I'm almost done,' I say. 'Otherwise I only type in the evening.' 'Well, all right.' She shakes her yellow-haired head. 'But not after eleven. You can hear every sound here. Say, wouldn't you like to hear Hitler's speech tonight? I listen to all of his speeches – they're wonderful. Manly, firm, resonant!' She gestures enthusiastically with her arm so you see her voluminous bosom. 'No,' I say alarmed, 'I . . . don't think I'll be home tonight.' But I *am* home because Nina has a visit from her forester, so I don't have anywhere to go. I sit and freeze even though I have my coat on, and I can't concentrate on writing because Hitler's speech roars through the wall as if he were standing right next to me. It's threatening and bellowing and it makes me very afraid. He's talking about Austria, and I button my coat at the neck and curl up my toes in my shoes.

16

'Can you dance the carioca?' I look up from my shorthand and say no. I look at the secretary who I'm taking shorthand for; he's really handsome, but he doesn't take his work seriously. He sits lazily leaning back in the chair, now and then taking a gulp of the beer at his side. He yawns noisily without holding his hand in front of his mouth. 'Well,' he says tiredly, 'where were we?' We're sitting in a large room on the top floor. Here there are lots of desks with many secretaries. Whenever they need a typist, they phone down to our office and the supervisor sends one of us up. I like this work, but the secretaries bring me to despair. They would rather talk, and in the meantime the case lies in a blue folder on which it says *'urgent!'* in red letters. There are applications for all kinds of things, and with each application there's a compelling letter implying that refusal of the enclosed will lead to suicide. Every single applicant writes about pressing, strictly personal reasons why *he* should be allowed to import his goods. I can dance the carioca just fine, but this is company time and I'm getting a high salary now, more than I've ever gotten before. 'Stop frowning,' says the secretary smiling, 'the wrinkles will end up being permanent.' I run down all the stairs and into the office to type up the letter. It's a rejection, and I try to make the tone of the letter kinder and less businesslike, just like I changed the letters to the brothers, but it isn't allowed here. I have to type it all over again and am requested to hold myself to the shorthand. There are about twenty of us young girls in the office, which looks like a schoolroom. There's a girl at every desk, and the desks are in three long rows. Farthest forward sits the supervisor, facing us like a teacher, and when the noise gets too intense, she hushes us sternly. All the other girls are very chic, with tight dresses, high heels, and a lot of make-up on their faces. One day one of them decides to make up my lips, my cheeks, and my eyes, and they all think I look much better that way. They say that I should wear make-up every day, and I start to borrow Nina's cosmetics when we go out in the evening. After I've typed up all of my poems, I can't stand sitting in my room with my teeth chattering from the cold. So I continue my nightlife with Nina, and even though it's rather monotonous, the days and nights fly by during this time, like a drumroll just before something's about to happen on stage. The terrible years at I. P. Jensen have passed; I'm eighteen; I've broken away from my family. One evening in the Heidelberg, I dance with a tall, blond young man who isn't like any of the usual young men and doesn't talk like them, either. He asks if he can treat me to a sandwich. I say that I'm with my girlfriend. He says that doesn't matter – then all three of us can have a sandwich. Nina looks at him approvingly and a little astonished when he introduces himself. His name is Albert and he's better dressed than the others. Maybe he's even a university student. We have sandwiches and beer, and I fumble with my knife and fork and watch to see how the others use the utensils. At home we cut up the food with the knife and then eat it with the fork. Albert asks me where I live and what I do. He asks me how much I earn and whether I can live on that. It's nothing special, but the other young men have never talked about anything but themselves. I have a tremendous desire to tell Albert everything about myself and my life. 'Maybe,' I say, 'I'll soon be able to earn more. I write poems, you see.' I don't like to say it, and especially not here, where there's so much noise, laughter, and music. But I don't feel that I can wait any longer and I don't know whether I'll ever see Albert again. 'Oh,' he says surprised, 'I didn't expect that. Are they good?' He smiles at me from the side, as if he's privately amused at me. That annoys me and I can feel that I'm blushing. 'Yes,' I say, 'some of them are.' 'Can you remember one of them by heart?' he says, munching. 'Yes, I can,' I say, 'but I don't want to say it here.' 'Then write it down,' he says calmly, pushing a napkin over to me. He takes a pencil out of his pocket and hands it to me. Which verse should I write? Which is the best of all? I feel that it's enormously important what I write, and after chewing on the pencil for a while, I write:

> I never heard your little voice.
> Your pale lips never smiled at me.
> And the kick of your tiny feet
> is something I will never see.

He looks thoughtfully at the verse for a long time and asks me what the poem is about. 'A child,' I say, 'stillborn.' He asks whether I've ever had a stillborn child, and I say no. 'I'll be damned,' he says then, regarding me with great curiosity. Nina is dancing with a young man and she winks at me encouragingly as they dance past the table. She thinks that I should make something of the situation, and I will too, in my own way. Albert follows my glance. 'Your girlfriend,' he says, 'is very pretty.' 'Yes,' I say, thinking that he wished it were her he had chosen and not me. But I don't care about that side of the matter now. 'Do you know,' I say stubbornly, 'where you can send a poem like this to be published?' 'Oh, sure,' he says, as if I'd asked about something perfectly ordinary. 'Do you know a journal called *Wild Wheat*? I don't, and he tells me that it's where young, unknown people can get their poems and drawings published. It's edited by a man named Viggo F. Møller, and he writes the name and address down on another napkin. 'I was out to see him recently,' he says so casually that it's clear that he's proud of it. 'He's very nice and he has a great understanding of young art.' I ask cautiously if he writes himself, and he says just as casually that in his spare time he has committed some verses to paper and a number of them have already been published in *Wild Wheat*. The news makes me totally speechless. I'm sitting next to a poet. It was more than I've ever dreamed of. I'm still silent when Nina returns. She lifts her fine eyebrows and thinks that Albert and I haven't gotten any further. 'In Heidelberg I lost my heart to the magic of a pair of eyes . . .' Everyone stands up and sings, as they swing the full beer steins back and forth. Albert has stood up too, and all of a sudden his posture expresses a certain impatience. I follow the direction of his glance and see, on the other side of the dance floor, a slight young girl, who's sitting alone and is very serious. When the music starts, Albert pays the bill, bows a little awkwardly to both of us, and asks the serious girl to dance. 'It was your own fault,' says Nina annoyed. 'He was really cute.' But actually I don't care. I've gotten hold of a corner of the world that I long for and I don't intend to let that corner go. I put the napkin in my purse and smile mysteriously at my girlfriend. 'I'm going home to type,' I say. 'If only the witch doesn't wake up.' 'You've gone from the frying pan into the fire,' Nina says. 'She's not a bit better than your mother.' I work my way to the cloakroom and get hold of my coat. I walk the whole way home even though it's bitter frost, and I feel very happy. A name and an address – how many years it can take to get that far. And maybe that's not even enough. Maybe this man won't want my poems. Maybe he'll die before they reach him. Maybe he's already dead. I should have asked Albert how old Viggo F. Møller is. I turn the name over and over and wonder what the 'F' stands for. Frants? Frederik? Finn? What if my letter never arrives because the postal service loses it? What if Albert has given me a totally wrong name and was putting one over on me? Some people think that kind of thing is so funny. Yet – deep inside I believe that this will work out. It's two in the morning when I tiptoe into my room. I fold the sofa blanket over several times and put it under the typewriter to dull the sound of it, and then I choose three poems that I send with a short, formal letter, so that the man won't think it's very important to me. 'Editor Viggo F. Møller,' I write, 'I am enclosing three poems in the hope that you will publish them in your journal, *Wild Wheat*. Respectfully and sincerely yours, T. D.' I run out to the nearest mailbox with the letter and look to see when it will be picked up. I want to figure out when the editor will get it and when he'll be able to answer it. Then I go home to bed, after first setting the alarm clock. I put all of my clothes on top of the comforter, but I still lie shaking from the cold for a long time before I fall asleep.

17

Every evening I rush home from the office and ask Mrs Suhr if there's a letter for me. There isn't, and Mrs Suhr is very curious. She asks if someone in my family is sick. She asks if I'm waiting for money in the mail, and reminds me of the five kroner that I owe her for the ruined chair. Once in a while she also asks me if I'm hungry, but I never am, even though I seldom eat dinner. Sometimes I eat at *Berlingske Tidende's* canteen with Nina. It's cheap, but it's only for employees. My landlady also says that I'm getting thinner and thinner and if I were her daughter she'd fatten me up all right. When I notice the smell from the dinner that she's cooking, I get hungry after all, but then, of course, it's too late. Usually I drink a cup of coffee at Østerport station before going home, and I eat a piece of pastry with it. But that's a luxury that I really can't afford because I'm on a very strict budget. So are all of the girls in the office, even though most of them live at home. Toward the end of the month, they all borrow from each other, and they'd borrow from me too if I had anything to lend them. They're not hurt if you refuse. Their poverty isn't oppressive or sad because they all have something to look forward to; they all dream of a better life. I do too. Poverty is temporary and bearable. It's not any real problem. Nina has her mother to borrow from and she has The Shrub. Nina's mother is a fat and friendly woman who doesn't take anything too much to heart. She makes a living cleaning for people and she lives with a man who is the father of Nina's twelve- or thirteen-year-old half brother. You can tell immediately that Nina didn't grow up in that home but is only visiting. She's also only visiting in Copenhagen, and it's incomprehensible to me that she really wants to live in the country. While I'm waiting for the letter, I don't go out in the evening, but sit freezing in my room, listening for sounds from the hallway. I know that express letters can be delivered outside of the normal delivery times. There's no reason whatsoever why I should receive an express letter, but I listen for the doorbell just the same. One evening there's a political meeting at Mrs Suhr's, and a bunch of boot-clad men swarm into the living room where there is soon a terrible uproar. In the living room they click their heels together and shout 'Heil!' at the picture of Hitler. There are also a number of women present. Their voices are shrill like Mrs Suhr's, and as usual I hope that none of them will catch sight of me. They sing the Horst Wessel song and stamp on the floor so that the wall shakes from it. Mrs Suhr comes into my room, her cheeks red and her hair sticking out in all directions. She's still wearing her kimono and looks as if she's come running out of a burning house. 'Oh,' she gasps, 'won't you drink a toast to the Führer with us? Come in and say hello to all of these splendid fellows. Join us in fighting for our great cause.' 'No,' I say terrified, 'I have something I have to finish. Overtime work from the office.' I set myself to tapping at the typewriter so that they'll think I'm working, while I think with sorrow and uneasiness about the darkness that is about to descend over the whole world. But I don't forget to keep an ear tuned toward the hallway. Express letter, telegram – you never know . . . Several days later Mrs Suhr is standing in the hallway with a letter in her hand when I let myself in. 'Well,' she says with sensation-hungry eyes, 'here's that letter you've been waiting for.' I grab it out of her hand and want to go into my room but she blocks the way. 'Open it now,' she says breathlessly, 'I'm just as excited as you are.' 'No,' I say with a pounding heart, 'it's strictly private, confidential. It's a secret message, I must tell you.' 'Oh God!' she puts her hand to her heart and whispers, 'Something political?' 'Yes,' I say desperately, 'something political. Let me get by.' She looks at me as if I were a modern-day Mata Hari and finally backs away, deeply impressed. At last I'm alone with my letter. It's much too thick, and I grow weak in the knees with fear that the editor is sending it all back. I sit down by the window and look down at the little courtyard. The dusk wraps itself around the trash cans and the lights are being turned on in the building opposite. I open the envelope with an effort, take the letter out, and read, 'Dear Tove Ditlevsen: Two of your poems are, to put it mildly, not good, but the third, "To My Dead Child", I can use. Sincerely, Viggo F. Møller.' I immediately tear up the two poems that, to put it mildly, are not good, and then read the letter once again. He wants to publish my poem in his journal. He is the person that I've waited for all my life. I have a copy of *Wild Wheat* that I bought with money I borrowed from Nina. In it there's a poem by a woman – Hulda Lütken – and I've read it many times because I can't forget that my father once said that a girl can't be a poet. Even though I didn't believe him, his words made a deep impression on me. I have to share my joy with someone.

I don't feel like talking about it at home, and Nina wouldn't understand what it means to me. The only one who might is Edvin. He was the first to say that my poems were good, after he made fun of them. But that doesn't matter; we were only children then. I take the streetcar out to Sydhavnen. Grete opens the door and smiles, surprised at seeing me. 'Come in,' she says hospitably, and then runs in and sits down on Edvin's lap, which apparently is her main occupation as a newlywed. I think he looks completely defenseless in the deep armchair. 'Hi,' he says happily, 'how are you?' He has to move Grete's head in order to look at me. 'How are Mummy and Daddy?' asks Grete between two kisses. My mother can't stand this affectionate form of address, but Grete is completely insensitive to the coldness my mother exudes. I don't care much for Grete either, because I had always imagined that Edvin would have a beautiful, proud, and intelligent wife and not a little, smiling housewife of the Rubenesque type. But that doesn't really matter because my feelings aren't nearly as strong or as passionate as my mother's. I tell Edvin what has happened and show him the letter. He asks Grete to make coffee while he reads it. 'Wow,' he says impressed, 'you should get paid for this. He doesn't write a damn word about that. Be careful he doesn't cheat you.' I haven't thought about that at all, not for a moment. 'He earns money selling the journal, you know,' explains Edvin, 'so he shouldn't have unpaid contributors.' 'No,' I say. Not even Edvin understands what a miracle has occurred – no one understands it. 'Now listen here,' he says. 'You call him up and ask him what you're going to get for it.' 'Yes,' I say because I would like to call him up. I would like to hear his voice, and this is an excellent excuse. Grete sets the table and chatters on about nothing, and Edvin tells her about the letter. 'Oh,' she says happily, 'then I'm related to a poet. I'll write that to my parents. Would you like a couple of slices of bread?' 'Yes, thank you,' I say and ask how Edvin's cough is. The doctor said that he'll cough as long as he is spraying cellulose lacquer. He'll cough until he finds some other occupation. The doctor also says that it sounds worse than it is. He won't die from it, not even get really sick. His lungs are just black and irritated. While we drink coffee, I look at my brother. He doesn't seem happy, and maybe marriage isn't what he had expected. Maybe he had imagined a wife that he could talk to about something other than love and the evening meal. Maybe he had imagined that they could do something else in the evening other than sit on each other's lap and declare how much they love each other. I think, at any rate, that it must be just terribly boring. 'Don't you need a new dress soon?' says Grete. 'I've never seen you in anything except that cossack dress. You should get a permanent,' she says, 'like mine.' Grete's hair sits on top of her head in lots of little curls, and she wears big hoop earrings that clink when she shakes her head. 'Isn't it strange to have such a handsome brother?' she says. 'I think it must be very strange for you.' Edvin gets tired of her conversation and quickly sits down in the armchair again. After the cups are carried out, Grete settles herself on his lap once more and twists his black curls in her fingers. I think my brother has married her in order to escape sitting in his rented room with the stern landlady, because what other way out did he have? I don't intend to live at Mrs Suhr's for the rest of my life either. Being young is itself temporary, fragile, and ephemeral. You have to get through it – it has no other meaning. Edvin asks me whether I've told them the news at home, and I say that I want to wait until the poem appears in the journal. Then I'll show it to them, not before. Edvin reads the poem and is deeply impressed. 'But you're still full of lies,' he says with wonder in his voice. 'You've never had any dead child.' He says that Thorvald has gotten engaged to a very ugly girl, and it annoys me a little. I could have had him but I didn't want him. Still, I liked it that he wasn't attached to anyone else. Before I leave, I borrow ten øre from my brother to make a call. I have to let myself out because Grete is in the middle of a long whispering in Edvin's ear. In the telephone booth on Enghavevej, I look up Viggo F. Møller's number and ask for it with my heart in my throat from excitement. 'Hello,' I say, 'you are speaking with Tove Ditlevsen.' He repeats my name inquiringly and then he remembers it. 'Your poem will come out in a month,' he says. 'It's excellent.' 'Will I get any money for it?' I ask, very embarrassed. But he doesn't get angry. He just explains to me that no one gets an honorarium because the journal runs on a deficit, which he pays for out of his own pocket. I hurry to assure him that it doesn't matter, it was just something my brother said. Then he asks me how old I am. 'Eighteen,' I say. 'Good God – not more?' he says with a little laugh. Then he asks me whether I would like to meet him and I say that I would. He'll meet me the day after tomorrow, six o'clock, in the Glyptotek café, so we can eat dinner together. I thank him, overwhelmed, and then he says goodbye. I'm going to meet him. I'm going to talk to him. He undoubtedly wants to do something for me. Mr Krogh said that people always wanted to use each other for something, and that there was nothing wrong with that. It's quite clear what I want to use the editor for, but what does he want to use me for? Next evening I go home anyway and tell everything. My mother is home alone. She's very happy to see me, and I have a guilty conscience because I come over so seldom. My mother has grown very lonely since Aunt Rosalia's death.

The building is just 'fine' enough that you don't simply go running over to visit other people, and my mother doesn't have a single girlfriend she can talk to and laugh with. She only has us, and we deserted her as soon as she and the law would permit it. We drink coffee together and I can see that her imagination is hard at work. 'You know what,' she says, 'that editor – he probably wants to marry you.' I laugh and say that she never thinks of anything except getting me married. I laugh, but when I get home and into bed, I think about whether he's married or not. If he's single, I have nothing against marrying him. Entirely sight unseen.

18

He has on a green suit and green tie. He has thick, curly gray hair and a gray mustache, the ends of which he often twists between his fingers. He has an old-fashioned wing collar, and his double chin hangs over it a bit. His eyes are bright blue like little babies' eyes, and his complexion is pink and white and transparent like a child's. He makes wide, sweeping movements with his small, fine hands that have dimples at the knuckles. He is warm and friendly, and I quickly forget my shyness in his company. He doesn't resemble Mr Krogh in appearance and yet he reminds me of him a little. He studies the menu for a long time before he chooses what to have and, without knowing what it is, I ask for the same. He says that he's very fond of food, and that you can probably tell by looking at him. I say politely no. I admit that I never notice what I'm eating and he says, laughingly, that you can certainly tell by looking at me. I'm much too thin, he says. We drink red wine with our meal and I make a face because it's sour. He says that's because I'm so young. When I get older, I'll learn to appreciate good wine. He asks me to tell him a little about myself, about how I found my way to him. I'm nervous and light-hearted and want to tell everything at once. I also mention Albert, and he shrugs his shoulders as if he's no one in particular. 'You never can tell with young people,' he says, twisting his mustache. 'You believe in some of them, and then they don't amount to anything. Others you don't believe in, and it turns out that they're good after all.' I ask him whether he thinks I'm any good, and he says that you can't tell. He says that those who don't amount to much are those young men who come with a poem and say, 'I wrote this in ten minutes.' If they say that, he knows that they're not any good. 'And what then?' I ask. 'Then I advise them to be streetcar conductors or something else sensible,' he says, wiping his mouth with his napkin. I'm glad that I didn't write anything about how many minutes it took me to write 'To My Dead Child'. I don't even know myself. I think the editor is a magnificent man and I think he's handsome. Maybe others don't think he's handsome, and Nina would think that he's too old and fat, but I don't care. He gives me the menu so that I can order dessert, and I ask for ice cream because everything else looks much too complicated. The editor wants fruit with whipped cream. 'I have a sweet tooth,' he says, 'because I don't smoke.' The waiter treats him very respectfully and calls him 'the Editor' the whole time. He calls me 'the young lady'. 'May I pour for the young lady?' I bravely drink the sour wine and grow warm and relaxed from it. It's getting to be dusk outside and the wind is blowing softly in the trees on the boulevard. They're already in blossom, and soon Tivoli will open. Viggo F. Møller says that he loves spring and summer in the city. The trees and the flowers bloom, and the young girls blossom too, like beautiful flowers out of the cobblestones. Mr Krogh said something similar, and he wasn't married. That's probably something that married men have no sense for at all. Finally I have the courage to ask him if he's married, and he says no with a little laugh. 'No one,' he says gesturing with his hand apologetically, 'has ever wanted to have me.' 'I was formally engaged once,' I say, 'but then he broke it off.' 'And now?' he asks. 'Aren't you engaged now?' 'No,' I say, 'I'm waiting for the right one to come along.' I try to look him deep in the eyes, but he doesn't see the meaning behind it. It's just that I've gotten used to the fact that everything is urgent, and I almost expect that he'll propose to me right then and there. You never know where a person will be tomorrow. He could get a letter from another young girl who writes poems – Hulda Lütken, for example – invite her out, and forget me completely. He must be the kind of man who can have whomever he chooses. With growing jealousy I ask how Hulda Lütken is, and he laughs loudly at the thought of her. 'She wouldn't like you,' he says. 'She's insanely jealous of other women poets, especially if they're younger than her. She's temperamental enough for ten. Once in a while she calls me and says, "Møller, am I a genius?" "Yes, yes," I say, "yes, you are, Hulda." Then she's satisfied for a while.' Then he asks me if I'd like to come to a *Wild Wheat* party next month. It's a party where the 'Top Wheat' and the 'Top Rusk' are chosen. Those are the poet and the illustrator who, during the year, have had the most contributions in the journal. I ask what I should wear, and he says a long dress. When he hears that I don't have one, he says that I can borrow one from a girlfriend. That makes me think of Nina, who got herself a long, backless dress for the dance at Stjernekroen. I say that I would love to go to that party. We have coffee in very thin cups and the editor looks at his watch, as if it's time to go. I would have liked to sit there for a lot longer. Outside, my daily life is waiting for me with its urgent matters at the office, the evenings at the taverns, the young men who accompany me home, and my cold room with the Nazi landlady. My only consolation in this existence is a handful of poems, of which there are still not enough for a collection. And I don't know, either, how to go about publishing a poetry collection. When the bill is paid, Mr Møller suddenly places his hand over mine on the colorful tablecloth. 'You have beautiful hands,' he says, 'long and slender.' He pats my hand a couple of times, as if he knows very well that I'm sorry to leave and wants to assure me that he won't disappear from my life right away. I notice that I'm about to cry, and don't know why. I feel like putting my arms around his neck, as if I'm very tired after a long, long trip and now have finally found home. It's a crazy feeling and I blink my eyes a little to hide that they've grown moist. Outside we stand together for a while and look at the traffic. He's shorter than me, and that surprises me because you couldn't tell when he was sitting down. 'Well,' he says, 'I guess we're going different ways. Stop by some day. You know the address.' He swings his green, wide-brimmed hat in an elegant arc, puts it on his head, and walks quickly down the boulevard. I stand there and watch him for as long as my eyes can follow him. I think that I'm always having to say goodbye to men – staring at their backs and hearing their steps disappear in the darkness. And they seldom turn around to wave at me.

19

I've been moved over to the State Grain Office on the other side of the street, and I like it much better. There are just the two of us women in the office. I take care of the switchboard and I write letters for the office manager, Mr Hjelm. He's a tall, gaunt man with a long, grim face that is never softened by anything resembling a smile. Whenever there's a pause in the dictation, he stares at me as if he suspects that I have something other than grain in my head. The other girl is named Kate. She's quick to laugh and childish and we have a lot of fun together when we're alone. I'm waiting for my poem to be published in the journal, because then I'll visit Viggo F. Møller – not before. I'm going to have summer vacation soon, and that's always been a problem for me. Nina wants us to join the Danish Youth Hostel group and go hiking in the country and stay at youth hostels. But I don't like people in groups and I'm not interested in it. But if my poem comes out soon, maybe I can stay with the editor during my vacation. While I wait, I still look at the little children and the lovers who are driven out of the buildings by the heat. I look at the dogs too, the dogs and their masters.

Some of the dogs have a short leash that's jerked impatiently every time they stop. Others have a long leash and their masters wait patiently whenever an exciting smell detains the dog. That's the kind of master I want. That's the kind of life I could thrive in. There are also the masterless dogs that run around confused between people's legs, apparently without enjoying their freedom. I'm like that kind of masterless dog – scruffy, confused, and alone. I go out in the evening less often than before, and Nina says I'm getting to be downright boring. I stay in my room now that the cold doesn't chase me out anymore. I read my poems over and over again, and sometimes I write a new one. The two that were, to put it mildly, not good, I've long ago removed from my collection. I think they were hideous, but if the editor had written that they were good, I would have believed him. Sometimes I go home for a visit. My father is unemployed again and there's a cool atmosphere between him and my mother. Usually he's lying on the sofa, sleeping or dozing, and my mother sits knitting with a disapproving look on her face. She thinks it's about time I visit the editor because she's more and more convinced that he wants to marry me. 'Fat people,' she says, 'are happy and good-natured. It's the lean ones that are grumpy.' She asks how old he is, and I say that he's about fifty. That too she thinks is fine because then he's sown his wild oats and will make a faithful husband. She says that soon I can probably quit my job and be provided for. I say nothing because all of this has to wait. 'We'll hold the wedding,' says my mother, and I think about what my editor will say about his mother-in-law. He's older than she is, I'm pretty sure; but that doesn't bother my mother. I always leave soon because now my mother is demanding something of me. My father says that there's no rush and that it's up to me whom I want to marry. 'You've never cared much about it,' says my mother, 'but now you can see what's happened to Edvin. That's what you get for your indifference.' Then the battle has turned away from me and I have no qualms about leaving them. One day when I come home from my parents', I find a written eviction notice from Mrs Suhr. 'Since it has become known to me,' she writes, to my astonishment, 'that you have participated in conspiratorial activities, I no longer wish to live under the same roof with you.' I remember the political letter that I received and my unwillingness to take part in her Nazi meetings. Then I find another room on Amager, not far from the editor's residence, and ride out there with my suitcase and my alarm clock in my hand. It's with a family that has grown children. A daughter has gotten married and it's her room that I move into. It's nicer and bigger than the other one and only ten kroner more. And on top of that, there's a stove. I immediately call Viggo F. Møller to tell him my new address, and he says it's good that I called because the journal has come out and he was just about to send it to me. He says it as if it were quite an everyday thing, as if I'd had dozens of poems published and this was just one of them. He says it in a friendly, ordinary tone, as if journals and books with my works were flooding the world so that it didn't matter so much whether such a trivial thing as a single poem got lost. But he is, of course, used to being around people like Hulda Lütken, people he's on a first-name basis with. Every time I think of her, I feel a stab of jealousy in my heart. I wonder whether Viggo F. Møller will ever tell peculiar things about me to other people? Will he say, 'Tove called recently, by the way, and said such and such. Ha, ha.' And twist his mustache and smile. The next day two copies of *Wild Wheat* arrive in the mail and my poem is in both of them. I read it many times and get an apprehensive feeling in my stomach. It looks completely different in print than typewritten or in longhand. I can't correct it anymore and it's no longer mine alone. It's in many hundreds or thousands of copies of the journal, and strange people will read it and may think that it's good. It's spread out over the whole country, and people I meet on the street may have read it. They may be walking about with a copy of the journal in their inside pocket or purse. If I ride in the streetcar, there may be a man sitting across from me reading it. It's completely overwhelming and there's not a person I can share this wonderful experience with. I rush home to show it to my father and mother. 'I think it's good,' says my mother, 'but you should have a pen name. The one you have isn't good. You should take my maiden name. Tove Mundus – that sounds much better.' 'Her name is good enough,' says my father, 'but the poem is much too modern. It doesn't rhyme in the right way. You could learn a lot from Johannes Jørgensen.' I'm not offended by my father's criticism because he has always wanted to protect us from disappointments. According to his experience, you should never expect anything from life, then you'll avoid disappointments. Still, he asks to be allowed to keep the journal, and he holds it in the same careful way as he does his books. On the way home, I go into a bookstore and ask for the latest edition of *Wild Wheat*. They don't have it but they can order one. 'We don't sell any of them as single copies,' the man explains to me, 'it's mostly by subscription.' 'That's too bad,' I say, 'you see, I've heard there's an excellent poem in it.' He takes down my name so I can get it in a couple of days. 'It's a very little journal, you know,' he explains talkatively. 'I think there are only five hundred copies printed. Strange that it can make a go of it.' Insulted, I go out of the store again. But I'm not the same as before. My name is in print. I'm not anonymous any longer. And soon I'll visit my editor, even though he didn't repeat his invitation on the phone. He has, of course, many other things to occupy him besides talking to young poets. A week after the journal came out, I'm called into Mr Hjelm's office. His long face is, if possible, even crabbier than usual and on the desk in front of him is *Wild Wheat* open to the page where my poem is. The thought flashes through my mind that he's going to praise me for it. 'I bought this journal,' he says, 'because I thought that it had something to do with grain. And then I see' – he strikes my poem with a ruler – 'that you apparently have other interests than the State Grain Office. I'm sorry, but unfortunately we can't use you here any longer.' He looks at me with his fish eyes and I don't know what to say. I feel bad because I was happy here, but there's also something comical about it that will make Kate and Nina laugh when I tell them. 'Yes,' I say, 'there's nothing to be done about it.' I edge my way out of the office and go in and tell Kate about being fired. She laughs that Mr Hjelm thought *Wild Wheat* was an agricultural journal, and I laugh too, but I'm still a girl who has lost her job and will now have the trouble of finding a new one. Kate says that I should report to the union and have them find a new position for me, and I think that's a good idea. The same evening I call Viggo F. Møller and he says that he would be happy to see me the following evening. Then it doesn't matter so much that I've been thrown out of the grain office. Maybe the editor can find a solution that is better than Kate's. I have so many expenses now that I can't allow myself to be unemployed.

20

'Wouldn't you like,' says Viggo F. Møller, 'to have a collection of poems published?' He says this as if it were nothing special. He says this as if it were quite common for me to publish poetry collections; as if it weren't what I've wished for, most fervently of all, for as long as I can remember. And I say with a thin, ordinary voice that yes, I would rather like that. I've just never thought of it before. But now that he mentions it, it would be great fun. I hope he can't tell how joyfully and excitedly my heart is pounding. It's pounding as if I were in love, and I look closely at this man who has caused such joy in my soul. He's sitting on the other side of the table, which is covered with a bottle-green tablecloth. We're drinking tea from green cups. The curtains are green, the vases and the pots are green, and the editor is wearing a green suit like before. The bookshelves reach almost up to the ceiling and the wall is completely hidden by paintings and drawings. It all reminds me of Mr Krogh's living room, but Viggo F. Møller doesn't remind me much of Mr Krogh. He's much less secretive and I'm welcome to ask him about anything I want to know. The sun is about to go down and there's a soft twilight in the living room that sets an intimate mood. I help my new friend carry the cups out to the kitchen and he asks me if I'd like a glass of wine. I say yes, thank you, and he pours wine into green glasses, lifts his and says, '*Skål.*' Then I ask him how you go about getting a poetry collection published, and he says that you send it to a publisher. Then they take care of the rest, if they accept the poems. It's very simple. I'm to show him all of the poems that I have so he can see if there are enough and if they're good enough. I don't care for the wine, but I like the effect. I'm very taken with the editor's soft, round arm movements, with his silver-gray hair and his voice, which wraps itself soothingly and refreshingly around my soul. I'm already fond of him, but I don't know what his feelings are for me. He doesn't touch me and doesn't try to kiss me. Maybe he thinks that I'm too young for him. I ask him why he's not married and he says gravely that no one wanted him. It's sad, he says, but now he figures that it's too late. He has a smile in his eyes when he says this, and I frown because he doesn't take me seriously. I tell him about my life, about my parents, about Edvin, and about how I've just lost my job because of the poem in *Wild Wheat*. The latter amuses him greatly and he says that it will amuse his friends too, when he tells them about it. His friends are celebrities, and some of them have asked him who the poor young girl is who wrote so beautifully about her dead child. So it's not just my family who thinks everything you write is true. 'Oh,' he says, slapping his forehead, 'I almost forgot. Did you see Valdemar Koppel's review of the journal in *Politiken* recently? He writes very positively about your poem.' He takes out the clipping and shows it to me. It says: 'A single poem, "To My Dead Child", by Tove Ditlevsen is justification enough for the little journal's existence.' 'Oh,' I say overwhelmed, 'how happy that makes me. May I keep it?' He gives it to me and he pours more wine into the green glasses. Then he says, 'It makes a strong impression on a young person to see their name in print for the first time.' 'I'm so glad that I met you,' I say. 'It's as if nothing bad can happen when I'm with you. When I'm here, I don't believe there'll be a world war.' Viggo F. Møller grows suddenly serious. 'It looks very bleak otherwise,' he says. 'I can probably do something or other for you, my dear, but I can't prevent the world war.' It's the wine that makes me say such things. All the grownups withdraw from me whenever they start thinking about the world situation. In comparison, my poems and I are just specks of dust that the smallest puff of wind can blow away. 'No,' I say, 'but you're not going to suddenly die and this building isn't going to be torn down.' I tell him about Editor Brochmann and Mr Krogh. The former he knew, but not the latter. 'No,' he says seriously, 'in that sense you can rely on me. Why don't we use our first names?' We toast our friendship and he turns on the lights in the green-shaded lamps. 'Call me Viggo F.,' he says then. 'Everyone calls me Viggo F. or Møller – no one calls me Viggo except my family.' His parents, he says, are dead, but he has a brother and a sister whom he rarely sees. 'Families,' he says, 'never understand artists. Artists only have each other to rely on.' He asks me if I'd like to sit next to him on the sofa, and I sit down by him. I sit close to him so that our legs are touching each other, but it apparently doesn't make any impression on him. Maybe I'm not pretty enough; maybe I'm not old enough. He tells me that he's fifty-three years old, and I say politely that he doesn't look it. He doesn't either, aside from the fact that he's fat. His skin is pink and white and totally free of wrinkles. I think my father looks much older. But for that matter I don't care a bit about how old people are. Viggo F.'s father was a bank director and his brother is, too. He himself works for a fire insurance company, which he doesn't care for, but you've got to earn a living somehow. He has also written books, and I'm embarrassed that I haven't read them. I haven't even run across his name in the library. My ignorance irritates me and I tell my new friend that I was supposed to go to high school but I wasn't allowed to. We couldn't afford it. Gently he puts his arm around my waist and a hot stream races through me. Is this love? I'm so tired of my long search for this person that I feel like crying with relief, now that I've reached my goal. I'm so tired that I can't return his tender, cautious caresses, but just sit passively and let him stroke my hair and pat my cheeks. 'You're like a child,' he says kindly, 'a child who can't really manage the adult world.' 'I once knew someone,' I say, 'who said that all people want to use each other for something. I want to use you to get my poems published.' 'Yes,' he says, continuing to caress me, 'but I don't have as much influence as you think. If the publishers don't want your poems, I can't do anything. But we'll take a look at them. I can advise you and support you, at any rate.' When I go out to the bathroom, I see that Viggo F. has a shower, and it overwhelms me. I ask him if I can take a shower, and he says yes, laughing. Otherwise I go once in a while to the public baths on Lyrskovgade, but it costs money, of course, so it's never been very often. Now I stand delighted under the shower, twisting and turning, and thinking that if we really get married, I'll take a shower every single day. When I come out of the bathroom, Viggo F. says, 'You have nice legs. Lift up your dress so I can see them properly.' 'No,' I say, blushing, because I have a run in one stocking. 'No, they're only nice from the knees down.' It's gotten to be twelve o'clock and I have to go home to my wretched room. Viggo F. offers to pay for a cab home, but I say that I can certainly walk the short distance. And I add, 'I can't figure out what I'm supposed to give the cabbie as a tip, anyway.' 'Remember to call him "driver", not "cabbie". That sounds too colloquial.' The remark hurts me and I get furious at my whole upbringing, at my ignorance, my language, my complete lack of sophistication and culture, words I hardly understand. He kisses me on the mouth when he says goodbye, and I walk through the mild summer night and recall all of his words and movements. I am not alone anymore.

21

I've been with many celebrities. I've seen them, I've talked to them, I've sat next to them, I've danced with them. As soon as I stepped in the door, I was moving on a completely different plane than usual. I walked in a glaring light and cast the rays of the celebrities back like a mirror. I reflected their images, and they liked what they saw. Flattered, they smiled and gave me many compliments. They even praised my dress, although it is Nina's and it's too big for me. But it hid my shoes, which are old and worn and need to be replaced. The celebrities constantly gathered in clusters around Viggo F.'s green shape, which appeared and disappeared like duckweed on a windy pond. It swelled back and forth before my eyes, and I repeatedly sought it out because it was my protection and my security among all the celebrities. Viggo F. introduced me to them with pride, as if he had invented me. 'My youngest contributor,' he said to the press photographers, smilingly twisting his mustache. I was photographed with him and some of the celebrities, and the picture was in *Aftenbladet* the next day. It wasn't very good, but Viggo F. said that it was important to be friendly toward the press. And I was friendly.

I smiled the whole evening to all of the celebrities who wanted to meet me, and in the end my cheeks hurt. My feet also hurt from dancing, and when I finally left, the whole thing was as unreal as a dream. I couldn't remember who had become the 'Top Wheat' and the 'Top Rusk'. But a young man I danced with said that everyone was chosen eventually. I, too, would someday be the 'Top Wheat', it was just a matter of writing a lot for the journal, regardless of whether it was good. The young man also asked me if I wanted to go to the movies some evening, but I turned him down coldly. I had quite different plans for my future. I've gotten a job as a temporary through the union and now I'm earning ten kroner a day. I've never had so much money in my hands before. I've paid the dentist bill and I've bought a light gray suit with a long jacket because the brown one had gone out of style. I don't spend much time with Nina anymore, because now I'm totally uninterested in meeting a young man who might want to marry me. After Viggo F. looked at my poems and selected some of them, I sent them to Gyldendal Publishing Company and now I'm going around waiting for an answer. 'If they don't want them,' says Viggo F., 'you just send them to another one. There are plenty of publishers.' But I'm certain that they'll want them, since Viggo F. says they're good. He knows the director, who is a woman. Her name is Ingeborg Andersen and she dresses like a man. 'But she's not the one who will decide,' says Viggo F., 'it's the consultants.' They are Paul la Cour and Aase Hansen, and I don't know either of them. I don't know any of the celebrities because I almost never read newspapers and have only read authors long since dead. I've never realized before that I was so dumb and ignorant. Viggo F. says that he'll take care of getting me a little education, and he lends me *The French Revolution* by Carlyle. I find it very exciting, but I would rather start with the present day. One evening when I'm visiting Viggo F., the doorbell rings and I hear a low female voice out in the hallway. Viggo F. comes in with a sparkling, plump, dark little woman who shakes my hand as if she means to tear it off, and says, 'Hulda Lütken. Huh . . . so that's what you look like. You're becoming so celebrated it's almost unbearable.' Then she sits down and speaks the whole time to Viggo F., who finally asks me to leave, because there's something he wants to talk to Hulda about. Later he explains to me – what he has already hinted at – that Hulda Lütken can't stand other female poets. While I'm waiting to hear from Gyldendal, I sometimes go home to visit my parents. My father says that of course it would be fun if I had a poetry collection published, but that you can't make a living as a poet. 'She won't have to, either,' says my mother, eager to fight. 'That Viggo F. Møller – he can support her.' I tell them about the shower and, in her thoughts, my mother also stands under Viggo F.'s shower. I tell them about the wine in the green glasses and, in her thoughts, my mother drinks from them too. They have cut out the picture from *Aftenbladet* and put it in the frame of the sailor's wife. 'It's good,' says my mother. 'You can really see that you've had your teeth fixed.' She says with pride, 'The doctor says that I have high blood pressure. I also have hardening of the arteries and a bad liver.' She's gotten a new doctor because the old one was no good. Whatever you said was wrong with you, he said that he suffered from the same thing. The new doctor agrees with all of my mother's suspicions and she is devoted to him. Since Aunt Rosalia died and both Edvin and I have moved out, she's very absorbed with her health, even though she never gave it a thought before. She's going through the change of life, the doctor said, and the people around her must be considerate of her. That's what she told my father, who never dares lie down on the sofa anymore, which she always has nagged him about. He sits up and reads and sometimes he falls asleep with the book in his hand. I never stay home for very long because I get tired of listening to my mother's alarming symptoms from her inner organs. But I feel sorry for her because she never had very much in this world, and the little she had, she lost. One day when I come home from work, there is a big, yellow envelope lying on the table in my room. My knees grow weak with disappointment because I know what it contains. Then I open it. They have sent my book back with a few apologetic sentences, to the effect that they only publish five poetry collections a year, and they've already chosen them. I take the letter and go over to Viggo F. with it. 'Oh well,' he says, 'it was to be expected. We'll try Reitzel's Publishing Company. Don't let yourself be beaten by something like this. Trust in yourself, otherwise you'll never get anyone else to.' We send the poems to Reitzel's and a month later they're sent back. I think it's starting to get interesting because I know that the poems are good. Viggo F. says that almost every famous writer has been through the mill – yes, there's almost something wrong if it goes too smoothly. Finally the poems have almost made the entire rounds, and it's hard to keep up my courage. Then Viggo F. says that it's a question of money. The publishers make almost nothing on poems; that's why they're reluctant to publish them. But *Wild Wheat* has a fund of five hundred kroner meant for cases like mine. He'll give the money to a publisher to publish the poems. He'll talk to his friend, Rasmus Naver, about the matter. Mr Naver agrees to publish the poems at his company, and I am happy. He comes over to Viggo F.'s to talk to him about it. He's a kind, gray-haired gentleman with a Fyn accent, and I smile at him sweetly the whole time so that nothing about me will make him give up the idea. He says that Arne Ungermann would probably draw the cover without a fee, and he likes the title: *Pigesind*, or 'Girl-Soul'. I like it too. Finally it's worked out and I don't know how to show Viggo F. my gratitude. I kiss him and ruffle his curly hair, but he is so absent-minded lately. It's as if he does want to do something for me, but he has something more important on his mind at the moment. One evening he tells me about the concentration camps in Germany and says that all of Europe will soon be one concentration camp. He also shows me a journal in which he has written an article against Nazism and he says that it will be dangerous for him if the Germans ever come to Denmark. I think about my poetry collection that will come out in October and have a strange feeling that it will never appear if the world war breaks out. 'If they go into Poland,' says Viggo F., 'the English won't stand for it.' I say that they have put up with so much. I tell him about my time at Mrs Suhr's. I tell him that every time I heard Hitler speaking through the wall on Saturday, he invaded some innocent country on Sunday. Viggo F. says that he can't understand why I didn't move out before, and I think that he doesn't know what it is to be poor. But I don't say anything. Arne Ungermann comes over one evening and shows me the cover drawing. It depicts a naked young girl with bowed head, and it's very beautiful. The figure is chaste and devoid of all sensuality. He and Viggo F. talk about the world situation and are very serious. Now I'm almost always at Viggo F. Møller's, and my mother thinks that I might just as well move in with him. 'When,' she says impatiently, 'do you intend to marry him?'

22

Edvin has left his wife. Now he's living at home in my old room behind the cotton curtain, and my mother is happy, even though he's going to move as soon as he can find a room. My mother says that she can understand why he left Grete, because she only had clothes and nonsense in her head and no man can put up with that. But my brother won't allow anyone to put Grete down. He says that the mistake was his. He didn't love her, and that wasn't her fault. That's also why he has let her keep the apartment. She gets to keep the furniture too, and Edvin will continue to make the payments. I like coming home now that my brother is there. We talk about my poetry collection, and Edvin can't understand why you don't get paid for something like that. 'It's a piece of work,' he says, 'and it's despicable that it's not paid for.' We also talk about Edvin's cough and about all of my mother's new illnesses. We talk about my work at a lawyer's office in Shellhuset, where I get to observe many disagreements between people. And we talk a lot about Viggo F. Møller and the world that he has opened for me. I have to tell my family everything about his apartment – how the furniture is arranged, how many rooms there are, and what books are on the bookshelves. I tell my father that Viggo F. writes books himself, and he says that he thinks he's read one of them once, but that it was nothing special. My father also says, 'Isn't he too old for you?' My mother protests and says it's not age that matters, and it never has bothered her that my father is ten years older than she is. She says the most important thing is that he can support me, so I can quit working. They all talk as if he has already proposed to me, and when I say that I don't know if he will have me, they brush the question aside as a minor detail. 'Of course he will have you,' says my mother. 'Why else would he do so much for you?' I think about that and come to the same conclusion. The different thing about me is that I write poetry, but at the same time there's a lot that is ordinary about me. Like all other young girls, I want to get married and have children and a home of my own. There's something painful and fragile about being a young girl who makes her own living. You can't see any light ahead on that road. And I want so badly to own my own time instead of always having to sell it. My mother asks me what Viggo F. makes at the fire insurance company, and she thinks it's strange that I have no idea. 'He's just a white-collar worker,' says my father, full of contrariness, invoking an indignant stream of words from both my mother and Edvin. 'If I were a white-collar worker,' says Edvin angrily, 'I would never have gotten this damned cough.' 'At any rate there's no risk,' my mother seconds him, 'of him being unemployed at any minute and loafing around with a book while decent people go to work. Feel my neck,' she says to me suddenly. 'It's as if there's a knot right here. I'll have to show it to the doctor. We'll hire a cook for the wedding – he's of course used to the best. Soup, roast, and dessert – I remember well how it was at the places where I worked. Couldn't you invite him home some day?' I don't know why I don't do that. My family is mine. I know them and am used to them. I don't like having them displayed to someone from a higher social class. Viggo F. has even asked me if he could meet my parents. He says he would like to meet the people who have produced such an odd creature as me. But I think that can wait until we get married. My father and Edvin also talk about the imminent world war. Then my mother gets bored and I lose my good humor. Suddenly it's a fact. England has declared war on Germany, and I stand with thousands of other silent people and follow the reader-board headlines flashing on *Politiken's* building. I stand next to my brother and my father and I don't know where Viggo F. is at this fateful hour. When we go home, I have a painful, sinking feeling in my stomach, as if I were very hungry. Will my poetry collection come out now? Will daily life continue at all? Will Viggo F. marry me when the whole world is burning? Will Hitler's evil shadow fall over Denmark? I don't go home with them but take a streetcar out to my friend's. There are a lot of celebrities at his house, and he doesn't seem to notice me. They're drinking wine from the green glasses and talking very seriously about the situation. Ungermann asks me what I think of his drawing, and I thank him for it. So the book will probably come out after all. I go home without really having talked to Viggo F., and at night I dream uneasily about the world war and *Pigesind*, as if there really were a fateful connection between them. But already the next day it's clear that daily life will go on as if nothing had happened. At the office the divorce cases, property line disputes, and other heated disagreements between people pile up. Excited people stand at the counter asking for the attorney, who is seldom there, and I have to listen to them present their special, terribly important case, and no one seems to remember that a world war broke out yesterday. My landlady tells me that pork has gone up fifty øre per kilo, and Nina comes over to confide in me that she's met a wonderful young man, and she's thinking of dropping The Shrub again. Nothing at all has changed, and when I go over to Viggo F.'s, he is again in a good mood, radiating calm and coziness in great, warm waves. 'In three weeks,' he says, 'your book will come out. Soon you'll have to read the proofs, but you shouldn't let it get you down. Reading the proofs, you never think it's good enough. It's like that for everyone.' Viggo F. isn't the least bit interested in ordinary people. He only likes artists and only spends time with artists. Everything about me that is quite ordinary, I try to hide from him. I hide from him that I like the new dress that I've bought. I hide the fact that I use lipstick and rouge and that I like to look at myself in the mirror and turn my neck around almost out of joint in order to see what I look like in profile. I hide everything that could make him have misgivings about marrying me. He's right about the proofs. When they arrive, I don't care for my poems at all anymore, and I find many words and expressions that could be better. But I don't correct very much because Viggo F. says that then the printing will be too expensive. In the days before the book comes out, I stay home in my room all the time that I'm not in the office. I want to be there when my book is delivered. One evening when I come home, there's a big package lying on my table, and I tear it open with shaking hands. My book! I take it in my hands and feel a solemn happiness, that isn't like anything I've ever felt before. Tove Ditlevsen. *Pigesind*. It can't be taken back anymore. It is irretrievable. The book will always exist, regardless of how my fate takes shape. I open one of the books and read some lines. They are strangely distant and foreign, now that I see them in print. I open another book because I can't really believe that it says the same thing in all of them. But it does. Maybe my book will be in the libraries. Maybe a child, who in all secrecy is fond of poetry, will someday find it there, read the poems, and feel something from them, something that the people around her don't understand. And that odd child doesn't know me at all. She won't think that I'm a living young girl who works, eats, and sleeps like other people. Because I myself never thought about that when I read books as a child. I seldom remembered the names of those who wrote them. My book will be in the libraries and maybe it will be in the windows of bookstores. Five hundred copies of it have been printed, and I've been given ten. Four hundred and ninety people will buy it and read it. Maybe their families will read it too, and maybe they'll lend it out like Mr Krogh lent out his books. I will wait to show the book to Viggo F. until tomorrow. Tonight I want to be alone with it, because there's no one who really understands what a miracle it is for me.

Dependency

PART ONE

I

Everything in the living room is green – the carpet, the walls, the curtains – and I am always inside it, like in a picture. I wake up every morning around five o'clock and sit down on the edge of the bed to write, curling my toes because of the cold. It's the middle of May, and the heating is off. I sleep by myself in the living room, because Viggo F. has lived alone for so many years that he can't get used to suddenly sleeping with another person. I understand, and it's fine with me, because now I have these early morning hours all to myself. I'm writing my first novel, and Viggo F. doesn't know. Somehow I think that if he knew, he would correct it and give me advice, like he does all the other young people who write in *Wild Wheat*, and then that would block the flow of sentences coursing through my brain all day long. I write by hand on cheap yellow vellum, because if I used his noisy typewriter, which is so old it belongs in the National Museum, it would wake him up. He sleeps in the bedroom looking out on the courtyard, and I don't wake him until eight o'clock. Then he gets up in his white nightshirt with the red trim, and with an annoyed look on his face, he walks out to the bathroom.

Meanwhile I make coffee for both of us and butter four pieces of bread. I put a lot of butter on two of them, because he loves anything fattening. I do whatever I can to please him, because I'm so thankful he married me. Although I know something still isn't quite right, I carefully avoid thinking about that. For some incomprehensible reason, Viggo F. has never taken me in his arms, and that does bother me a little, as if I had a stone in my shoe. It bothers me a little because I think there must be something wrong with me, and that in some way I haven't lived up to his expectations. When we sit across from one another, drinking coffee, he reads the newspaper, and I'm not allowed to talk to him. That's when my courage drains away like sand in an hourglass; I don't know why. I stare at his double chin, vibrating weakly, spilling out over the edge of his wing-tip collar. I stare at his small, dainty hands, moving in short, nervous jerks, and at his thick, gray hair which resembles a wig, because his ruddy, wrinkle-free face would better suit a bald man. When we finally do talk to one another, it's about small, meaningless things – what he wants for dinner, or how we should fix the tear in the blackout curtains. I feel glad if he finds something cheerful in the newspaper, like the day when it said people could buy alcohol again, after the occupying forces had forbidden that for a week. I feel glad when he smiles at me with his single tooth, pats my hand, says goodbye and leaves. He doesn't want false teeth, because he says that in his family men die at fifty-six, and that's only three years away, so he doesn't want the expense. There's no hiding the fact that he's stingy, and that doesn't really match the high value my mother put on being able to provide. He's never given me a piece of clothing, and when we go out in the evening to visit some famous person, he takes the streetcar, while I have to ride my bicycle alongside it, speeding along so I can wave to him when he wants. I have to keep a household budget, and when he looks at it, he always thinks everything is too expensive. When I can't get it to add up, I write 'miscellaneous', but he always makes a fuss about that, so I try not to miss any expenses. He also makes a fuss about having a housekeeper in the mornings, since I'm home anyway, doing nothing. But I can't and won't keep house, so he has no choice. I feel glad when I see him cut across the green lawn toward the streetcar, which stops right in front of the police station. I wave to him, and when I turn away from the window, I completely forget about him until he shows up again. I take a shower, look in the mirror, and think to myself that I am only twenty years old, and that it feels like I have been married for a generation. It feels like life beyond these green rooms is rushing by for other people as if to the sound of kettledrums and tom-toms. Meanwhile I am only twenty years old, and the days descend on me unnoticeably like dust, each one just like the rest.

After I get dressed, I talk with Mrs Jensen about lunch and I make a list of what needs to be purchased. Mrs Jensen is taciturn, introverted and a bit insulted that she's not alone in the house anymore, like she used to be. What nonsense, she mumbles, that a man of his age would marry such a young girl. She doesn't say it so loud that I have to answer, and I can't be bothered to listen to what she says. I'm thinking about my novel all the time, which I know the title of, though I'm not completely sure what it will be about. I'm just writing; maybe it will be good; maybe not. The most important thing is that I feel happy when I'm writing, just as I always have. I feel happy and I forget everything around me, until I pick up my brown shoulder-bag and go shopping. Then I'm gripped again by the morning's vague gloom, because all I see in the streets are loving couples walking hand in hand and looking deep into one another's eyes. I almost can't bear the sight of it. I realize I've never been in love, except for a brief episode two years before, when I walked home from the Olympia Bar with Kurt, who was going to be leaving the following day for Spain to take part in the civil war. He might be dead now, or maybe he came back and found himself another girl. Maybe I didn't really have to marry Viggo F. to make it in the world. Maybe I only did it because my mother wanted me to so badly. I poke a finger into the meat to see if it feels tender. This is something my mother has taught me. And I write on my little notepaper what it costs, because I'll forget before I get home. When the shopping is done and Mrs Jensen has left, I put everything out of my mind so I can hammer away at the typewriter, now that it won't disturb anyone.

My mother comes and visits me regularly, and together we can be pretty silly. A couple of days after I got married, she opened up the closet and looked through Viggo F.'s clothes. She calls him 'Viggomand', because she has just as much trouble as other people calling him by his real name. I can't do it either, because there is something immature about the name Viggo when it's not referring to a child. She held all his green clothing up to the light and found a set that was so moth-eaten, she thought it couldn't be worn anymore. Mrs Brun could use this to sew me a dress, she concluded. It was never any use to oppose my mother when she made a decision like that, so offering no resistance, I let her leave with the clothes, hoping that Viggo F. wouldn't ask about it. Sometime later we visited my parents. We don't do that very often, because there's something about the way Viggo F. talks to them that I can't stand. He speaks loudly and slowly, as if to mentally disabled children, and he searches carefully for subjects he thinks might interest them. We visited them, and suddenly he prodded me with a confidential elbow in my side. What a coincidence, he said, twirling his mustache between his thumb and forefinger. Did you notice that the fabric of your mother's dress exactly matches a set of clothes I have hanging in the closet at home? Then my mother and I dashed from the room and burst out laughing.

During this period I feel very close to my mother, and I'm not harboring any deep and painful feelings about her anymore. She is two years younger than her son-in-law, and they never talk about anything except how I was as a child. I don't recognize myself at all in my mother's early impressions of me; it's like they're talking about a different child altogether. When my mother comes to visit, I stuff my novel away in my locked drawer in Viggo F.'s desk. I make coffee and we drink it while we chat. We talk about how good it is that my father has gotten steady work at the Ørsted factory, about Edvin's cough, and about all the alarming symptoms from my mother's internal organs, which have plagued her ever since Aunt Rosalia's death. I think my mother is still pretty and youthful. She's petite and her face is nearly wrinkle-free, just like Viggo F.'s. Her permed hair is thick as a doll's, and she always sits on the edge of her chair, with a straight back and her hands on the handles of her purse. She sits the same way Aunt Rosalia always did when she only was going to stay 'a brief moment', and then didn't leave until several hours had passed. My mother leaves before Viggo F. comes home from the fire insurance company, because he is usually in a bad mood then and doesn't like it if anyone is here. He hates his work at the office and he hates the people there, too. He has something against everyone, I think, unless they happen to be artists.

After we've eaten and gone over the household budget, he

usually asks how far I've come with *The French Revolution*, which is supposed to be part of my basic education, so I make sure that I have read at least a few new pages in it. After I've carried out the dishes, he lies down to rest on the divan, and I glance at the blue globe outside the police station, which illuminates the deserted courtyard with a glassy light. Then I roll down the shades, sit down and read Carlyle until Viggo F. wakes up and wants coffee. While we drink it, and if we don't have to go out to visit some famous person, a strange silence spreads between us. It's as if everything we might have said to one another was used up before we were married, as if we spent all the words that ought to have lasted the next twenty-five years; because I don't believe he's going to die in three years. The only thing occupying my thoughts is my novel, and since I can't talk about that, I don't know what to talk about. A month ago, just after the occupation started, Viggo F. was alarmed because he thought the Germans were going to arrest him, since he had written an article in the *Social-Demokraten* about the concentration camps. So we talked about what might happen. And in the evening his equally frightened friends, who had similarly troubled consciences, came by. But now they all seem to have forgotten about the danger, and they live mostly as if nothing ever happened. Every day I'm afraid that he will ask me if I have finished reading his manuscript for the new novel he'll be sending to Gyldendal Publishing. It's lying on his desk, and I've tried to read it, but it's so boring and wordy and full of knotty, incorrect sentences, that I don't think I will ever be able to get through it. That also makes the atmosphere between us tense – that I don't like his books. I've never said that out loud, but I've never praised them either. I've just said that I don't understand much about literature.

Though our evenings at home are sad and uniform, I still prefer them to the evenings with the famous artists. When I am with them I'm gripped by shyness and awkwardness, and it's as if my mouth were full of sawdust, because it's impossible for me to come up with clever answers to their jovial remarks. They talk about their paintings, their exhibitions or about their books, and they read aloud poems they have just written. For me, writing is like it was in my childhood, something secret and prohibited, shameful, something one sneaks into a corner to do when no one else is watching. They ask me what I am writing at the moment, and I say, Nothing. Viggo F. comes to my rescue. She's reading right now, he says. You have to read an awful lot to be able to write prose, and that will be the next thing. He talks about me almost as if I weren't present, and I'm relieved when we finally get up to go. When he's with famous people, Viggo F. is a completely different person – cheerful, self-confident, witty – just like he was with me in the beginning.

One evening, out at the home of the illustrator Arne Ungermann, they mentioned wanting to gather together all the young people who are published in *Wild Wheat*, since they are most likely very lonely, scattered around Copenhagen. They would probably be happy to get to know one another. Then Tove could be the head of the association, says Viggo F., giving me a friendly smile. Thinking about that makes me happy, since otherwise I only see young people when they venture out to us with their work, and they barely even glance at me then, since I'm married to this important man. My elation frees up my tongue and I say it could be called 'The Young Artists Club'. The idea draws general applause.

The next day I find the addresses in Viggo F.'s notebook, and in a few brief phrases I write a very formal letter in which

I suggest a meeting at our home one particular evening in the near future. Then I deposit all the letters in the mailbox beside the police station, imagining how happy they will be, because I think that they're poor and lonely like I was not long ago, and that they're sitting in ice-cold, rented rooms all around the city. It occurs to me that Viggo F. knows me quite well after all. He knows I'm tired of only being around old people. He knows that I often feel suffocated by life in his green rooms, and that I can't spend my entire youth reading about the French Revolution.

2

The Young Artists Club is now a reality and my life has regained color and substance. Every Thursday evening about a dozen of us meet, in a room in the Women's Building that we got permission to use as long as we each buy a cup of coffee. It costs one krone per person, without cake, and those who don't have money borrow it from those who do. The meeting starts with a lecture by a famous older artist – a 'Big Fish' – who thereby does Viggo F. a friendly favor. I never hear a word of the lecture, because I'm too preoccupied with having to stand up and thank them when it's over. I always say the same thing: Let me thank you for that excellent lecture. It was very kind of you to come. Usually, to our relief, the Big Fish declines our offer to stay for coffee. Then the rest of us pass the time, chatting cheerfully about everything under the sun, but rarely naming who brought us together. At the most, one of them might say to me incidentally, Do you happen to know if Møller liked the two poems I sent him recently? They all call him Møller and speak of him with veneration. Thanks to him they're not unknowns; thanks to him, if they're lucky, once in a while they'll get to see their names in a review of *Wild Wheat*, which has always enjoyed attention from the media. There are only three girls in the club – Sonja Hauberg, Ester Nagel and myself. The two of them are pretty, serious, dark-haired, dark-eyed and from wealthy homes. Sonja studied literature, and Ester works in a pharmacy. All of us are about twenty years old except for Piet Hein, who is the only one who doesn't seem to respect Viggo F. very much. Piet Hein makes a fuss over the fact I have to be home by eleven, and that I can never go with him afterwards to the Hungarian Vinhus. But I always arrive home on time, because Viggo F. is sitting up, waiting for me, to hear how the evening went. He waits there with coffee or a glass of wine, and at those times I see him through my friends' eyes. This usually makes me want to show him my half novel, but in the end I can't bring myself to do it. Piet Hein has a face as round as a pie, and a sharp tongue, which frightens me a bit. When he walks me home at night through the blacked-out moonlit city, he stops at the canal or in front of the stock-exchange building with its green copper luminous roof, opens my hands like a book, and kisses me long and deep. He asks me why I married that troglodyte, when I'm so beautiful I could have almost anyone I choose. I answer obliquely, because I don't like it when anyone makes fun of Viggo F. I don't think Piet Hein knows what it's like to have been poor and to have had to use nearly every second of your life just to survive. I have more compassion for Halfdan Rasmussen, who is short, skinny, badly dressed, and living off public support. He and I had the same kind of upbringing and we speak the same language. But Halfdan is in love with Ester, Morten Nielsen with Sonja, and Piet Hein with me. We figured this out within a few Thursdays. I'm not sure if I'm in love with Piet Hein. When he kisses me I get aroused, but he also confuses me when he wants me to do a ton of things all at once, like: marry him, have children, and meet a girl he knows because he thinks I need a girlfriend. When Piet takes me in his arms, he calls me 'Kitten'.

One evening he brings the girl to the club. Her name is Nadja and she is obviously in love with him. She is taller than me, thin, slightly stooped and with an uneven, sloppy expression on her face, as if she lives too much for other people, so she never has time for herself. I really like her. She works at a garden center and she lives with her father, who is Russian and divorced. She invites me over, and I go to visit, after telling Viggo F. about her. Their apartment is large and grand, and Nadja entertains me with stories about Piet Hein while we drink tea. She says that he likes to have two girlfriends at once. When she first got to know him he was married, and he made sure that she became friends with his wife before he left her. But they aren't friends anymore. It's just something he cooked up, says Nadja calmly. She asks me about my life and suggests I get divorced from Viggo F. That idea had also just occurred to me. I tell her about our nonexistent sex life, and she says it's a sin and a shame that he has doomed me to childlessness. You should get advice about it from Piet, she says. As long as he's hot for you, he'll do anything you ask.

So I do that, one evening while we're standing quietly by the canal, the water sloshing against the wharf with a soft, lazy sound. I ask Piet how a person gets divorced, and he says that he'll take care of all the practical matters. All I have to do is tell my husband. Piet says he'll pay for me to live in a boarding house, and that he'll take better care of me than Viggo F. does. I say, I might be able to support myself; I'm writing a novel. I say this matter-of-factly, as if I have written twenty novels and this is just number twenty-one. Piet asks me if he can read it, and I say no one can read it until it's finished. Then he asks if he could invite me over to his place for dinner one night. He lives on Store Kongensgade in a little apartment, where he set himself up when he got divorced. I say yes, and then I tell Viggo F. that I'm going out to visit my parents. It's the first time I've lied to him, and I feel ashamed when he believes me. Viggo F. is sitting at his desk, laying out *Wild Wheat*. He's cutting out drawings, stories and poems from the proofs, then gluing them into the pages of an old issue. He does this so delicately, and his whole body, with the big head bent beneath the green lamp, radiates something resembling happiness, because he loves that journal the way other people love their families. I kiss him on his soft, damp mouth and suddenly I get tears in my eyes. We have something together – not much, but something – and now I am starting to destroy it. I'm sad that my life is about to get complicated as never before. But I also think how strange it is that I never go against what anyone else wants; not really. I might be home a bit late, I say. My mother isn't feeling well. So don't wait up.

Well, says Piet jovially, wasn't that good?

Yes, I say, happily. Since my affair with Aksel I've been wondering if maybe there was something wrong with me in that department, but there isn't. Piet and I have had food and drink, and I'm a bit tipsy. We're lying in a wide canopy bed that Piet got from his mother, who is an eye doctor. The room is furnished with funny lamps, modern furniture and a polar-bear skin on the floor. In a vase by the bed there's a rose which is already starting to lose its petals. Piet gave it to me. He has given me a blue flannel dress too, which has to hang at his place for the time being. I can't just take it home. I pick up the rose and sniff it. It doesn't want to just be grafted anymore, I laugh. I can use that, exclaims Piet, jumping out of bed completely naked. He sits down at his desk, grabs a pen and paper and scribbles something down. When he's done he shows it to me. It's a grook for the *Politiken* newspaper, for whom he writes these four-line witty stanzas every day. It reads:

> I placed a rose by my lover's bed
> It blushed, sweet aroma wafting
> First one petal fell then two and more
> Now it doesn't believe in grafting.

I praise him for it, and he says that I should get half the honorarium. For Piet, being a writer is not something to hide or be ashamed of. To him it is as straightforward as breathing.

This is going to be a tough pill for Møller to swallow, he says with satisfaction. When you got married, all his friends bet on how long it would last – more than one year or less. No one thought it would last longer than one year. And then Robert Mikkelsen provided the pre-nuptial agreement, because they all thought you would take half his property.

I'm shocked. I say, You are so wicked. And conniving.

No, says Piet, it's just I don't like him. He's a parasite of the arts without being an artist himself. He can't even write.

Feeling ill at ease I say, That's not his fault. And I don't like it when you talk about him like that; it puts me in a bad mood. I ask what time it is, and my brief happiness slips away. A wet, silvery stillness fills the room, as if something fateful is about to happen. I don't hear what Piet says. I'm thinking about Viggo F., bent beneath his desk lamp, laying out his journal. I'm thinking about the bet his friends made and about the impossibility of saying to him that we have to split up. Sometimes, Piet says tenderly, you get very distant, and I can't reach you. You are so fascinating and I think I'm in love with you. Can I write to you? He asks, Does the mail arrive after he leaves? Yes, I say, you can write to me. The next day I get a love letter from Piet: Dear Kitten, You are the only girl I could ever imagine marrying. I get anxious and I telephone Viggo F. What is it? he asks, a bit shortly. I don't know, I say. I just feel very alone. Alright, he says. I'll be home tonight, okay?

Then I take out my novel and I write and write and forget about everything. The novel is nearly finished. The title is going to be *A Child Was Harmed*. In one way or another it's about me, even though I may never experience the things the people do in the book.

3

And this, says Viggo F., twirling his mustache, a sign that he is in a good mood – have you hidden this from me all this time? He's sitting with my manuscript in his hand, looking up at me with his bright blue eyes, which are so clear it's like they've just been washed. Everything about him is clean and dapper, and he gives off the scent of soap and shaving lotion. His breath is fresh as a baby's, because he doesn't smoke.

Yes, I say, I wanted to surprise you. Do you really think it's good?

It's stunning, he says. There's not a comma out of place. This will be a huge success.

I can tell I'm blushing with happiness. In that moment I couldn't care less about Piet Hein or my divorce plans. Once more Viggo F. is the person I have dreamed of meeting my entire life. He pulls out a bottle of wine and pours it into the green glasses. Cheers, he says, smiling. And congratulations. We agree again to try Gyldendal first, even though they didn't want my poems. They have recently accepted the novel by Viggo F. that I couldn't get through. He just said that I was too young to have a feel for his writing, and that it couldn't be helped. This one evening we enjoy each other's company as it was before we were married, and the thought of what I will soon say to him seems distant and unreal, like the thought of what could happen in ten years. That was the last evening we were really close. We were alone together behind the black-out curtains in the green living room, sharing something the world had not yet seen, and we talked about my first novel until it was past our bedtime, and we both yawned between drinks of wine. Viggo F. never gets drunk, and he can't stand when other people do. He threw out Johannes Weltzer many times, when, tipsy, enthusiastic and sweating, he paced our floor while talking about the novel he was writing. He'll talk it to death, says Viggo F., who thinks Johannes has only written one good sentence in his whole life. It was: 'Dear to me are restlessness and long trips.' The expectation that one should drink in moderation, similar to the expectation that one should leave at the appropriate time, is always hanging in the air. We have company quite often. At those times I go shopping in a delicatessen on Amagerbrogade, because like my mother, I hardly know how to prepare food other than the most basic things.

One day I tell my mother I'm planning to get divorced. I tell her about Piet Hein, about all the gifts he has given me, and about how he is going to take care of my future. My mother wrinkles her brow and thinks for a long time. On the street where I grew up no one ever got divorced. The couples there might argue and fight like cats and dogs, but they never mention divorce. That must be something that only happens among higher society; no one knows why.

But will he marry you? she asks finally, rubbing her nose with her index finger, as she always does when something is troubling her. I say that he hasn't talked about it, but that he probably will. I say that I can't bear staying married to Viggo F., and that every day I feel heartsick when it's time for him to come home. I say that the marriage has been a mistake for both of us. Yes, she says, I understand, in a way. It does look rather dumb when you two walk down the street, since he's so much shorter than you. My mother lacks the ability to put herself in other people's shoes, which keeps her from hurting my feelings, and that suits me fine.

Now I go home with Piet Hein every Thursday after the meeting. I tell Viggo F. that the discussions after the lecture last so long, and that as chairperson it wouldn't be proper if I were the first to leave. I tell him not to wait up for me, but to just go to bed. When he's asleep, nothing can wake him up, and he doesn't know how late I come home. But why, says Piet impatiently, why don't you tell him? I keep promising to tell Viggo F. the next day, but in the end I doubt that I will ever be able to get the words out. I'm afraid how he will react. I'm afraid of arguing and scenes, and I always think with horror about when my father and brother fought every night, so there was never any peace in our little living room. If you can't tell him, says Piet one evening, you can just move out, just like that. You can't take anything but your clothes with you anyway. But I can't do it. It would be too mean, too brutal, too ungrateful. Piet also asks me to pay more attention to Nadja, who is miserable because he left her. I visit her frequently. She sits in a metal chair, stretching out her long legs and rubbing her face irritably, as if she wanted to rearrange her features. She says that Piet is dangerous, created to make women unhappy. Now that he has left her, she's going to change her life. She's going to attend the university and study psychology, because she has always been more interested in other people than in herself. And that will save her. She says sadly, He'll leave you, too. One day he'll come to you and say, I've found someone else. But I'm sure you'll take it on the chin. Take it on the chin is his favorite expression. She also says that I'm going to get divorced anyway, and that Piet is as good an excuse as anyone. I don't pay too much attention to what she says, because when it comes down to it, she's bitter about being deserted.

Sometimes Piet Hein bothers me, like when I'm lying with his arm around me, and he's conjuring up plans for my future. It bothers me that he wants to rummage in my life and arrange it, as if I were unable to take care of it myself, and I wish he would just leave me alone. I wish I could move back and forth between him and Viggo F. without losing either of them and with no radical upheavals. I've always avoided change and been comforted by things staying the way they are. But it can't go on. Now I'm able to look at loving couples in the street again, but I turn away from the sight of mothers with small children. I avoid looking in baby carriages or thinking about the girls from my old street, who were so proud that they waited until they were eighteen to have children. I suppress all those kinds of thoughts because Piet is careful not to get me pregnant. He says that women authors shouldn't have children; there are plenty of other women who can. On the other hand, there aren't so many who can write books.

My misery gets dramatically worse toward five o'clock in the afternoon. While I'm standing in the kitchen turning on the potatoes, my heart starts hammering and the white tile wall behind the stovetop flickers before my eyes, as if the tiles were starting to fall off. When Viggo F. walks in the door with his dark, irritated face, I start talking feverishly as if to defend against something horrible; I don't know what. I talk incessantly while we eat, even though he only responds with one-syllable words. I'm anxious that he will say or do something terrible, irreversible, something he never said or did before. When I get his attention, my heart slows a bit, and I'm able to breathe easy again, until there's another pause in the conversation. I talk about all kinds of things: about when Mrs Jensen, after I showed her a drawing that Ernst Hansen did of me, said, Is that drawn by hand? I talk about my mother, about her blood pressure which is too high now, though before it had always been too low. I talk about my book which has been returned from Gyldendal with a strange response, insinuating that I have been reading too much Freud. I don't even know who Freud is. Now I've sent the book to a new publisher by the name of Athenæum, and every day I look forward to hearing a response. One evening Viggo F. notices my restlessness and says that I've turned into quite a chatterbox. I tell him I'm not feeling all that well and that I think there's something wrong with my heart. Nonsense, he laughs, not at your age. It must be some kind of anxiety. He gives me a worried look and asks if anything is bothering me. I assure him there's nothing wrong, that I'm snug as a bug in a rug. Then he says, I'll call Geert Jørgensen and make an appointment for you. He is a head psychiatrist. I saw him myself once many years ago. A very sensible man.

So I sit across from the doctor, a large knobby man with huge eyes that look like they are about to leave their sockets. I tell him everything. I tell him about Piet Hein and about not telling Viggo F. that I want to get divorced. Geert Jørgensen smiles at me cheerfully, while he plays with a letter opener on the desk.

Isn't it, he says, quite interesting to be caught between two different men?

Yes, I say, surprised; because it is.

You have to let Møller go, he says matter-of-factly. It's a crazy marriage. As you may know, I'm the head psychiatrist at Hareskov Sanatorium. I'll recommend to your editor that you stay there for a little while. Then I'll take care of the rest. As soon as you're out of his sight, your heart trouble will pass.

Right then and there he calls Viggo F., who has nothing against the idea. The very next day I pack my suitcase and go to Hareskov, where I get a private room with a view out to the woods. I talk to the head doctor again, who says that Piet Hein may not visit me before everything is taken care of. He'll call Piet and tell him to stay away. At the sanatorium there are only women my mother's age, very dainty and well dressed. I feel weighed down by my shabby clothes, while I think about all the outfits Piet has given me that I can't use yet. The days pass without drama, and my heart returns to normal. I rent a typewriter from a shop in Bagsværd, and with it I write a poem:

The Eternal Triangle

In my life there are two men
who cross my path incessantly –
the one man is the man I love,
and the other man loves only me.

But I don't really know if I love Piet Hein, just as he has never said that he loves me. He sends me chocolates and letters, and one day he sent me an orchid in a cardboard box. I placed it in a narrow vase and set it on the nightstand without giving it a second thought. On the day that Viggo F. has to go and talk to Dr Jørgensen, he first comes up to my room. He barely says hello before he sees the orchid. He gets pale and sits down on the edge of a chair. Shocked, I see his lower lip trembling. That there, he says, his voice shaking, pointing at the orchid, Who sent that? Is there someone else?

Uh, no, I say immediately, It was sent anonymously, from some secret admirer.

While I say that, I'm thinking of my mother, whose quickness with a remark I have admired my whole childhood.

4

Now it's fall, and I'm wearing a black coat with an ocelot collar while I walk around in the woods. I walk by myself, because my world seems completely different from that of the other women. I only have superficial conversations with them at mealtimes. Piet Hein visits me every day. He brings me chocolate or flowers, and we walk around in the woods for hours, while he tells me how he is looking for a good boarding house for me, and what a great job I did getting rid of Viggo F. I don't feel like I've gotten rid of him just because I don't see him anymore, but I can't explain that to Piet, who is practical, worldly and unsentimental. He kisses me as if he were my happy owner under the multi-colored trees whose leaves float down over us, and he doesn't think I look as happy as I ought to. I showed him a letter I received from Viggo F., but Piet just laughed and said, what else could we expect from a disappointed, bitter man. Viggo F. had written: Dear Tove, I have received a message from the publisher that they have accepted your book. I am enclosing the accompanying check. And then his signature. I turned the paper over and over, but there was nothing else. The letter upset me, even though I was glad that they wanted my book. It upset me because I'm thinking back on our last good evening, and what we had together, which is now ruined. Dr Jørgensen tells me that Viggo F. doesn't want to get divorced, because he thinks I'll regret what I'm doing with Piet Hein. Viggo F. never liked Piet because of his sarcastic nature, and they only met one another a few times. I got a letter from Ester too. She wrote that they miss me in the club, and she asked me if I would mind if she acts as chairperson in my absence. She couldn't get Viggo F. to reveal where I was, but by twisting stone-faced Piet's arm she was able to obtain my address. If I had been home with Viggo F., I would have paid for dinner at an expensive restaurant to celebrate the occasion. But I don't feel like treating Piet to dinner, because it's hanging in the air that he should be the one to treat me. And I think uneasily about my future, because there was a kind of security in those green rooms. There was security in the thought of being a married woman, who went shopping and made dinner every day, and now it's all ruined. Piet never talks about getting married, and doesn't seem to care if Viggo F. wants to get divorced or not.

Eventually Piet locates a suitable boarding house and I move in with a renewed feeling of being a young girl whose existence is fragile, fleeting and unsure. I have a nice bright room with good furniture, and I'm tended to by a maid with a cap on her head. I bought a typewriter with my advance and I'm transcribing poems on it, because I've started writing poetry again. Piet says I should try selling them to one of the magazines that publish things like that, but I'm afraid they won't accept them. In the evening, when Piet and I lie talking in my narrow bed, I think how strange it is that he never says a single word about himself. His eyes are dull as raisins, and when he smiles, all his clean white teeth show. I still don't know if I'm in love with him. I feel weighed down by the thought that he's just amusing me, while I'm longing for a home and a husband and a child just like all young women do. The boarding house is located on River Boulevard and members of the club come up often and visit me when they are in the area. Then we have coffee, which I order by pushing a button. We talk about Otto Gelsted's lecture at the club. It was about the political engagement of artists, and the discussion fell flat, because none of us are politically engaged. Morten Nielsen sits on the edge of my divan with his hands supporting his big angular face like a cradle. He says, Maybe I should join the freedom fighters. I think it's a stupid idea, because the occupying forces are so powerful, but I don't say that I don't agree. Maybe I've inherited my father's dislike of God, king and homeland, because I don't have the urge to hate the German soldiers tramping around the streets. I'm too busy with my own life, my own uncertain future, to be able to think patriotically right now. I miss Viggo F. and I forget that it made me sick to be in the same room with him. I miss showing him my poems and I'm jealous of my friends who visit him and show him their writing. But the head psychiatrist said that I should leave him alone. One day Ester visits me and says that she has agreed to be Viggo F.'s housekeeper. She got fired from the pharmacy where she worked because she was always late, so she's glad. She's written half a novel, which now she hopes to have time to finish. She says that since I moved out, Viggo F. can't stand being alone.

After I lived in the boarding house for a month, Piet visited me one afternoon. He seemed excited and a bit nervous. He didn't kiss me as usual, but he sat down, drumming lightly on the floor with the silver-handled walking cane that he had picked up recently. There is something I have to tell you, he says, looking at me askance with his raisin eyes. He hangs the cane on the back of the chair and wrings his hands, as if he's cold or is relishing something. He says, I'm sure you'll take this on the chin, won't you? I promise to take it on the chin, but his entire manner frightens me. In this moment he seems like a complete stranger who has never held me in his arms. Quickly he continues, I met a young woman recently, very pretty, very rich. We fell in love immediately, and now she's invited me over to Jylland – to a mansion. It's in her family. I'm leaving tomorrow; I hope you're not upset.

I feel dizzy – what about my rent and what about my future? No tears, he says, opening his hands in an authoritative motion. For God's sake, take it with a stiff upper lip. We're under no obligation here, right? I'm unable to answer, but it feels as if the walls are starting to lean in, and I want to hold them back. My heart is pounding violently like it did back when I felt sick with Viggo F. Before I can say or do anything, Piet is out the door again, so fast it's as if he left through the wall. Then the tears come. I lie down on the divan, sobbing into the pillow, thinking about Nadja and how I should have listened to her warnings. It's hard to stop crying, so maybe that means I was in love with him after all.

Then there's a knock on the door and Nadja walks in, wearing a dingy trench coat over long pants. She sits down calmly on the divan and strokes my hair. Piet asked me to look in on you, she says. Stop crying; he's not worth it. I dry my eyes and stand up. You're right, I say. It was exactly like he did to you. And the chin? she asks, laughing. Were you supposed to take it on the chin? I laugh too, and the world gets a bit brighter. Yes, I say, with a stiff upper lip. He's so funny. Yes he is, admits Nadja, and there's something about him that girls fall for, but then afterwards they have no idea what it was. Afterwards all you can do is laugh at him. She sits there with a pensive look on her benevolent face with its heavy Slavic features. He writes good letters, she says. I've saved all of them. Did he write to you too? Oh yes, I say, walking to the dresser. I take out a whole bundle of letters that I've tied up with a red bow. Let me see them, says Nadja, if you don't mind? I give them to her, and she reads a couple of lines of the first one and immediately throws her head back and starts laughing, so she can hardly stop. Oh God, she says, reading: Dear Kitten, You are the only girl I could ever think of marrying. That is so insane, she says, gasping for air, that is exactly the same thing he wrote to me. She reads some more and realizes that it is word for word the same letter she has at home. You know what, she says, he must have them duplicated someplace. Heaven knows how many Kittens he has, spread around the country. When he leaves that mansion woman, he'll send you there to comfort her. I get serious again and explain to Nadja that I can't stay living here, because it's too expensive, and I'm flat broke. Then she suggests, just like Piet, that I try and sell my poems, because she thinks it would be too sad if I had to work in an office again. Go over to the *Red Evening Post*, she says. Piet sold them a ton of poems, all the ones the *Politiken* didn't want. You have to live by the pen now. All that about being taken care of is nonsense. That must be something you were brought up with.

The next day I visit the editor's office with three poems. I'm shown in to the editor, an old man with a long white beard. While he reads the poems, he pats me on the behind, absent-mindedly and mechanically. Then he says, These are good. You can go out to accounting and withdraw thirty kroner. After that I sell poems to the *Politiken's* magazine and to Hjemmet, and I write a column for Ekstra Bladet about the

Young Artists Club. So I'm able to stay in the boarding house. Through Ester I learn that Viggo F. is missing me terribly, and that she has to sit and talk with him for hours every night before he goes to bed. I ask her to ask him if he wants to see me, but he doesn't. He doesn't even want her to mention me. I miss him more than I miss Piet Hein, and apart from the sporadic visits by my friends from the club, I never see anyone.

One evening Nadja comes over, dressed, as usual, as if she had just escaped a burning house. You need a circle of friends, she says. You're so alone in the world. I know some young people, out by the south harbor, who would love to meet you. They're all students at Høng Business School, and on Saturday they're having a party. Won't you come? The most charming of them is the dean's son. His name is Ebbe, and he looks just like Leslie Howard. He's twenty-five, and he's studying economics, when he's not drinking. I used to be totally infatuated with him, but he never knew it. He's attracted to poetic, blonde, long-haired girls like you. Now listen to me, I say, you're acting like a matchmaker or something. I'll come on Saturday, because you're right, I do need to get out with other young people who aren't artists. I happily prepare my divan, and I go to bed with a faint yearning in my heart to be lying with someone's arm around me. I think about this Ebbe fellow before I fall asleep. I wonder what he looks like? Would he really fall for someone like me? The streetcars roll by, whining through the night, as if they were driving across my living room. People are sitting inside them, going out to have fun, completely normal people, who want to place glorious events between the evening and the morning, when they have to get up early for work. Apart from my writing I'm completely normal too, dreaming about a normal young man, who is attracted to blonde, long-haired girls.

5

On the way out to the south harbor, Nadja tells me a little about 'The Lantern Club', as they call themselves, no one knows why. It's made up of students who have come to Copenhagen to get their degrees from Høng Business School, but they don't do much other than hold parties, get drunk, and lie around with hangovers. We're riding our bicycles into the wind; it's rainy and cold. I'm dressed up as a little girl, with a short dress, a bow in my hair, knee socks and flats. I have a wool sweater over my dress, and over that a trench coat just like Nadja's, with a red scarf around my neck with the ends trailing behind me. That's supposed to be in fashion this year. Nadja is dressed as an Apache girl, and her long black silk pants flap against the bike chain guard with loud smacks. She tells me this group is very free-thinking. They're all dirt poor and only get a little money from home. The party will be at Ole and Lise's, who are married with an infant. Ole is going to be an architect, and Lise works in an office, while her mother, who is a widow and lives next door to them, watches the baby. They live off mushrooms from the landfill, she says, which is nearby. She also says that it's a pot-luck dinner, but that girls don't have to bring anything. They don't let any new men into the group, she says, but they always need girls. When we arrive, everyone is sitting around a table in a long bright room with fine old furniture. They're eating open-faced rye-bread sandwiches – most of them topped with ramona, a kind of carrot mixture with a poisonous color. They are also drinking pullimut, because that is the only alcohol anyone can get. The mood is already pretty high, and everyone is talking at the same time. I say hello to Lise, a pretty, thin girl with a madonna-like face. She welcomes me and then they sing an invented song with unintelligible references to everyone there. Ole stands up and delivers a speech. He has a flat, dark, immense face with two deep furrows from his nose to his mouth, which make him look much older than he is. He is constantly pulling up his pants, as if they were too big for him, and he isn't dressed up like the rest of us. He says he's proud to have a writer in the house, and he says he's sorry that Ebbe is at home with his mother, nursing a fever of 39°C. He just caught the flu. Then the table is moved to the side, and Nadja and Lise carry out the dishes. The record player is turned on, and we start dancing. I dance with Ole, who stoops over me, pulls up his pants, gives a shy laugh and says that he'll go over and get Ebbe. Ebbe lives across the street, and Ole says that Ebbe has been looking forward to meeting me. He says that a little fever won't stand in the way. Then he and another guy go out into the night to bring back Ebbe. The mood is quite loose; everyone is a bit drunk. Lise comes over and asks if I want to see the baby, and we go into the baby's room. It's a six-month-old boy, and I feel a pang of jealousy when she starts nursing him. She's no older than I am, and I feel like I've been wasting my time, since I don't have a baby too. The little boy has a slight shadowed hollow in the back of his neck, just under his hairline. It pulses rhythmically as he drinks. Suddenly the door opens; it's Ole, standing there pulling on his curly black hair. Ebbe's here, he says. Tove, don't you want to say hello? I go with Ole into the living room, where the noise is tremendous. A cover from a record is hanging from the chandelier, and streamers of all different colors are intertwined between the furniture and dangling from the shoulders and hair of the people dancing. Standing in the center there's a young man wearing a blue robe over striped pajamas, and a gigantic scarf is wrapped several times around his neck. This is Ebbe, says Ole proudly, and I shake Ebbe's hand, which is sweaty with fever. He has a drawn, gentle face with fine features, and I get a strong feeling that he is the leader of their clique. Welcome to the Lantern Club, he says. I hope—Then he looks around with a helpless expression and loses his train of thought. Ole claps him on the back. Don't you want to dance with Tove? he asks. Ebbe looks at me for a second with his slanted eyes. Then he extends his palm and says quietly: *Die Sternen, begehrt Mann nicht.** Bravo, exclaims Ole, no one else in the world could have thought of saying that. Ebbe dances with me anyway. His hot cheek finds mine and our steps get a bit unsteady. Then the others suddenly gather around him, hand him a glass, pull on his robe, and ask about his health. Another guy dances with me, and for a moment I lose sight of Ebbe. The gramophone is blasting, and Ole is sitting in the corner with his ear pressed to a homemade speaker, listening to the BBC broadcast. Now everyone is drunk, and a lot of them are sick. Nadja grabs them one by one, leads them

* 'A man should not covet you, O stars', adapted from Goethe's 'Trost in Tränen'.

to the toilet and holds their heads while they throw up. She loves doing that, says Lise, laughing. Lise is dressed as Columbine, and you can see her large plump breasts beneath all the ruffles. I wonder if it's true that you get a nice bust from nursing, and I dance with Ebbe again, who desires the stars after all, because he suggests that we take a break in another room. We lie down on a bed and he takes me in his arms, as if that is something they just do in this group, with no lead-in maneuvers of any kind. I feel happy and loved for the first time in my life. I stroke his thick brown hair, which curls at his neck, and I look into his strange, slanted eyes, which have brown dots in the blue. He says it's because his mother has brown eyes, and that always comes through in one way or another. He asks if he can come visit me at my boarding house, and I say yes. He reaches down on the floor for a bottle he brought in with us, and we both take a drink from it. Then we fall asleep. Early in the morning I wake up and I don't know where I am. Ebbe is still sleeping, and his short, turned-up eyelashes brush lightly against the pillowcase. Suddenly I see another couple in a child's bed by the other wall. They're sleeping in one another's arms and I don't recognize them from the night before. A motley pile of dress-up clothing is lying on the floor. I get up carefully and walk into the living room, which resembles a battlefield. Nadja is already cleaning up, wiping up vomit in the corners. She looks cheerful. That damned pullimut, she says. No one can take it. Isn't he sweet – Ebbe – completely different than that creep Piet. In the baby's room, Lise is sitting, nursing. Watch out for Ebbe, she says smiling, looking up at me. He's a heartbreaker.

I put on my trench coat, tie the red scarf around my neck, and walk in to say goodbye to Ebbe. Oh God, my head, he moans. As soon as I get over this flu I'll come and visit you.

Are you a little bit crazy about me? I say yes, and he apologizes for not walking me out. I can see he's flushed with fever and I say that's perfectly alright. Then I ride my bike home alone. It's not quite daylight yet. The birds are chirping as if it were spring, and I'm thinking, happily, that a college student is in love with me. I have a funny feeling that it might last a lifetime.

When Ebbe is over the flu, he starts coming to visit me every evening, and I neglect the club meetings, because I don't want to miss him. He never stays overnight, because he's afraid of his mother. She's the widow of the college dean. Ebbe has an older brother who also lives at home and can't bring himself to move out, even though he's twenty-eight. When Ebbe leaves, he winds his long scarf so many times around his neck that it reaches all the way up to his nose, because we're having a bitterly cold winter. I get wool in my mouth when he kisses me goodbye.

I start visiting Lise and Ole quite frequently, and I visit Ebbe's mother too. She is little and old, and she describes everything as if it were a problem. Now that my husband is dead, she says, I only have my two boys. She looks at me with her vibrant black eyes, apparently afraid that I am going to take one of the boys away from her. Ebbe's brother's name is Karsten. He's studying to be an engineer and he's always speculating about how he's going to tell his mother that he wants to move out, but he doesn't have the courage. Ebbe's mother is the daughter of a Lutheran priest and she asks me if I believe in God. When I say no, she looks at me sadly and says: Ebbe doesn't either. I hope you both will turn your souls toward the Lord. Ebbe looks embarrassed when she says things like that.

When Ebbe and I go to bed he never uses protection. I've

told him that I want to have a baby, and that I'll take care of it. Every month I put a red cross on my calendar, but time passes and nothing happens. Then my novel comes out, and the next morning my landlord comes running in with the *Politiken*. You're in the paper today, she says, panting. Something about a book. Read it. I open up the paper and I can't believe my eyes. In the most prominent position in the newspaper, next to the 'Day to Day' column, Frederik Schyberg has a review across two columns. The title reads: 'Refined Innocence'. It's an effusive review, and I am giddy with joy. Soon afterwards a telegram arrives from Morten. It reads: Thank goodness for Schyberg and the real genius. Later in the day Morten comes by in person, and while we drink coffee he says that rumors are flying at the club. People are saying I used Viggo F. for a while and then dumped him when I could take care of myself. I tell Morten there is something to that, but it still makes me feel bad, because it's not the whole truth. The next day there's a grook about me in the *Politiken*. It reads:

> I do not swing my poet's hat
> for just any Tove this or that
> but I am thoroughly charmed
> An undebatable debut
> and such great prospects in view
> that I'm afraid a child was harmed.

Evidently he still thinks about his Kitten. But he married his mansion woman and he never comes to the club anymore.

Suddenly, nothing else matters, because I'm a few days late. I discuss it with Lise, who tells me to go to the doctor with a urine sample and have it tested. The doctor promises to call when the results come in, and over the following days

I hardly leave the telephone. Finally he calls and tells me in a totally normal voice: the result was positive. I'm going to have a baby. I can hardly believe it. A tiny clump of mucus inside me is going to expand and grow every day, until I get fat and shapeless like Rapunzel was when I was a child. Ebbe isn't nearly as happy as I am. We have to get married, he says, and I'd better tell my mother. I ask if he has anything against us getting married and he says, No, it's just that we're so young and we have no place to live. He gets a helpless look in his eyes at the thought of all the things to consider, and I kiss his fine, delicate mouth. I feel like I have enough strength for all three of us. Then I realize that I'm not even divorced yet, and I write a nice letter to Viggo F. asking him for a divorce since I'm pregnant. Offended, he writes back: I only have one thing to say: Good grief! Go to a lawyer and get it done, and the sooner the better. When I show the letter to Ebbe, he says: He's ridiculous. What did you ever see in him?

In the following weeks, Ebbe is often drunk when he comes to visit me. He unwinds his scarf with stiff movements, and his tongue wags nonsensically when he tries to say something. I'm no good, he says. You deserve someone better. I haven't told my mother yet. Finally he pulls himself together and tells her. She cries as if it were a disaster and says that now she has nothing to live for. Lise says that Ebbe can't bear tears or reproaches. She says that he's a good but weak person, and that I'm the one who will have to call the shots in our marriage. Even though I don't do anything about it, I don't like hearing that. And besides, I have morning sickness and I throw up every morning. Nadja visits me and says things even more directly. Ebbe is a lush, she says, and he doesn't do a thing. He is terribly sweet, but I'm afraid you're going to be providing for him.

6

We move into a room at Ebbe's mother's house until the divorce is finalized, because we want to be together all the time. Ebbe spends the mornings at the State Pricing Advisory, where a lot of students kill time and earn a little pocket money. He sits with another economics student named Victor. Ebbe has as many friends as there are stars in the sky, and I will never meet all of them. When he and Victor arrive at work in the morning, they sing the psalm of the day from a hymnal booklet which they then use to roll their cigarettes. Finding tobacco is very difficult, and sometimes they roll their cigarettes with ersatz tea. Meanwhile, I'm writing my next novel. I have recently submitted the manuscript of a poetry collection called *Little World*. Ebbe thought of the title. He's quite interested in my work. He wanted to get a degree in literature, but his father, who died two years ago, said that that was a peasant's fantasy. So now he's studying economics, which doesn't interest him in the least. But he loves literature, and he's always reading novels when we're not talking together. He introduces me to books that I never knew existed. And every afternoon when he returns from work, he wants to see what I've written. If he critiques it, there's always substance to his advice, and I follow it. I don't see my family much these days. My brother has moved in with a divorced woman who has a three-year-old child. Ebbe and I visited them, but he and Ebbe don't have much in common. Ebbe is an upper-class young man from the suburbs, and Edvin is a Copenhagen painter's helper, who breathes cellulose lacquer into his damaged lungs every day because he has no other choice. My parents' world is also very remote from Ebbe's. Ebbe talks with my father about books, and with my mother about me, just like Viggo F. used to do. But there's nothing condescending in Ebbe's attitude to them. After we've finished eating dinner with his mother and Karsten, we lie on the bed in our room, talking about the future, about the baby we are going to have, about life, and about our past before we knew one another. Ebbe loves questions that have no definitive answer. For example, he has a theory of why Negroes are black, and another one about why Jews have hooked noses. Once he propped himself up on his elbow and stared at me with an expression of moral intensity. I'm thinking, he said solemnly, about joining the underground resistance. It's not looking so good after the fall of France. I say that he can leave that to people who don't have a wife and child to think of. He seems to forget about the idea. I feel good these days: I'm going to get married, I'm going to have a baby, I'm in love with a young man, and soon we're going to have our own home. I tell Ebbe that I'll never leave him, and that I can't stand it when life gets so complicated, like it's been recently. He lifts my chin and kisses me. It could be, he says, that if you're complicated, your life gets to be like that too.

Finally the divorce goes through, and we rent an apartment

on Tartinisvej, near Lise and Ole and Ebbe's mother. The south harbor is at the end of long Enghavevej like a nail on the end of a finger. This neighborhood is also called 'Music Town' because all the roads are named after composers. The apartment buildings are not very tall, and most of them have little yards out front with grass and trees. Between the last road and open country lies the landfill, and when the wind is just right, the stench carries to the apartments, so we can't keep our windows open. Across from the house where Lise and Ole live, on Wagnervej, there are lots of cabins where people live all year round. One of the cabin ladies cleans Lise's house. And every Saturday, Lise takes the lady's five children upstairs to the bathroom and soaps and scrubs them clean, so the apartment fills with their drawn-out cries. Lise does things like that without thinking twice, and she reminds me of Nadja that way. Nadja has moved in with a sailor who's a communist, and now she's constantly airing communist views, though she was very conservative back when she was seeing Piet. I know this from Ebbe, because I don't go out in the evenings anymore. I'm too tired by eight o'clock because of my pregnancy.

Our apartment is a room and a half, and our full-size bed covers nearly the entire half-room floor. We got the bed from Ebbe's mother. Ebbe's father's desk stands in the other room, along with a dining-room table we bought used, four chairs that we got from Lise, and a divan along one wall. Over the divan we lay a brown blanket, and in a moment of inspiration, Ebbe hangs another brown blanket on the wall behind it. He got a piece of red felt from Lise, and he cut a heart out of it. He glued the heart onto the hanging blanket and stood back to admire his work. In our house, he says, we'll never have drinking parties. Out of consideration for his mother, we aren't moving into our apartment until we're married. Otherwise she would think our sinfulness was too overt.

We're getting married on one of the first days of August, and we ride our bicycles to City Hall holding hands. We arrive too early, so we walk over to Frascati and have coffee. While we drink it, I sit there observing Ebbe's face and I think there is something soft and naive about it, something defenseless, so I feel like protecting him. Suddenly I say: Your top lip really sticks out. I don't mean anything hurtful by it, but he looks at me belligerently. It doesn't stick out any more than yours, he says. Insulted I say, Mine hardly sticks out at all. Yours covers almost your whole face. His face turns red with anger. Don't criticize my looks, he says. The girls in school were crazy about me. Lise only married Ole because I wasn't interested in her. Irritated, I say, You are so conceited. Meanwhile I'm thinking in wonder: we're fighting, and we've never done that before. Silently Ebbe pays the waiter. His dark jacket sleeves are too long; he borrowed his wedding suit from his brother. In the Lantern Club they don't wear shabby clothes because they're poor; it's because being well-dressed is seen as ludicrous. Ebbe runs his index finger around his stiff collar, which is also too big, and he walks in front of me with long strides, back to City Hall, without saying a word. Then he stops and flips his hair back with a toss of his head. He says, If you don't take back that thing about my top lip, I won't marry you. I start to laugh. No, I say, that's too childish. Are we seriously going to become enemies over whose top lip sticks out more? It can be mine then. I pull my top lip down over my bottom lip and try to stick out my eyes so I can see it. It's a half mile long, I say. Come on, we're going to get married.

And we do. We move into the apartment and we hire a woman to clean, because I'm starting to earn a lot of money.

Her name is Mrs Hansen, and when she comes to interview for the job, Ebbe says emphatically, Can you peel carrots? She says she thinks she can. Ebbe explains to her that carrots are very healthy, considering so many things are unavailable now. Since then she has always been amused that there are never any carrots in the house. The days pass like a drum roll before a solo. I read books about pregnancy, motherhood and caring for an infant, and I can't understand why Ebbe isn't as interested in all of this as I am. He says he almost can't believe that he's going to be a father. He also can't believe it when he sees my name in the newspaper. He doesn't understand that he's gotten married to a famous person, and he doesn't know if he likes it. Twisting his hair around his fingers, Ebbe sits in the evening solving equations. He loves when they work out and he says that he probably should have been a mathematician. I tell him that Geert Jørgensen once said to me that no normal man would ever find me attractive. Ebbe says, So who's normal? while he pats his pockets to find his notebook or his tobacco pouch or his keys. He is quite absent-minded and is always losing his things. He walks with his head bent back, as if he is trying to keep his eyes focussed and his chin up, so he frequently trips over things on the street. He often goes to parties at Ole and Lise's, and he comes home drunk and wakes me up in the middle of the night. I get angry and brush him away, because I really need my sleep these days. He always apologizes the next day. Sometimes I go to visit my mother, or she visits me. I talk with her about giving birth, and she says that Edvin and I were born in a cloud of soap bubbles, because she tried to force us to come out by eating pine-oil soap. She says, I never liked children.

The days pass, weeks pass, months pass. I'm going to give birth at Dr Aagaard's private clinic at Hauser Square, and I have my check-ups with him. He's a nice older man who eases my many anxieties about the birth. I'm told that I should come back when there are five minutes between contractions. But the due date passes and nothing happens. I bought a sealskin coat, and I have to keep moving the buttons farther and farther out until they're dangling on the very edge of the jacket. Ebbe has to tie my shoes for me, since I can't reach them. I don't think I've ever seen a pregnant woman as fat as me. I'm afraid that I'm going to have a huge baby with water on the brain. I read about that somewhere. Often I borrow Lise's little boy Kim and take him for walks. He's sweet and laughs a lot, and I think about the poem by Nis Petersen: I collect the smiles of little children. In the middle of all this I get interviewed by Karl Bjarnhof for the *Social-Demokraten*. I get a shock when I see the headline: 'I want money, power and fame'. Did I really say that? The entire interview gives an unflattering impression of me. I'm portrayed as a vain, ambitious and superficial person, who only thinks about herself. Otherwise journalists have always treated me well, and I wonder what I could have done to Karl Bjarnhof. Then I remember that he's one of Viggo F.'s friends, so maybe he's angry because I left Viggo F.

This winter is very cold, and there's a layer of ice on the streets. I feel impatient, waiting for the contractions to start, so to bring them on I run, arm in arm with Ebbe, panting around the house after dark. The buttons on my coat spring open; nothing else happens. Finally one morning I have a stomachache and I ask Mrs Hansen if it could be contractions. She thinks it probably is, and it gets worse as the day progresses. Ebbe holds my hand as the contractions come. That evening we go to the clinic and he says goodbye with a sad, helpless expression.

*

She's so ugly, I say, surprised, looking down at the little bundle of a baby in my arms. Her face is pear-shaped, with two dark marks on her temples from the forceps. There's not a hair on her head. The doctor laughs. That's just because you've never seen a newborn baby before, he says. They're never cute, but the mother usually thinks so anyway. I'll call your husband now. Ebbe arrives with a bouquet of roses in his hand. He's carrying them awkwardly, and I realize that he's never given me a gift before. Then he sits down next to me and looks into the cradle, where they've put the baby. She's pretty chubby, he says, and I feel offended. I say, Is that all you have to say? The birth took twenty-four hours, and I swore I would never have a baby again. I yelled and screamed in pain, and all you have to say is that she's chubby? Ebbe looks ashamed and makes it even worse by saying that maybe she'll get prettier as she grows. Then he asks when I'm coming home, because he misses me. I bend over the cradle and touch the tiny fingers. I say, Now we are a father, mother and child – a normal, regular family. Ebbe asks, Why do you want to be normal and regular? Everyone knows you're not. I don't know how to answer him, but I have wanted that as far back as I can remember.

7

Something terrible has happened. Ever since Helle was born I've lost all desire to go to bed with Ebbe, and when I do it anyway I feel absolutely nothing. I tell Dr Aagaard about it, and he says that it's not unusual – I'm just drained from nursing, child-rearing and working like a madwoman, so there's nothing left over for Ebbe. But it makes Ebbe unhappy, because he thinks it's his fault. He talks it over with Ole, who advises him to buy van de Velde's *Ideal Marriage*. He buys it and reads it blushing, because this book is the present-day pornographic bible. He reads about all the positions and we try a new one every night. In the morning we're both sore from attempting to be acrobats, and it doesn't help in the least. I talk about it with Lise, who tells me confidentially that she never got anything out of sex before she had Kim. She looks at me thoughtfully with her gentle madonna-eyes: How about taking a lover? she asks. Sometimes it brings a couple together if one of them has someone else. She has a lover herself – a lawyer. He works at the police station, and they walk around together every day for hours, while she tells Ole that she's working overtime. Ole knows, but then doesn't know at the same time. Ole has had a child by another woman, and before the child was born Lise thought seriously about adopting it. Then it turned out the baby was deaf and dumb, so now she's glad she didn't do it. I tell her I don't want a lover, because I won't be able to work if my life becomes all messy and complicated again. And I realize more and more that the only thing I'm good for, the only thing that truly captivates me, is forming sentences and word combinations, or writing simple, four-line poetry. And in order to do this I have to be able to observe people in a certain way, almost as if I needed to store them in a file somewhere for later use. And to be able to do this I have to be able to read in a certain way too, so I can absorb through all my pores everything I need, if not for now, then for later use. That's why I can't interact with too many people; and I can't go out too much and drink alcohol, because then I can't work the next day. And since I'm always forming sentences in my head, I'm often distant and distracted when Ebbe starts talking to me, and that makes him feel dejected. This, together with all the attention I give to Helle, makes him feel like he's being abandoned, outside my world, where he used to be included. When he comes home in the afternoon he still likes reading what I've written, but now his comments have become meaningless and unfair, as if he's trying to hit me in my sorest spot. One day we start arguing, because in my book *The Street of Childhood*, there's a character named Mr Mulvad who likes to solve mathematical equations, and Ebbe is furious. That's me, he says. All my friends will recognize it and laugh at me. He demands that I remove Mr Mulvad from the book. It's true that Mr Mulvad is a strange fish, because I'm not that skilled at characterizing men yet. But I don't want to delete him. I don't understand, says Ebbe. Why can't you make your characters like Dickens did, for example. You take yours from real life. That's not art. I ask him to stop reading what I write, since he doesn't understand it anyway. He says he's sick and tired of being married to a writer, who's frigid on top of everything. I gasp for air and break down in tears. I've never fought with anyone since I fought with my brother back when we were children, and I can't stand being at odds with Ebbe. Helle wakes up crying, and I pick her up. Can't he solve equations, I say pitifully. Otherwise I don't know what a guy like that would do in his free time. Ebbe puts his arms around me and Helle together and says, I'm sorry, Tove. Please stop crying. He can solve equations, and I didn't mean what I said. It's just bothering me, that's all.

One afternoon, not long after that fight, Ebbe doesn't come home at the usual time, and I realize how dependent I am on him. I pace the floor and I'm unable to do anything productive. Ebbe goes out often in the evenings, but he always comes home first. As it gets later, I nurse Helle, get her dressed and go over to see Lise, who has just come home from work. She says Ole isn't home either, and that they're probably out together. Then they probably met some other friends and lost their way home. It wouldn't be the first time that had happened. You're so conventional, she says, smiling. Maybe you should have married the kind of man who always comes right home with his paycheck and never drinks. Then I tell her about our fight and I say that our marriage isn't going so well anymore. I confide in her that I'm afraid he's going to find someone else; someone who isn't a writer and isn't frigid. He might do that for one night, she says, but Ebbe would never dream of leaving you and Helle. He is really proud of you; it's obvious when he talks about you. You just have to understand that it's so easy for him to feel inferior. You're famous, you earn money, you love your work. Ebbe's just a poor student who's being more or less supported by his wife. He's studying for a degree he doesn't fit, and he has to get drunk to cope with life. But it will be a relief when your sex life gets going again. And it will; you're just exhausted from nursing. She picks Kim up onto her lap and starts playing with him. When Ole graduates, she says, I want to become a child psychologist. I can't stand working in an office. Lise loves other people's children as well as her own. She loves other people in general, and friends are always coming by and confiding things in her they wouldn't tell even the people closest to them. When do you think he'll come home? I ask. I don't know, she says. Once Ole was gone for eight days, but then I started to get nervous. After putting Kim to bed, Lise sits with her legs pulled up and her chin on one knee. Her entire person radiates peace and friendship, and I feel a bit better. Sometimes, I say, I don't think I can deal with other people at all. It's as if all I can see in the whole world is myself. That's nonsense, says Lise. You really do love Ebbe. I say, Yes, I do, but not in the right way. If he forgets his scarf, I don't remind him. I don't go out of my way to make nice food for him or anything like that. I think I can only like other people if they're interested in me; that's why I'll never suffer from unrequited love. That might be so, she says, but Ebbe is interested in you. I tell her about Mr Mulvad and the equations, and she starts laughing. I didn't know Ebbe solved equations; that's funny. I say, No, that's not what I mean. When I'm writing I don't care about anyone. I can't. Lise says that artists have to be self-centered, and that I shouldn't think about it so much. I walk home through the pitch-black streets, which the stars don't have the power to brighten. I'm glad I have the baby carriage to lean on. It's not quite eight o'clock, and I'm hurrying because that's the curfew. Everyone is supposed to be home by eight. That means Ebbe won't be coming home tonight, wherever he is. I change Helle, put her in pajamas and tuck her into bed. She's four months old and she gives me a toothless smile, while clutching my finger with her whole hand. It's a good thing that, for now, she doesn't care if her father is home or not.

The next morning Ebbe comes home in terrible shape. His jacket is buttoned crooked and his scarf is all the way up to his eyes, even though it's spring and mild weather. His eyes are red from drinking and lack of sleep. I'm so glad to see him alive that I'm not interested in yelling at him. He stands there swaying in the middle of the floor and does a few awkward steps of the 'baboon dance', a solo dance he always does at a certain point in his drunkenness, while everyone around him claps. He stands on one leg and swings around, but loses his balance and reaches for a chair. I cheated on you, he says, in a gravelly voice. Dejected, I say, With who? With a pretty girl, he says, who isn't pregnant, no, fri-frigid. Someone Ole knew from the Tokanten Pub. I ask, Are you going to see her again? Well, he says, plopping down in a chair, that depends on a lot of things. If you make that Mulvad guy play solitaire instead, then maybe I won't see her anymore. Otherwise, I don't know. I walk over to him, remove the scarf from his mouth and kiss him. Don't see her anymore, I say emphatically, I'll have Mulvad play solitaire instead. He hugs me around my waist and lays his head against my groin. I'm a monster, he mumbles. Why do you want to have anything to do with me? I'm poor and a drunk and I'm good for nothing. You're beautiful and famous and you could have anyone you want. But, I say wholeheartedly, we have a child together. I don't want any man but you. He stands up and embraces me.

I'm so tired, he says. I can't solve our problems by getting drunk. That damned van de Velde; it gives me a backache. Then we laugh and I help him out of his clothes and into bed. Then I sit at my typewriter and I forget, while I'm writing, that my husband has gone to bed with someone else. I forget everything, until Helle starts crying because she's hungry.

The next day I write a poem that starts like this: Why does my lover walk in the rain, without a coat and without a hat? Why does my lover leave me at night, no one could understand that. When I show it to Ebbe, he says it's good, but that it wasn't raining, and that he had a coat on. I laugh and tell him about the time Edvin read my poems and said that I was such a liar. Ebbe says that he'll never lose his way home again, since it makes me so miserable. It's the damned pullimut, he says. To get a beer at a pub, you have to buy a glass of pullimut too, and that gets people drunk. I'm jealous and I ask what the girl looked like. He says that she wasn't anywhere nearly as pretty as me. The kind that chases artists and students, he says. There are so many of them you could use them to feed the sharks. He adds: If we hadn't had Helle, everything between us would still be fine. I say, It'll return to normal; I think it's getting better. But it's not true. Something essential, something incredibly good and valuable between us has been destroyed, and it's worse for Ebbe, since he can't just write away his problems and sorrows. Before we fall asleep that night, I stare into his slanted eyes, whose brown dots glow in the light of the lamp. Whatever happens, I say, promise me you won't leave me and Helle. He promises. We'll grow old together, he says. You'll get wrinkles, and the skin under your chin will droop like my mother's, but your eyes will never age. They will always be the same with the black line around the blue. That was what I fell in love with.

We kiss and lie in each other's arms, chaste as brother and sister. After the van de Velde period passes, Ebbe doesn't try to have sex with me anymore, even though I'm not opposed to it and I have rarely turned him away.

8

One day at the end of May, Ester visits us. She says the club meetings are falling apart, partly because of the curfew, partly because of unwillingness from the restaurant, for which we haven't exactly been a goldmine, and partly because of complications with the members. Sonja can't seem to finish her novel, which Morten Nielsen edits and edits. She has also let Professor Rubow read a few chapters. Halfdan has a poetry collection coming out from Athenæum, which have also praised Ester's own new novel, which will be published in the fall. I've delivered my manuscript, 'The Street of Childhood', and now that I'm not currently writing, I have a huge void inside me that nothing can fill. It feels like everything is going into me but nothing is coming out again. Lise says that now I have to enjoy life for a while, that I deserve it after all that hard work. But for me life is only enjoyable when I'm writing. From sheer boredom I hang out for hours with Arne and Sinne, who live on Schubert Street. They're the couple who were lying in the child's bed, that first night Ebbe and I met. Arne is an economics student like Ebbe, and he gets so much money from home that he doesn't have to work. Sinne is the daughter of a farmer from the Limfjord area, and she is buxom, red-haired and full of energy. She's started studying for an associate's degree, because she can't stand how little she knows. I tell her that I've grown used to my ignorance and that I'm terrible at learning things. I tell her I got divorced from Viggo F. before I ever even finished *The French Revolution*.

Ester doesn't live with Viggo F. anymore. She says she got tired of hearing how much he missed me and how bitter he was that I left him. She moved back home, but that's not so good either. Her father is a bankrupt grocer who brings his lovers home, one after the other. Her mother has gotten used to it. You know what, Ester says, I'm sick and tired of all that forced free-thinking. I am too, and I ask her what a couple of weirdos like us should be doing when we aren't writing. Then she tells me her real reason for coming. Back from when she worked at the pharmacy, she knows a painter named Elisabeth Neckelmann. Elisabeth lives with another woman who wears a collar and a suit and uses an amber cigarette holder, because she only likes women. And she likes me, says Ester calmly, and she asked if I might want to live in her vacation home for a while. I think it sounds nice, but I can't live there with Halfdan, because we won't have any income. Would you stay there with me? The country air would be good for Helle. When I hesitate before answering, Ebbe interrupts: I think you should go, he says, a little separation can revitalize a marriage. He adds that he'll have more peace and quiet for studying without Helle bothering him. His exams are soon, and he has a lot of catching up to do. So I agree to Ester's offer. I like her because she's so calm, friendly and sensible, and because she has the same mission in life as I do. Ebbe promises to come visit me there, as often as he can, even though the house is far from Copenhagen, somewhere in southern Sjælland. Ester and I decide to bicycle out there the next day, and in the evening Ebbe goes to bed with me for the first time in a long while. But he does it angrily and uncaringly, as if he's irritated that he's still attracted to me. It'll be different, I say, feeling guilty, after I finish nursing. I get milk on him and he laughs. He says, Yeah, it's not that easy going to bed with a dairy.

The house sits in lowlands, with a wheat field behind it and grass sticking up and wild raspberry canes along the slope up to the road, where a pair of crooked pine trees hide the walk. Inside the house there's a large living room, with an old-style stove at one end, and a little room with two beds, where we lie so close to one another I can hear Ester's quiet breathing if I wake momentarily in the middle of the night. I sleep with Helle and I feel cosy and glad with her warm little body next to mine. During the day she lies in her carriage out in the sunshine, but she doesn't tan, just like me. We both have fair skin. Meanwhile Ester gets a tan within a couple of days. It makes her teeth look like they've become whiter, and the whites of her eyes resemble wet porcelain against her taut brown skin. I wake up first in the morning, because Ester needs more sleep than I do. With lots of difficulty, I light the stove with wood we buy from the farmer nearby, who also sells us milk and eggs. The stove puts out more smoke than fire, and I have to light it several times before it really catches. Then I make tea, and butter some bread, and sometimes I serve Ester breakfast in bed. You're going to spoil me, she says happily, rubbing the sleep out of her fall-brown eyes. Her long black hair falls down over her smooth forehead. The days pass with long walks, talks, and playing with Helle, who has just got her first tooth. I've never been out in the country before, and I'm amazed at the silence, which is like nothing I have ever experienced.

I feel something resembling happiness, and I wonder if this is what is meant by enjoying life. In the evening I go for a walk alone while Ester watches Helle. The aromas from the fields and pine forest are stronger than on the day we arrived. The lighted windows in the farmhouse shine like yellow squares in the darkness, and I wonder what the people there do to pass the time. The man probably sits listening to the radio; and the wife probably darns socks which she pulls up out of a woven basket. Soon they'll yawn and stretch and look out at the weather and say a few words about the work awaiting them in the morning. Then they'll tiptoe to bed so as not to wake the children. The yellow squares will go dark. Eyes will shut all over the world. The cities go to sleep, and the houses, and the fields. When I come back to the house, Ester has made some dinner, like fried eggs or something like that. We don't go to much trouble. Then we light the petroleum lamp and talk for hours, with long pauses in between, which aren't tense and sizzling like the silences between Ebbe and I have become. Ester tells me about her childhood, her unfaithful father and her gentle, patient mother. I tell her about my childhood too, and our pasts come alive between us like a section of a wall teeming with life. These quiet days are only interrupted when Ebbe or Halfdan comes to visit. Sometimes they ride their bicycles out here together, and they arrive hot and panting. We have a nice time while they're here, but I like being alone with Ester better. She's like a boy in her faded short-sleeved shirts and long pants and her pouty mouth with the small, upturned top lip.

On warm mornings we wash all over out by the edge of

the field. Ester's body is brown and strong with large firm breasts. She's a bit taller than I am, with broad shoulders. I squeal when she pours the cold water over me, and my skin turns blue with goosebumps. But Ester doesn't mind at all when it's her turn, and she lets the sun dry her shiny smooth limbs, stretched out in the grass like a crucifix. I think I could live this way for the rest of my life. It's too complicated to think about Ebbe and our constant problems.

The grain is golden, standing there swaying in the wind, heavy with ripe kernels. I'm awakened very early by a cuckoo calling outside the house, first near, then distant, as if amusing itself by teasing us. Finally one of us tumbles out of bed, dizzy with sleep, opens the top half of the Dutch door, and claps to scare it away. An hour later the harvester starts cutting out in the field, and the sun lifts its yellow forehead up behind the pine woods. I lie there looking at Ester while I nurse. I'm thinking that soon we will leave and each go back to our husbands. I think about Ruth too, my childhood friend, and a warm feeling leads my thoughts aimlessly around in space. When Ester wakes up, I ask her, Do you think I should stop nursing? Sure, she says smiling. Helle doesn't seem to be lacking anything, but some solid food wouldn't be bad. Though you'll lose your nice-looking bosom.

I come home to a sunburned Ebbe, who passed his first semester with the lowest grades possible; but he made it. He is sincerely glad to see me again, and when he hugs me I can tell that my frigidity is passing. I tell him, and he says, Then nothing in the world will ever come between us again. I don't think it will either. But in the following days I think about Ester's little boyish face with the pouty mouth, and how in some indecipherable way she is the reason that Ebbe and I have become close again.

9

In the fall my new book comes out, and it gets good reviews everywhere except in the *Social-Demokraten*, where Julius Bomholt rips it apart across two columns under the headline: 'Escape from Worker Street'. He writes that the book contains 'not a single glimmer of gratitude'. 'It also lacks', he adds, 'a description of our young healthy boys in the Danish Social Democratic Union (DSU).' I cry into my ersatz tea, blubbering: But I've never met anyone from the DSU so how could I ever describe them? Ebbe does what he can to comfort me, but I'm not used to being criticized like that, and I sob as if a member of my closest family just died. He used to be so nice to me, I say, when Viggo F. and I visited him. Ebbe says that he's probably angry because I left Viggo F., just like Barnhof was, and the review does seem cruel, as if there were a personal grudge behind it. Graham Greene writes somewhere, Ebbe continues, looking up at the ceiling like he always does when he's really thinking, that there is something wrong with a person who has never had a flop. So I let him comfort me. I cut out all the reviews except the bad one, which doesn't matter anyway, and I bring them over to my father. He glues them in my scrapbook, which is already half full. Then he says to me reproachfully, Couldn't you have left out the part about me lying there sleeping with the rear end of my pants worn shiny and turned toward the living room? I am not always asleep and my pants are not worn shiny. My mother says, No one knows that it's you. The mother in the book doesn't resemble me at all. Then she tells me that she lent their copy of my book to a woman from the ice-creamery when she asked her what it was like having a famous daughter. My mother says, Before that she never gave me the time of day.

This is a brief happy period, when Ebbe doesn't go out in the evening and doesn't drink too much. On the other hand, it's not going well between Lise and Ole. They're fighting over pressing financial problems, because Ole has student debt and Lise doesn't earn very much at the department where she works. They would die of starvation if it weren't for the mushrooms from the landfill, which Lise picks at dusk, and she tells me she wants to get a divorce and marry her lawyer. He's married with two children. And Arne wants to divorce Sinne, because she has a lover who sells on the black market and earns fifty kroner a day, an outrageous amount. In the evening I lie in Ebbe's arms and we promise one another that we will never separate and never cheat on each other.

I tell Ebbe that I've always hated change. I tell him how sad I was when we moved from Hedebygade over to Westend where I never felt at home. I tell him that I'm like my father. When my mother and Edvin changed the furniture around at home, my father and I always moved it back. Ebbe laughs and strokes my hair. You're a goddammed reactionary, he says. I am too, even though I'm a radical. Then his gentle, dark voice spins an unending spool of comfort and constancy into my ear.

He's developing his theories about why Negroes are black and why Jews have hooked noses, and about how many stars there are in the sky; unanswerable questions to which I fall asleep like a child to a repetitious lullaby. Outside is the evil complicated world, which we cannot bear and which wants to brush us aside. The police have been taken over by the Germans, and Ebbe has become a CB'er.* It's supposed to be a kind of replacement for the police. They have blue uniforms with slanted shoulders, and Ebbe's uniform cap is too large for him. I think he looks like the Good Soldier Švejk in it, and when he says that he ought to join the resistance, I can't take him seriously.

When Helle is nine months old, panting and grunting with effort, she stands up in her playpen. She grips the bars, swaying and screeching with joy. When I bend over to congratulate and praise her, my mouth starts watering and I have to run and throw up. I tell myself that I probably ate something that didn't agree with me, but the thought that I could be pregnant makes my legs tremble. If that's the case, I know it will ruin everything between Ebbe and me.

You're in the second month, says Dr Herborg, my public-healthcare doctor, and he sits down, while the curtain that is always hanging between me and reality turns gray and perforated, like a spider web. A button is missing from the doctor's shiny white coat, and he has a long black hair sticking out of one of his nostrils. But I don't want to have this baby, I say emphatically. It was a mistake. I must have put my diaphragm in wrong. He smiles and looks at me unsympathetically. Dear

* A member of the Civil og Beskyttelse, the civilian defense and rescue corps formed when the Germans dissolved the Danish police during the occupation.

Lord, he says, how many children do you think are born by mistakes? The mothers love them anyway. I ask carefully, Can't I have it taken out? and immediately the smile disappears from his face like a rubber band gone limp. I do not do that, he says coolly, and you may know that it is illegal. Then I ask him, following Lise's advice, if he can refer me to someone who does do it. No, he says, that is also illegal. So I go and visit my mother, who I know will understand. She's sitting in the kitchen playing solitaire. Oh, she says, when she hears my reason for coming, it's not so hard to knock it out of there. Just go to the pharmacy and buy a bottle of amber oil. Drink it down and that'll work. It's worked for me twice, so I know what I'm talking about. I buy the amber oil and I sit across from my mother on the kitchen chair. When I take the top off the bottle, a nauseating smell surrounds me and I run out to the bathroom and throw up. I can't do it, I say, I can't get that down. My mother doesn't have any other ideas, so I walk to the government office where Lise works and I stand outside against the building, waiting for her. I can see the green roof of the stock exchange, glinting weakly in the twilight, and I remember my walks with Piet through the dark city on the way home from the club meetings. Back then I wasn't pregnant, and if I had stayed with Viggo F. I wouldn't have become pregnant either. People go by without noticing me. Women walk past alone, or holding their children's hands. Their faces are relaxed and introspective, and they probably don't have anything growing inside them that they don't want. Lise, I exclaim as she walks toward me. He won't do it. What in the world am I going to do? On the way to the streetcar I tell her about my mother's horrible amber oil, which is a remedy that Lise has never heard of. I go in with her to pick up Kim from her mother's. Her mother is an authoritative woman wearing a floor-length dress with a cap on her head because she has a bald spot. I recall that she has given birth to ten children, because Lise's father always wanted there to be a baby in the cradle, and no one ever cared what she thought about that. When we're back at Lise's, she says that I mustn't panic; there must be a solution. She's going to ask a young woman at her office who had a pregnancy terminated illegally about a year ago. Unfortunately the woman is sick at the moment, but as soon as she's back at work, Lise will get the address for me. Dr Leunbach isn't doing them right now, says Lise, because he was just in jail for it. Maybe Nadja knows of someone, she says, but I don't remember where she and her sailor live. But I can't just wait around, I say desperately, I have to do something. I can't work, and I've lost all feelings toward Ebbe and Helle. Lise says that there are probably lots of doctors in the same situation as Leunbach. She says that if I have to do something, I could call them one by one from the phone book, and maybe I'll get lucky. In the meantime, the woman from the office might get better; so I shouldn't lose hope. She looks at me solemnly: Do you really think it would be so terrible, she asks, if you had another child? Lise doesn't understand either. I don't want anything to happen to me that I don't want, I say. It's like getting caught in a trap. And our marriage won't be able to bear another period of nursing frigidity. I can't stand it as it is when Ebbe touches me.

When I get home, Ebbe tells me that he's contacted the resistance and he's going to be trained as a freedom fighter, to prepare for the day when the Germans capitulate and pull out of the country. No one thinks it will happen without a fight. No one thinks they're going to win either, not after their defeat at Stalingrad. I could not care less, I tell him irritably, if you want to play soldier; I have other things to deal with. Ebbe says he isn't so crazy about the idea of getting rid of the baby. People can die from that, he says, and in any case he won't help me find a doctor to do it. I can't be bothered to talk to him. He doesn't understand. I don't know what I ever saw in him.

The next day I begin my doctor odyssey. I can only do a couple of visits a day, because they all have consultations at the same times. I sit across from these white coats in my worn-out trench coat with my red scarf around my neck. They look at me coldly and in disbelief: Who in the world took it upon themselves to give you my address? Dear woman, there are women who are much worse off than you. You're married and you only have one child. One of them says, You don't want me to commit a crime, do you? There's the door.

I return home, miserable and humbled. I pick up Helle from Ebbe's mother's house and I nurse her, without paying her any attention. I put her in bed, and then pick her up again. The telephone rings and a voice says, Hello, this is Hjalmar, is Ebbe home? I hand Ebbe the phone, and he answers with one-syllable words. Then he puts on the coat he inherited from his father with the silly strap in the back. He slips on his high rubber boots because it's raining and a cap that he otherwise never wears, pulled down over his forehead. Under his arm he is holding a briefcase uncomfortably, as if it were filled with dynamite. His face is pale. Do I look suspicious? he says. No, I say flatly, though even a child would think there was something fishy about him from miles away. After he leaves, I scan the telephone book some more, page after page. But finding an abortion doctor this way is like trying to find a needle in a haystack, and I give up after a couple of days. I realize I'm in a race against time, because I know no one will do it if I'm more than three months pregnant. It's not easy to see Lise in the evening, because she's with her lawyer after work, and she doesn't think we should ask Ole, because he has the same attitude as Ebbe. Men seem to be excluded from my world right now. They're foreign creatures, it's as if they came from another planet. They're not in touch with their bodies. They don't have any tender, soft organs where a blob of slime can attach itself like a tumor and, completely independent of their volition, start living its own life. One evening I go to visit Nadja's father and ask where she and her sailor live. It's a basement apartment in Østerbro, and I go right over there. They're sitting eating, and Nadja kindly asks if I will join them. But the smell of food makes me nauseous, and I can hardly eat anything these days. Nadja has had her hair cut, and she's affected a swinging gait, as if she were on the deck of a ship. The sailor's name is Einar, and he repeats the same phrases again and again: That's right, that's the way to do it, etc. Nadja talks like that too. When she finds out why I came by, she says that she can get me some quinine pills. She used them for a miscarriage herself once. But it could take a couple of days to work, she says. It's not that easy. But I know where you're coming from, she says. You hate the thought of it growing eyes and fingers and toes and you can't do anything about it. You stare at other children and you don't see any redeeming qualities in them. You can't think of anything but being alone in your own body again.

Slightly relieved, I tell Lise that Nadja has promised to get me some quinine pills, but Lise isn't so enthusiastic. She says, I've heard that some people go blind and deaf from those. I say that I don't care, as long as I get rid of this.

Finally, the young woman we had been waiting for comes back to work at the office, and Lise gets the address of the doctor who helped her. For the first time in a long time I feel happy, walking home with the note in my hand. The man's name is Lauritzen and he lives on Vesterbro Street. People call him 'Abortion-Lauritz', so it must be right. I can look at Helle and Ebbe again. I put Helle on my lap and play with her, and I say to Ebbe: When you go out and meet Hjalmar, don't wear a cap and you should hold that briefcase as if it had books inside. You are so bad at that. But he calms me down by saying that he's not going to be taking part in any sabotage operations, so there's not much chance the Germans will capture him. Tomorrow at this time, I say, I will be happier than I have ever been in my entire life.

The next day I put on the lined fustian jacket that I bought from Sinne, because it's getting cold out. Sinne had it sewn from some old comforters from her family, but when everyone and his brother started wearing fustian jackets, she didn't want it anymore. I'm also wearing long pants. I bicycle to Vesterbro Street, which is already decorated for Christmas with pine garlands and red ribbons along the sidewalk. I've been told not to tell anyone and not to say where I got the address from. There are a lot of people in the waiting room, mostly women. A woman in a fur coat is pacing, wringing her hands. She pats a little girl on the head as if it were something her hands did all on their own, and then she continues pacing. She turns and approaches a young woman and asks, May I please go in before you? I'm in a lot of pain. Okay, says the woman amenably, and when the door to the consultation room opens and someone yells: Next! she runs inside and slams the door shut. A few moments later the woman comes out a changed person. Her eyes are beaming, her cheeks are red, and there is a strange distant smile on her lips. She pulls aside the curtain and looks down at the street. How beautiful, she says, to see all those decorations. I can't wait until Christmas. Amazed, I watch her go. My respect for the doctor has grown. If he can help such a miserable person in just a couple of minutes, who knows what he could do for me.

What seems to be the trouble? the doctor says, looking at me with his tired, friendly eyes. He is an older, gray-haired man with an undefinable, slovenly appearance. There's a salami sandwich on his desk, with both ends of the bread curled up. I tell him that I'm pregnant but that I don't want another baby. Well, he says, rubbing his chin, I'm sorry to disappoint you. I'm not doing that for the time being, because it's getting hot around here.

My disappointment is so immense, so paralyzing, that I bury my face in my hands and burst out crying. But you're my last chance, I sob; I'm almost three months pregnant. If you don't help me, I'll kill myself. That's what so many women say, he says quietly, removing his glasses to get a better look at me. Now, he says, you're Tove Ditlevsen, aren't you? I admit it, but I don't see that it makes any difference. I read your last book, he says, it was good. I'm an old Vesterbro boy myself. If you'll just stop crying, he says very slowly, I might be able to whisper an address to you. I am about to hug him in gratitude when he writes an address down on a slip of paper for me. You can get an appointment with him, he says. All he does is poke a hole in the amniotic sac. If you start to bleed, you have to call me. And if I don't start bleeding? I ask, anxious that this is going to be more complicated than I thought. That wouldn't be good, he says, but it usually does. We'll cross that bridge when we come to it.

When I come home I tell Ebbe about it, and he pleads with me to give up my mission. No, I say vehemently, I would rather die. Ill at ease, he paces the living room, looking at the ceiling as if he could find a convincing argument up there. I call the doctor, who lives in Charlottenlund. Tomorrow six o'clock, he says in a grumpy, toneless voice. Just come right in; the door will be open. Bring three hundred kroner with you. I tell Ebbe not to worry. If anything happens I'll be at the doctor's, so he'll be careful. When it's all over, I say, things will return to normal, Ebbe. That's why I need to have this done.

10

I take the streetcar to Charlottenlund, because I don't want to ride my bicycle, not knowing what kind of condition I'll be in after my appointment. It's two days before Christmas, and people are loaded down with packages covered in bright wrapping paper. Maybe this will all be over by Christmas Eve, so we can have Christmas at my parents' house again. I would love that. I'm sitting next to a German soldier. A heavy-set woman with packages has just made a big show of getting up and moving over to the opposite side. I feel bad for the soldier, who probably has a wife and children at home, where he would rather be, instead of traipsing around in a foreign country that his leader decided to invade. Ebbe is sitting at home, more nervous than me. He bought me a flashlight so I can find the address in the dark. We looked in a book to find out what an amniotic sac was. When it breaks, the book said, the water comes out and the birth starts. But there's supposed to be blood, not water. Neither of us really understands.

The doctor greets me in the entry, where a bare lightbulb dangles from a hook in the ceiling. He seems nervous and grouchy. The money, he says flatly, holding out his hand. I give it to him, and he nods toward the examination room. He's about fifty, small and shriveled, and the corners of his mouth droop, as if he has never smiled. Come on up, he says, slapping his hand on the examination table with the hanging straps for patients' legs. I lie down with an anxious glance at the side table which has on it a row of shiny pointed instruments. Will it hurt? I ask. A bit, he says, only a second. He talks like a telegram, as if he's trying to limit the use of his vocal cords. I shut my eyes, and a sharp pain darts through my body, but I don't make a sound. Done, he says. If you notice blood or fever, call Dr Lauritzen. No hospitals. Don't mention my name.

Sitting in the streetcar on the way home, I'm afraid for the first time. Why is it so secretive and complicated? Why didn't he just take it out? My insides are as quiet as a cathedral; there's no sign that a deadly instrument has just penetrated the membrane which was supposed to protect what wants to live against my will. When I get home Ebbe is sitting there, feeding Helle. He's pale and nervous. I tell him what happened. You shouldn't have done that, he says repeatedly. You're putting your life in danger and that's wrong. We lie awake most of the night. There's no sign of blood or water, no fever, and no one has told me what to expect. Then the air-raid siren sounds. We carry Helle down to the cellar in her bed; this never wakes her up. People are sitting there, half asleep. I talk to the woman who lives downstairs; she's stuffing the mouth of her sleepy, cranky child with cookies. She's young, with a weak, immature face. Maybe she tried to have an abortion too, with that child, or a later one. Maybe lots of women have done what I'm doing now, but no one talks about it. I haven't even told Ebbe the name of the doctor in Charlottenlund, because I don't want him to get in trouble if something happens to me. He helped me as my last resort, and I feel a solidarity with him, even though he was an unpleasant man.

I get cold sitting down here, and I button my fustian jacket up to my neck. I'm so cold my teeth start chattering. I think I might have a fever, I say to Ebbe. The air-raid siren stops, and we go back up to the apartment. I take my temperature, which reads 40°C. Ebbe is beside himself. Call the doctor, he says vehemently. You have to go to the hospital right away. The fever makes me feel like I'm tipsy. Not now, I laugh, it's the middle of the night. Then his wife and children will find out. The last thing I see before falling asleep is Ebbe pacing the floor, furiously running his fingers through his hair. I can't believe this, he mumbles in despair, I can't believe this. Meanwhile I'm thinking: your buddy in the resistance, Hjalmar, he puts your life in danger too, you know.

Early the next morning I call Dr Lauritzen to tell him my fever is 40.5°, but there's no blood or water. It'll come, he promises. Go to the clinic right away; I'll call and tell them you're on your way. But not a word to the nurses, okay? You're pregnant, you have a fever, that's all. And don't be scared. It'll all work out.

It's a nice clinic on Christian IX Gade. The head nurse receives me – a nice, motherly older woman. We might not be able to save the baby, she says, but we'll do what we can. Her words make me wonder, and when I'm shown to a double room, I prop myself up on my elbow and look at the woman in the other bed, who is five or six years older than me and has a sweet, trusting face above the white shirt she's wearing. Her name is Tutti, and to my surprise, she's Morten Nielsen's girlfriend. He's the father of the baby she was going to have. Tutti's divorced, an architect, and she has a six-year-old daughter. Within an hour it's like we've known each other our whole lives. A little Christmas tree stands in the middle of our room with tinkling glass decorations and a star on top. It seems ludicrous, given the circumstances. When I was a child, I say to Tutti in my fevered reverie, I thought that stars really had five points on them. The light goes on, and a nurse arrives with two trays for us. I still can't take the sight or smell of food, so I don't touch it. The nurse asks, are you bleeding? No, I say. Then she leaves a pail and some pads, in case it starts during the night. Dear God, I think in desperation, just let me bleed one drop of blood. After they take away the trays, Ebbe arrives, and then Morten. Hi there, he says, surprised, What are you doing here? Then he sits down on Tutti's bed and they disappear, whispering and embracing. Ebbe has brought me twenty quinine pills which he got from Nadja. Only take them if you have to, he says. After he leaves, I tell Tutti that Nadja once forced a miscarriage by taking quinine. She doesn't see any reason not to take them, so I do it. The night nurse comes in, turns off the ceiling light and turns on the nightlight. Its blue glow illuminates the room with an unreal, ghostly hue. I can't fall asleep, but when I say something to Tutti, I'm unable to hear my own voice. Tutti, I yell, I'm deaf! I can see Tutti moving her lips, but I can't hear anything. Say it louder, I tell her. Then she shouts, You don't have to yell; I'm not deaf. It's those pills, but I think it's just temporary.

There's whooshing in my ears, and behind the whoosh there is a cottony, charged silence. Maybe I've become permanently deaf, for no reason, because there's still no blood. Tutti gets out of bed and walks over to me and shouts in my ear, They just want to see blood. So I'll give you my used pads, and you just show it to them tomorrow morning. Then they'll scrape you out. Talk louder, I say, and finally I'm able to understand what she said. During the night she walks over and places her used pads in my pail. When she passes the Christmas tree, the glass decorations clink together and I know they're tinkling, but I can't hear them. I think about Ebbe and Morten and their desolate expressions amid this woman's world of blood, nausea and fever. And I think of my childhood Christmases, when we walked around the tree singing: Out of the depths we come – instead of singing psalms. I think about my mother. She has no idea I'm lying here, because she can never keep a secret. I also think about my father who has always been hard of hearing, because it runs in his family. Deaf people must live stifled, isolated lives. I might need a hearing aid. But my deafness doesn't mean much next to Tutti's act of mercy. She shouts in my ear, They know full well what's going on here. They just have to keep up appearances.

Towards morning I fall asleep, exhausted, until the nurse comes in and wakes us. My oh my, you've been bleeding a lot, she says with fake worry, looking down into the pail with the night's harvest. I'm afraid we won't be able to save the baby. I'll call the doctor right away. To my relief, I realize that my hearing has come back. Are you sad? asks the nurse. A little, I lie, trying to put on a downcast face.

In the afternoon the doctor comes in, and I'm wheeled to the operating room. Don't feel so bad, he says cheerfully. At least you have one child already. Then they place a mask over my face and the world fills with the smell of ether.

When I wake up, I'm lying in bed with a clean, white shirt on. Tutti smiles over at me. Well, she says, are you happy now? Yes, I say. I don't know what I would have done without you. She doesn't know either, and she says that it's all behind us now. She says Morten wants to marry her. She's madly in love with him and she adores his poetry, which has just been published and has been praised everywhere in the press. Besides you, she says tactfully, he's the most talented young person today. I think so too, but I've never been close to him. Ebbe arrives with flowers like I've just given birth, and he's so happy, because now it's over. We have to be more careful in the future, he says. I go and ask Dr Lauritzen to show me how to put my diaphragm in correctly. Still I harbor a strong resistance to that piece of hardware, a resistance that will remain with me my whole life. My temperature drops quickly to normal, and I'm ravenously hungry now that my nausea has disappeared, as if by a stroke of magic. I miss Helle's little pudgy body with the dimples on her knees. When Ebbe brings her in to me, I think with horror, what if it were her that we had just denied access to life? I bring her up into the bed with me and play with her. She is more dear to me than ever.

In the evening the doctor comes into our room without his coat on, holding two children by the hand. They are ten or twelve years old. Merry Christmas, he says jovially, and squeezes our hands. The children shake hands with us too, and when they're gone, Tutti says: He's so nice. We should be thankful that someone dares to do this.

On Christmas Eve I wake up, take out a pencil and paper from my bag and write a poem in the weak glow of the nightlight:

> You who sought shelter
> with one weak and afraid,
> For you I hum a lullaby
> between the night and day – – –

I don't regret what I did, but in the dark, tarnished corridors of my mind there is a faint impression, like a child's footprints in damp sand.

II

The days pass, the weeks pass, the months pass. I've started writing short stories, and the veil between myself and reality is solid and secure again. Ebbe has started going to hear lectures, and now I'm not so anxious when he's out with Hjalmar. To my relief, he's not as interested in my writing as he once was, so I can create my male characters in peace. But after the episode with Mulvad I'm still careful not to include any obvious similarities to Ebbe. After Helle is in bed in the evening, he reads poems to me from Sophus Claussen or Rilke. Rilke makes a deep impression on me, and I would never have discovered him if it weren't for Ebbe. He's also very interested in Viggo Hørup at the moment. Ebbe poses dramatically with his foot up on a stool and his hand on his heart: My hand, he recites in a deep voice, will always be lifted against the politics that I deem the meanest of all – that which attempts to band together the wealthy and set the upper classes against those who have little to prevent them from being crushed into the dust. In the evening when we are lying in one another's arms, he tells me about his childhood, which is just like every other man's. There is always something about a garden with some fruit trees, and a slingshot, and a cousin or girlfriend they're lying with in a hayloft – but then a mother or aunt comes and ruins it. It's a boring story after you've heard it a few times, but they're so captivated while they tell it. And anyway, what we say to one another doesn't matter all that much, as long as things are good between us.

We've moved to a new apartment on the first floor of the building where Lise and Ole live. It has two and a half rooms, and there's a little yard out front, where Helle can run and play. She's two now, and a cascade of blonde curls has suddenly replaced her baldness. She's so easy that Lise says we don't really know what it's like to raise a child. When I'm writing in the morning, I set her to playing with her blocks and dolls, and she has learned not to bother me. Mama's writing, she says ceremoniously to her doll, and afterwards we will all go for a walk.

She's already speaking in complete sentences. A couple of days before we were going to move into the new apartment, Mrs Hansen called to me from the kitchen. The HIPOs* have blocked the street, she says. Look over there, there's a bonfire. I pull aside the curtain and look down. Across the deserted street HIPOs are tossing pieces of furniture out of the top window of the building facing ours, and burning them in a big bonfire. Down below there's a woman with her hands up, standing against the building wall with two children. Men shouting commands are holding them there with their machine guns. Mrs Hansen says, Those poor people – but luckily this damned war will soon be over.

Just as I'm about to leave my lookout, a woman comes

* The Hilfspolizei, a Gestapo-backed pseudo-police force of Danish citizens that patroled and terrorized Copenhagen in 1944.

running at full speed around the corner and I see, to my horror, that it's Tutti. A HIPO man shouts at her and shoots into the sky, and she disappears into our entry. When I let her in, she falls on me sobbing: Morten is dead, she says, and at first the words don't quite register. I get her to sit down, and I can see that she's wearing two different shoes. Dead how? I ask. Is it true? I just saw him two days ago. Tutti tells me between sobs that it was a stray bullet, an accident, completely meaningless, and unbearable. He was sitting across from an officer who was going to show him how to use a pistol with a silencer. Suddenly the gun went off and hit Morten right in the heart. He was only twenty-two, says Tutti, looking at me desperately. I loved him so much. I don't think I'll ever get over this.

I can see Morten's angular honest face before me, and I remember his poem: I have known death since I was a boy. It's so strange, I say, how he wrote so much about death. I know, says Tutti, calming down a little. It was as if he knew that he wouldn't be allowed to live.

Later that day, Ester and Halfdan come by, and they're both shocked. I know that Halfdan was very close with Morten. But what I can't get out of my mind is that the same thing could happen to Ebbe. Now it feels gravely serious when he goes out to meet Hjalmar, and I feel anxious until I see him again. We move into the new apartment and we visit Lise and Ole during curfew. After a tuberculosis exam, which all students have to go through once a year, Ole is told that he has 'something in his chest'. If it weren't for that, he says, he would train to join the resistance too. The doctor decided that Ole has to live for a few months at a college in Holte for students with tuberculosis, and Lise isn't too upset about their separation. Now she can put off their divorce and see her lawyer in peace.

Then arrives the fifth of May, Liberation Day, with jubilant crowds cheering in the streets, as if they've sprouted up from between the paving stones. Strangers embrace one another, bawl out the freedom song and cheer hurray every time a car carrying resistance fighters drives past. Ebbe is in full uniform, and I'm worried what will happen to him, because no one knows if the Germans will pull back without a fight. Upstairs, at Lise and Ole's, the pullimut bottles are on the table for the last time, and there are lots of people there, and we don't know them all. We dance, celebrate and enjoy ourselves, but this historic event doesn't really penetrate my consciousness, because I always experience things after they've happened; I'm rarely in the present. We tear down the blackout curtains and stomp them to pieces. We're acting like we're happy, but really we're not. Tutti is still grieving for Morten; Lise and Ole are separating; and Sinne has just left Arne, who is so depressed that he doesn't get out of bed. Nadja, who is always hunting for a man, but always the wrong one, is trying to get together with Ebbe's brother Karsten, who she would fit like a ring in his nose. Meanwhile I'm thinking about my abortion and I'm always calculating how old the baby would have been by now. Something has gone wrong for each one of us, and I think that our youth has disappeared along with the occupation. Helle and Kim are sleeping in the nursery, and when they cry so loud that we can hear it over our own noise, Lise goes in and sings them back to sleep. Outside in the sky, the spring night revolves and the elegantly suspended moon observes a drunken and dead-tired crowd, who can't bear to leave and go home.

A couple of days later, Ebbe comes home pale and agitated. He tells me how the traitors and collaborators are being treated at Dagmarhus, the previous Gestapo headquarters.

He takes off his uniform and puts on his civilian clothes. When I take a walk with Helle at Vesterbro Square, I see a group of unarmed German soldiers come shuffling, out of step and with exhausted, hopeless faces. They are quite young, some of them only fifteen or sixteen. When I get home I write a poem about them. It starts:

Tired German soldiers
trudging in a strange city,
not looking at one another,
spring light on their foreheads.
Tired, hesitating, shy,
in the middle of a strange city
they approach defeat.

One day Lise comes down to visit us and tells me that Ole is inviting a lot of young women to a 'Tubercular Ball' which they are holding at the Rudershøj dormitory. Ebbe is upset that he can't go, but there are already more than enough men, so it's no use. I'm happy to be invited, because my short-story collection is finished, and I don't know what to do with myself when I'm not writing. Lise says that the dean's wife's son will be there to lure his mother to bed early.

When we get there, the party is in full force. People are dancing to a local band, and none of the students look any worse than Ole, who is the picture of health. A big-chested woman comes rushing up to welcome us. She is evidently the dean's wife. I dance with lots of different men in a large, open room with a parquet floor and high-backed chairs along the walls. The dormitory is located in a large park, which is veiled that evening by a rainy haze, greenish, black and silvery under a misty moon, sailing between the clouds. A bar has been set up in a kind of foyer, with a counter and high chairs and a bartender who is pouring real liquor and not pullimut. For some reason I feel happy and free, and I have a feeling that something special is going to happen before the night is over. I'm drinking whiskey, and I get drunk, jolly and impetuous. On one of the barstools, Sinne is sitting on a young man's lap. I sit next to them and say traitorously, You're betting on the wrong horse; she's engaged to a black marketeer. The young man brushes Sinne off as if she were a fleck of dust. I never thought, he says to me, that poets could be so beautiful. Then, from the shade of the lamp, his face emerges, and I find myself observing it with the attention of a painter of miniatures. He has thinning reddish hair, relaxed gray eyes, and teeth so crooked it looks like they are in two rows. It turns out he is the dean's wife's son, and has completed his medical degree. I'm surprised to meet a student who has actually finished. He dances with me, and we trip over one another's feet and have to give up, laughing. Then we take a walk in the park. The night is clearing and the air is like damp silk. He kisses me beneath a silver-gray birch tree, then suddenly his mother comes rushing out to us with her undulating violet silk bust and waving arms. Young people nowadays, she pants. The contents of her mind are expressed primarily in half-intelligible sentimental outbursts. Then her son, whose name is Carl, remembers his promise to the students to take his mother home to bed, and he mutters something to me about us getting together later, and he disappears into the building with her.

Then the party gets wilder. People are dancing, drinking and carrying on. Pair after pair disappear up the stairs and don't reappear. I'm more drunk than I have been in a long time, and when Carl returns he suggests that we go up to his room so he can get some sleep. I think that sounds like a fine idea. I've forgotten about Ebbe, and about my promise to be faithful to him.

In the morning I wake up with a horrible headache. I glance at the man sleeping next to me and realize that he is quite ugly with all those teeth and that underbite which doesn't hide them. I wake him and say that I'm going home. I'm irritated and sluggish, and I put on my clothes without a word. I decide I never want to see him again, and when he asks if he can walk me home, I say, No thanks, I would rather go alone. When I go down to the messy ballroom, I sit down for a moment on one of the bar chairs. Down the stairs comes Sinne on the heels of a very tall young man, who is holding her bra in one hand. Without taking the least notice of him she walks over to me and asks, Dear God, what did we drink? He was hideous, over six feet tall, and probably only had half a lung. Then she grabs the bra and disappears with a sleepy yawn.

I leave the battlefield and bicycle home to Ebbe, who is furious that I stayed out all night. You probably slept with someone else, he says. I plead my innocence, but actually find it humorous that it should matter so much. There are other forms of loyalty that mean so much more. When I go to bed, I realize that I didn't have my diaphragm in. Otherwise I have always been so careful since my abortion. Then I think that if something does happen, at least he's a doctor, so that should make it easier than last time.

12

Good God, I say. He has an underbite and sixty-four teeth in his mouth instead of thirty-two. And I don't know if it's his or Ebbe's. Lise, what should I do?

I pace the floor, and Lise watches me with two deep furrows on her forehead. You get pregnant just walking through a draft, she says with a sigh. But if he's a doctor he should be able to get rid of it without all the trouble you went through last time. But do I have to see him again? I say. He's so hideous, and what do I tell Ebbe? Things have never been as good between us as they are now. Lise explains to me patiently that I have to see him again. I have to call his mother and find out where he lives. And I can tell Ebbe anything – that I'm going over to visit Nadja or Ester, or that I'm going to visit my parents; he's not suspicious. So we have coffee, and Lise tells me that she's not doing so well either. Her lawyer won't get a divorce after all, but he still wants to be with her. Isn't it terrible, she says, these men with two women. Both of them are suffering, and the man won't choose. She brushes her short brown hair away from her cheek and looks miserable, and it makes me feel bad that I'm always dumping my own problems on her. If I'm not writing, I say, then I'm pregnant. That makes us laugh, and we agree that I have to do something. I'll have to get Carl's address and visit him and have him get rid of it.

The next day Carl calls me himself and asks if we can get together soon. I say yes, and I agree to come and visit him the following evening. He lives at the Biochemical Institute, where he also works. He's a scientist. I tell Ebbe that I'm going to visit Nadja, and I ride my bicycle through the twilight down Nørre Allé, where the trees are as motionless as a drawing. It's summer, and I'm wearing a white cotton dress that I bought from Sinne. Carl's room looks like any student's dorm: a bed, a table, a couple of chairs and some shelves full of books. He's bought sandwiches, beer and schnapps, but I don't touch any of it. We sit at the table and I say: I'm pregnant, and I don't want to have a child when I don't know who the father is. I see, he says, relaxed, looking at me with his serious gray eyes, which are the only pleasant thing about him. I can help you with that. Come tomorrow evening and I can do a curettage. He says this as if it's something he does every day, and he seems like the kind of person that nothing in the world could bother. I smile, relieved, and say: Can you give me anesthesia? I'll give you a shot, he says, so you won't feel a thing. A shot? I ask. What is it? Morphine or Demerol, he says. Demerol is the best. Morphine makes a lot of people throw up. So I calm down, and I eat and drink with him after all. I'm only eight days late, and my morning sickness hasn't started yet. Carl has small, thin, quick hands, which remind me a little of Viggo F.'s. He has a nice voice and he's well spoken. He tells me he went to boarding school at Herlufsholm, that his mother got a divorce when he was two, and that as far back as he can remember, he always wanted her to remarry.

He also tells me that his father, as far as he knows, is in a home for alcoholics, but that he's had no contact with him since he left them. He also tells me that, since we met, he's been reading everything I've written; and he adds, smiling, that we could have a fine child together. He would like to marry me. I already have a very suitable husband, I say, and a lovely daughter, so that will have to wait. Okay, he says, rubbing his chin as if he were checking for stubble. It probably wouldn't be such a great idea to marry me anyway, he says. I have to tell you that I am a little crazy. He says this in complete seriousness, and I ask what he could possibly mean by that. But he can't really explain it. It's just a feeling he has. He says there's a lot of mental illness on his father's side, and also that his mother isn't too bright. I laugh and don't give it another thought. When I'm leaving, he gives me a gentle kiss, but doesn't try to get me to go to bed with him. I think I'm in love with you, he says, but it's probably no use.

When I come home, Ebbe is reading poetry by Thøger Larsen while puffing on his pipe, which he has started doing after reading that cigarettes can cause cancer. He doesn't want Helle and me to lose him to an early death. He asks how Nadja is doing, and I tell him the truth – that she's gotten engaged to a student from the University of Copenhagen, and that she spouts the most reactionary opinions, as if she were from before the reign of Frederik VI. He chuckles and says that she should get married and have children. We're getting old, he says, tapping out his pipe in the ashtray. He is twenty-seven and I'm twenty-five. When I think about my childhood, he says, I feel just like Thøger Larsen. Listen to this:

> Be glad if you meet a withered glimpse
> in dreams from the spring of your youth.

A ray of grace. Your father is near.
Your mother is in the kitchen.

My mother, I object, is over fifty, and I don't think she's old at all. My mother is sixty-five, he says, and I've never thought she was young. It makes a difference. I don't really follow him when he talks about how old he is, and everything I have to hide from him is also creating distance between us. When we go to bed, I say that I'm exhausted and that I have to go straight to sleep. Tomorrow, I say, I want to visit Ester and Halfdan. When he says he'd like to come, I say that we can't always have Lise watching Helle, and his mother doesn't really like watching her either. But I promise him not to stay too long.

The next evening, while I'm sitting in a streetcar on the way to Carl's, I tell myself that it's not definite that I'm pregnant. It could be just a fluctuation in my period; that's not so uncommon. I say this because I don't want another shadow to crop up next to Helle, another one whose age I will always have to calculate. I know that some women get scraped out just to clean their inner parts. When I arrive, I see that Carl has obtained a high table for the occasion. It stands in the center of the room, and there's a white sheet over it. He has also put his pillow on it, so I can be comfortable. He's wearing a white lab coat, and he washes his hands and scrubs his nails, while he pleasantly asks me to make myself comfortable. There are some shiny instruments on the bookshelf next to the table. When he's washed his hands, he takes a syringe from the glass shelf over the sink. He fills it with a clear liquid and lays it next to the instruments; then he ties a rubber hose around my upper arm. You'll feel a little prick, he says calmly. You'll hardly feel it. He taps lightly on the inner side of my elbow, until a blue blood vessel protrudes. You have good veins, he says. Then he gives me the injection, and a bliss I have never before felt spreads through my entire body. The room expands to a radiant hall, and I feel completely relaxed, lazy and happy as never before. I roll over on my side and close my eyes. Leave me alone, I hear myself say, as if through many layers of cotton. You don't have to do anything to me.

When I wake up, Carl is standing there washing his hands again. I still have the blissful feeling, and I have the sense that it will disappear if I move. You can get up and put your clothes on, he says, drying his hands. It's done. I do what he says, slowly, without telling him how happy I feel. He asks if I want a beer, but I shake my head. He says I need some fluids, and he takes out a soda which I force myself to drink. He sits down on the bed next to me and kisses me carefully. Was it painful? he asks. No, I say. What was it you gave me? I ask. Demerol, he says, a painkiller. I take his hand and put it up to my cheek. I'm in love with you, I say. I'll come back soon. He looks happy, and in that moment I think he is almost handsome. He has a solid, durable face, made to last his whole life. Ebbe's face is fragile, scarred in many places, and might be used up by the time he's forty. It's a strange thought, and I don't know how to express it. When I come back, I say slowly, can I have another shot of that? He laughs and rubs his protruding chin. Sure, he says, if you think it's so wonderful. You don't have the makings of an addict. I wish I could marry you, I say, stroking his soft, thin hair. What about your husband? he says. I'll just move out, I say, and take Helle with me. While I ride home in the streetcar, the effects of the shot wear off slowly, and it feels as if a gray, slimy veil covers whatever my eyes see. Demerol, I think. The name sounds like birdsong. I decide never to let go of this man who can give me such an indescribable blissful feeling.

When I get home, Ebbe wants to know how Ester and Halfdan were, but I only give him one-word answers. When he asks me what's wrong, I tell him I have a toothache. I roll over on my side in bed, with my back to him, touching the little bump on my elbow from the injection. I am preoccupied with the single thought of doing it again. I could not care less about Ebbe or anyone else but Carl.

PART TWO

I

Ebbe has since died, but whenever I try to recall his face, I always see him the way he looked that day I told him there was someone else. We were sitting at the table, eating with Helle. He put down his knife and fork and pushed back his plate. He was pale, and a nerve in his cheek was vibrating slightly, but that was the only sign of any disturbance. Then he got up from his chair, walked over to the bookshelf, took out his pipe and carefully started filling it. Then he paced the floor, puffing violently on the pipe while staring at the ceiling, as if he could find an answer up there. Do you want a divorce? he asked in a flat, calm voice. I don't know, I said. For the meantime Helle and I can move out for a while. Maybe we'll come back. Suddenly he put down his pipe and picked up Helle in his arms, which he rarely did. Daddy sad, she said, putting her cheek against his. No, he said, forcing himself to smile, go on and finish eating. He put her back down in her high chair, picked up his pipe again, and resumed pacing. Then he said: I don't understand why people absolutely have to get married or live together. It forces you to see the same person every day for a generation, and there's something unnatural about that. Maybe things would be better if we only visited one another. Who's the other man? he asked, without looking at me. He's a doctor, I said. I met him at the Tubercular Ball. He sat down again, and I saw how his forehead was bathed in sweat. Then he said, still looking at the ceiling: Do you think he can give you an outlook on life? When Ebbe was upset, he always said stupid things. I don't know what you mean by that, I said. I don't think an outlook on life is something people give one another.

When we went to bed, Ebbe held me in his arms for the last time, but he could tell I was distant and distracted. Right, he said. You're in love with someone else. This is something that happens to people, not even unusual in our circles. Still it feels totally unreal. And it's crushing me, even though I'm not showing it. That's one of my problems, that I don't dare to show how I feel. If I had shown you how much I love you, maybe this would never have happened. Ebbe, I said, gently touching his eyelids, we'll visit each other, and maybe you'll get to know Carl. Maybe we can all be friends. No, he said with a sudden vehemence, I never want to lay eyes on that man. I only want to see you and Helle. I propped myself up on my elbow and observed his handsome face with its soft, weak expression. What if I told him the truth? What if I told him I was in love with a clear liquid in a syringe and not with the man who had the syringe? But I didn't tell him; I never told that to anyone. It was like when I was a small child and a secret was ruined if you told a grownup. I rolled over on my side and went to sleep. The next day Helle and I moved to a boarding house that Carl had found for us.

It was a boarding house for older, single women. Our room was furnished with cretonne-covered wicker furniture, a rocking chair with a pillow attached to the back, a tall iron bed from the 1880s and a small feminine writing desk, which nearly collapsed when I set my heavy typewriter on it. Even Helle's little crib seemed too robust in these fragile surroundings, not to mention herself. That first day she played ship with the overturned rocking chair and then she started chewing on a horribly ugly life-sized statue of Christ, which was behind the desk. She was craving calcium at the time. Her piercing child's voice rang through the convent-like hush with a provocative intensity, and one by one the old ladies turned up at my door, asking for a bit of quiet. I don't know why I ever was allowed to move in. When I started writing on my typewriter the next day, the whole boarding house was in an uproar, and the manager, who was an old lady herself, came in to ask if all that racket was really necessary. The residents in her boarding house were all people who had retreated from life, she said. Even their families considered them dead. At any rate no one ever visited them; their families were just waiting to inherit whatever bit of money they might have left. I paid attention to what she said, because I wanted to stay. I liked the location and the room, and the view of the two maple trees, between which hung an old ragged hammock whose rope weave was still covered with snow, though it was nearly March. The woman had a sickly, mild face with pretty, gentle eyes, and she picked Helle up and carefully put her on her lap, as if the vibrant girl might break from the least handling. I agreed not to use the typewriter between one and three in the afternoon, when the ladies were resting, and I promised to visit them once in a while, since their families had deserted them. I liked being with the ladies who either were not completely deaf, or whose fate in this end-station had not made them angry and bitter. And there was always one of them who could watch Helle while I saw Carl in the evenings, which I often did. I sat on his ottoman with my arms under my chin and my knees pulled up, watching him while he worked. He had lots of flasks and beakers in wooden stands around the room. He tasted the contents of the beakers and slid his tongue thoughtfully between his lips. Then he wrote his observations in a large notebook. I asked what he was testing. Piss, he said calmly. Yuck, I said. Then he smiled and said, There is nothing as sterile as piss. He had a strange, careful way of walking, as if he were trying to avoid waking someone, and the desk lamp imparted a copper-like glow to his thin hair. The first three times I visited him he gave me a shot every time and let me lie there passively, dreaming away, without bothering me. But the fourth time he said, No; we'd better take a break. It's not candy, you know. I was so disappointed I got tears in my eyes.

When Ebbe visited me and Helle, he was almost always drunk, and his face was so blank and defenseless that I couldn't bear to look at him. While I sat looking at the two maple trees, with whose branches the sun and wind drew shifting patterns of shadow on the lawn, I thought that I was not a woman whom any man ought to marry. Ebbe played with Helle a little, and she said: Daddy is nice. Helle doesn't like Carl. It took a long time before she would let Carl touch her.

I had delivered a short-story collection and lost my desire to write for the time being. All I could think about was how to get Carl to give me another shot of Demerol. I remembered that he had said it was a painkiller. Where could I say it hurt? From an old untreated infection, one of my ears oozed once in a while, so one day when I was lying on his bed while he tiptoed around the room, chatting intermittently with me and with himself, I put my hand on my ear and said, Ow, I have a terrible earache. He came and sat next to me on the bed and asked sympathetically: Does it hurt badly? I grimaced as if I were in pain. Yes, I said, I can't stand it. I get this once in a while. He moved the lamp so he could look inside my ear. It's oozing, he said, surprised. Promise me you'll have an ear doctor look at it. He patted my cheek. Relax, he said. I'll give you a shot. I smiled thankfully at him, and the fluid went into my blood, lifting me up to the only level where I wanted to exist. Then he went to bed with me, like he always did, when the effect was at its peak. His embrace was strangely brief and violent, with no foreplay, no tenderness; and I didn't feel anything. Light, gentle, untroubled thoughts glided through my head. I thought warmly about all my friends who I almost never saw anymore, and I fantasized that I was having conversations with them. How is it possible, Lise said to me recently, that you could be in love with him? I said, Who can ever understand someone else's love? I lay there for a couple of hours, and the effect wore off, so it was more difficult to find that blank, untroubled state. Everything returned to being gray, slimy, ugly and intolerable. When I said goodbye, Carl asked when my divorce would be finalized. Anytime, I said, figuring that once I was married to him it would be even easier to get him to give me shots. Wouldn't you like to have another baby? he asked as he walked me out, down the stairs. Sure, I said immediately, because a child would bind Carl to me even more, and I wanted him with me for the rest of my life.

2

In the divorce I was given our apartment, which I moved into together with Helle and Carl. Ebbe moved back in with his mother, and I visited him there sometimes, when he called and asked me to come. He never set foot in our apartment again, for fear of running into Carl. But Lise and Ole visited us, as did Arne and Sinne, who were back together, since her black marketeer was doing time. Back when I was with Ebbe, I thought it was so friendly with all of us visiting one another unannounced, but now it really irritated me. It bothered Carl too, because he was jealous of all my friends. Whenever they came over to visit, he would sit with his shy, quiet smile, rarely saying a word. One day Lise asked me cautiously, Isn't he a little strange? I replied brusquely that he worked hard during the day and he was tired in the evening. And what about you? she asked. You've changed since you met him; you've lost weight, and you don't look so healthy anymore. Listen, I said to her angrily, you never like anyone except the students from Høng, and you think anyone who's not chatty and extroverted is strange. She was so hurt by what I said that she stayed away from me for a long time.

One evening shortly after Carl and I had gotten married, Arne and Sinne invited us over for a big dinner. Sinne had had half a pig sent from her family's farm, and they were going to have a party. Carl said he wasn't going to go, and that he thought I should stay home too. When a person has work that requires concentration, he said, with that apologetic tone that never revealed his true intention, it's not good to be overloaded with human interactions. These are my friends, I protested. I see no reason why I shouldn't go to the dinner. Will you stay home, he said gently, if I give you a shot? Bowled over, and for the first time a little frightened, I said, Sure, sure I will. The next morning I felt so miserable that I couldn't even get up and make coffee for him. The light seared my eyes, and I could barely separate my dry, cracked lips. It felt as if my skin couldn't bear the pressure of the sheet and the blanket. Everything I cast my eyes on was ugly, hard and sharp. I pushed Helle away from me and snapped at her, which made her cry. What's wrong, asked Carl. Is it your ear again? Yes, I whined, putting my hand to my ear. Dear God, I thought in desperation, please let him believe me just one last time. Don't let him leave for work before giving me a shot. Let me see it, he said gently, and he took an ear speculum and a little flashlight down from the top shelf in the closet, where he kept the instruments from the curettage. It looks pretty good, he mumbled, and since you're going to the ear doctor twice a week, it should be under control. While he looked in my ear, I lay there without blinking to get my eyes to tear up. I'm rather worried, he said, filling the syringe. If this keeps up, there might be no way around an operation. I'll speak with Falbe Hansen about it. He was the ear doctor Carl had found for me. Why are you giving Mama a needle? asked Helle, who had never seen this before. I'm giving her a vaccine against diphtheria, he said, just like you had. It's supposed to be in your shoulder, she said. Why are you putting it in her arm? That's the way you do it with grownups, he said. Limp and distant and peaceful I watched while Carl drank his coffee and spooned out Helle's oatmeal for her. Lazy and blissful I said goodbye to Carl, but far back in my foggy brain anxiety began gnawing. Operation! There was nothing wrong with my ear. Then I forgot about it again and lay there fantasizing about a novel I was going to write. It was going to be called *For the Sake of the Child*, and I was writing it in my mind. Long, beautiful sentences flowed through my thoughts as I lay on the divan, looking at my typewriter, powerless to make one single movement towards it. Helle crawled around on me and had to dress herself. I said that she should go upstairs and get Kim, so they could play together outside in the yard. When the effect of the shot wore off, I broke out in sobs and pulled the comforter up to my chin because I was shivering, even though it was the start of summer. This is awful, I said out into the air, I can't take this. What am I going to do? So I got dressed, with difficulty, because my hands were shaking, and every piece of clothing scratched my skin. I thought of calling Carl, so he could come home and give me another shot. The hours in front of me seemed like years, and I didn't think I could survive them. Then I got a bad stomachache and I had to go to the toilet. I had gotten diarrhea and I had to run out there every five minutes.

Later in the day I felt a bit better. I even sat in front of my typewriter and started that novel which had been haunting my thoughts for a long time. But the words didn't come easy and flowing like they usually did, and I had trouble keeping my thoughts on the subject. I kept looking at my watch to see how long it would be until Carl came home.

Around noon, John came over to visit. He was a friend of Carl's, a tubercular medical student who was living at Rudershøj with my mother-in-law. I didn't like him, because whenever he visited us, he tended to sit in a corner and stare at me with his big X-ray eyes, as if I represented a difficult problem that he had to solve at all costs. He and Carl usually talked over my head about incomprehensible scientific questions, and I had never been alone with him before. I'd like to talk to you, he said solemnly, if you have a moment. I let him come in, while my heart started thumping with a strange, indefinite fear. John sat on my desk chair, while I sat on the ottoman. When he sat down, he gave the impression of being tall, because his face was large and squarish, his shoulders broad and his body long and stooped. But he had short legs and they didn't get much longer when he stood up. He and Carl had lived together at Regensen, and they had helped one another write their theses. He sat quietly for a while, wringing his big hands as if he were cold. I looked down at the floor, because I couldn't stand his penetrating stare. Then he said, I'm worried about Carl, and maybe about you too. Why? I said, on guard. We're doing fine together. He bent over to catch my gaze, and I looked at him, obstinate and afraid. Has Carl ever told you, he said, about his institutionalization a year ago? Ill at ease, I said, What kind of institutionalization? In a psychiatric ward, he said; he had a psychosis. Why can't you talk Danish, I said, irritated. What's a psychosis? It's a short-lived mental illness, he said, leaning back in the chair. It lasted three months. I forced myself to laugh. I said, Are you telling me that he's crazy? Crazy people get locked up, because they're scary. I'm not scared of him. John released me from his unnerving gaze, and he looked out in the yard at the children playing. There's something wrong, he said.

I have a feeling he's getting sick again. When I asked why, John said that Carl has recently ignored all his work in order to study nothing but ear maladies. At the institute there were textbooks piling up about ear anatomy and ear illnesses, and he was studying them as if he were trying to become an ear doctor. That's crazy, said John emphatically. Just because you have a little earache once in a while? Anyone else would leave it to an ear doctor and trust that he would do what he could. But he cares about me, I said, and I could feel myself blushing. He cares about me, and he wants to help me get better, that's all. Then I laughed at his serious mortician's face. Some friend you are, I said, running over to tell his wife that he's stark raving mad. I'm not saying that at all, he said irresolutely. I just want you to know that three of his cousins are in a mental institution. I wouldn't recommend having any children with him. When he says that, I realize that my period is a few days late. Well you know what, I say, I think your warning has come too late; I think I might be pregnant. The thought of it makes me happy, and I ask if John wants a beer or a cup of coffee, because I don't feel like listening to him anymore. But he doesn't want anything; he's going to a lecture. I follow him out to the door, and he sticks out his hand to shake mine, something my friends and I never do. I'm being admitted to Avnstrup in a few days, he says, to have one of my lungs taken out of action. For a person like me, health is not something you take for granted. He hesitates a second more before he leaves. And you, he says, just like Lise did, you don't look as good as you used to. Are you eating enough? I assure him that I am, and I breathe easy again once he's finally gone. I decide, even though he didn't ask me to, not to tell Carl that he was here.

When Carl came home, I told him that I was probably

pregnant. He was happy and revealed his plan for us to build a house on the outskirts of the city. I asked if we had enough money for that, and he said that he was expecting a large grant to come through soon. Then we could live in our own house, concentrate on our work, and not see so many people and never go anywhere. I thought that sounded marvelous, because I was starting to feel that it was becoming necessary for us to live without interference from other people. When he asked about my ear, I said that the pain had gone away. John's visit had frightened me. Then I said, without knowing why, that I always had trouble sleeping when I was pregnant. He thought about it, rubbing his chin. I'll tell you what, he said. I'll give you some chloral. It's a good sedative with no side effects. It tastes awful, but you can just drink it in some milk.

The next day he came home with a large brown bottle of medicine. I'd better pour it for you, he said. It's easy to take too much. A few minutes after drinking it I was feeling good, not like after Demerol, more like I had had too much alcohol. I blabbed on about our house, how it would be furnished, and the baby we were going to have. Then in the middle of this I fell asleep and didn't wake up until the next morning. Can I have that every night? I asked. Sure, of course, he said. It can't do any harm. Then he thought of something. Let me feel behind your ear, he said, pressing on my skull. Does that hurt? he asked. Yes, I said. Lying to Carl had become such a habit that I couldn't resist. He bit his top lip pensively. I'm going to talk with Falbe Hansen about that operation after all, he said. I asked if I would be anesthetized with Demerol. He said no, but that afterwards I could have as much as I wanted to numb the pain. After he left, I walked to the bathroom and stared at my face in the mirror for a long time. It was true. I didn't look good. My face was drawn, and my skin was dry and rough. I wonder, I said to my reflection, which of us is crazy. Then I sat down at my typewriter, because that was my one remaining hope in a more and more uncertain world. While I wrote, I thought: all the Demerol I want; and the operation, which would be the prerequisite for entering that paradise, didn't matter to me one bit.

3

But the doctor wouldn't do the operation. After the X-rays were taken, Carl and I rode to his office on the motorcycle he had just bought. He stood next to Falbe Hansen in his leather jacket, which flared out in the back like a duck's ass. And with his helmet in his hand, he stared at the pictures the doctor held up one after the other. There's nothing abnormal, said Falbe Hansen. I walked over and stood next to Carl, and while the ear doctor spoke, he stared at me the whole time with a cool look in his gray eyes. If she's in pain, he said slowly, then it must be from rheumatism, and nothing can be done for that. It usually goes away by itself. Then Carl talked about bones, hammers, anvils, stirrups and God knows what, while I felt the earth burning beneath me, because this man knew I was lying. Falbe Hansen's attitude got even more icy. You won't get anyone to operate on it, he said, sitting down at his desk with a distracted expression. That ear is completely healthy. I have had it dried out, and your wife doesn't need to come back and see me anymore.

Don't worry, Carl said gently while we walked back through the hospital grounds. If the pain keeps up, we'll find someone else to operate. Maybe the conversation did make some kind of impression on him, because when we got home he said: I'll write a prescription for you for some pills called methadone. It's a strong painkiller; then it won't matter if I'm home or not. He wrote the prescription on a piece of my typewriter paper, and then he cut the edges carefully. He admired his work with a smile. He said, It looks kind of fake. If they want to check on it, you can just give them my number at the institute. What do you mean fake? I said. It looks like you wrote it yourself, he chuckled. That's how some real addicts do it. He often used the expression 'real addicts' when making comparisons to me. Then I realized that I thought I saw a real addict once. I told him about the day I was sitting in Abortion-Lauritz's office and a woman was pacing adamantly and begging to go into the office first. Then when she came out, just a few minutes later, she was completely changed, talkative and lively, and with shining eyes. Yes, said Carl, that probably was a real addict. When I was alone I looked more carefully at the prescription and I thought he was right: anyone could have written this. Then I went to the pharmacy and got the pills. When I came home I took them right away to see how they worked; maybe they would take away my nausea. It was a Saturday afternoon. Lise was free early and she came over to pick up Kim, who played with Helle almost every day. Our relationship had cooled since that day when she asked me if Carl was strange, but I asked her to stay for a while, so we could chat, like in the old days. I felt happy and positive and accommodating, and she said she was glad to see I was my old self again. I said, That's because I'm writing. That's the only thing that really works for me. I made us coffee and while we drank it I asked how she was. I was feeling guilty for neglecting her for so long. Not so good, she said. Married men are a load of crap, but I can't get away from him. Ole had had a jealous neurosis, and he went to a psychoanalyst named Sachs Jacobsen who Lise thought was incompetent. Then last Sunday morning Lise had bought nice rolls, since Kim was sick, and Ole made a big stink about it. The next day Sachs Jacobsen called Lise on the phone at work. She was German. Well your husband must doch need his warm buns, she said. We had a good laugh about it, and our old friendship was quietly being restored. I wanted to tell her something private too, so I told her about Carl's obsession with my ear and his plan to get me an operation. That's terrible, she said, visibly horrified. Don't do that, Tove. You can get deaf from an operation like that. That happened to one of my aunts. And you never had an earache before you met Carl. No, I said, but I get them now sometimes. Then I thought about the important letter that Carl had received a few days before. It was from a girl in Skælskør who was informing him that she was going to have a baby of his in a month or so, and that she hadn't written before, because she thought it was a tumor. The baby was going to be given away for adoption in consideration of her very respectable family. Carl had suggested to me that we adopt it, and I had tepidly said yes, since I didn't think one child more or less made any difference. Besides – but this I didn't tell Lise – it would be very difficult for him to leave me if I adopted his child. That sounds like a good idea, said Lise, who, like Nadja, made a habit of saving people, helping them, and relieving them of their burdens. You'll have plenty of room when you move out to your new house. Then I'll do it, I said, as if I were talking about taking a walk in the woods. And Carl has promised me house-help too. I can't write and also take care of three children. Lise thought that sounded sensible. Then you'll have someone to make food for you too, she said, tapping absent-mindedly on her front teeth with her index finger. You need that. Look how thin you've become. Then she fetched Kim from the yard and went back to their place. I went into the bathroom and took two more pills. Then I sat down to write, and for the first time in a long time the words just flowed, just like in the old days, I forgot everything around me, including the reason for my peace of mind, which was inside a bottle in the bathroom.

In October of 1945 we brought home the newborn girl from the National Hospital. She was tiny and only weighed about five pounds. She had red hair and long golden eyelashes. That day I had taken four pills, because they didn't have as strong an effect on me anymore. I thought it was wonderful having a newborn in my arms again, and I promised myself that I would care for her as if she were mine. She needed a bottle every three hours, night and day, and at night Carl got up and fed her. I couldn't wake up from my chloral-sleep. When my mother came to see the new baby, she glanced in the crib and said: Well, you couldn't call her pretty. She thought it was insane that I would take on more children than absolutely necessary. My mother-in-law came to visit too. She just about fainted with emotion. Dear God, she said, putting her hands to her heart, she looks so much like Carl. Then she went on at length about how her cook had left her, and how difficult it was to find another one. She was always having trouble with her cooks. What should I do for my hot flushes? she asked her son, who always had to get tipsy to be able to endure her visits. He smiled. That sounds nice, he said, with this cool summer we're having. He never took her seriously, and when she went to kiss him, he did a little skip to avoid her embrace. Then at the last second he turned his cheek, so she could give him a kiss. Whenever she came over, he had me put on a dress with long sleeves to hide the needle marks on my arms. Not that it matters that much, he said, but it doesn't look so great.

Jabbe was installed in our apartment, and for the moment had to sleep in the kids' room. Her name was Miss Jacobsen and she was from Grenå, but since Helle called her Jabbe, the rest of us did too. She was a large, strong, skilled girl who loved children. She had a simple, reliable face with protruding eyes that were always a bit damp, as if she were constantly moved to tears. She woke up early in the morning to bake rolls for breakfast, which she served me in bed, while Carl slept beside me. You have to eat, she said. You're too thin. My appetite improved a little, now that the food was being served to me, and it seemed that everything was getting better. I worked well on methadone, and I was happy to get a shot just once in a while. Ebbe called me frequently when he was drunk. He wandered the bars with Victor, whom I had never met, although many of my friends knew him. Ebbe really wanted me to meet this Victor. But whenever I said to Carl that I was thinking of going over to visit Ebbe, the syringe came out and he went to bed with me in his coarse, careless way. I love passive women, he said. When he acknowledged that Ebbe had a valid reason to see his daughter, we arranged it so I could drop her off at Ebbe's mother's once in a while, and then she brought her back after the visit.

I gave birth to Michael at a clinic on Enghave Street, and Carl helped bring the child into the world. Afterwards, while I lay in the private room with our infant in my arms, he gave me a shot and sat by my bed for a long time, observing his child, who was immediately put back into the crib. This is going to be an incredible child, he said proudly; the son of an artist and a scientist – a good combination. I'm looking forward to the house being finished, I said sluggishly, while the familiar sweetness flowed into all my extremities. We will always stay together, Carl said with conviction. It won't be like with the others. Viggo F. and Ebbe didn't understand you like I do.

A short while later we moved out to the finished house which was located on Ewaldsbakken in Gentofte. It was a completely custom-built brick house with two stories. On the ground floor was the children's room, the maid's room, the dining room, the bathroom and the kitchen. Upstairs, Carl and I each had our own room. Mine was large and bright, and from my desk I could see down into the beautiful yard with many fruit trees in the lawn, which Carl mowed every Sunday morning. That summer was relatively happy. We had created a civilized frame around our life, a dream that I had always harbored deep down. Whatever I earned I gave to Carl, who managed our finances skillfully and economically as far as I could tell. But one day that fall when I asked him for a new prescription for methadone, he said, while pacing the floor with his tentative, careful steps: Let's stop for a few days. I'm afraid you may be taking too much of it. Later that day I felt very sick, which I had experienced a few times before. I was shaking and sweating and I had diarrhea. On top of that I was gripped by severe anxiety, which made my heart pound in panic. I knew I needed to have some of those pills, and I soon found a way to get them. For some reason I had kept one of Carl's old prescriptions, and I quickly copied it. I sent an unsuspecting Jabbe down to the pharmacy, and she came back with the pills, as if they were only a bottle of aspirin. After I had taken five or six of them – that's what I needed to have the same effect that two gave me at the start – I realized with a vague dismay that, for the first time in my life, I had done something criminal. I decided never to do that again. But I didn't hold to it. We lived in that house for five years, and, for most of the time, I was an addict.

4

If I hadn't gone to that dinner, my ear wouldn't have been operated on, and maybe from then on a lot of things would have been different. That was a period when Carl was only giving me shots once in a while. I stayed high on methadone, and the marks on my arms were getting fainter. My craving for Demerol was fading too. Whenever it reappeared, I reminded myself that I couldn't write under its influence, and I was completely preoccupied with working on my new novel. Life on Ewaldsbakken had taken on a nearly normal character. During the day I was with Jabbe and the children quite a bit, and in the evening, after we had eaten dinner, Carl and I went up to my room where we drank coffee, and Carl read his scientific books without saying much. A strange void stretched between us, and I realized that we were unable to hold a conversation. Carl had no interest in literature, and didn't seem to be interested in anything but his line of work. He sat with his pipe gripped between his uneven teeth, sticking out his lower jaw so it looked like it was supporting the rest of his face. At times he would raise his eyes from his book, smile to me shyly and say, So Tove, are you doing okay? He never told me about his childhood, as other men had, and if I asked about it, he gave me an empty, meaningless response, as if he couldn't remember anything about it. I often recalled Ebbe's evening ramblings, his recitations of Rilke poems in German and his dramatic Hørup passages. Lise, who made her way over to our place once in a while, told me that he was still grieving over losing me and that he was going to the Tokanten Pub and other places with Victor instead of doing his coursework.

Ester and Halfdan came by sometimes as well, when Carl wasn't home. They lived in an apartment on Matthæusgade. They had a little girl who was a year younger than Helle, and they were incredibly poor. They asked me why I had deserted all my old friends, and why I never came to the club anymore. I said that I was busy, and that it wasn't good for artists to socialize. Ester smiled sadly and said, Have you forgotten when we were at the Neckelhuset? But I was suffering from isolation and I longed for someone I could really talk to. I was a member of the Danish Authors' Association, but every time there was an event or a meeting, Viggo F. would call me to ask if I were going, because then he would stay away; so I never went. I was also a member of the exclusive PEN Club, whose director was Kai Friis Møller, one of my most effusive reviewers. He called me one day leading up to Christmas and asked if I would come to a dinner with him, Kjeld Abell, and Evelyn Waugh at Knights Restaurant. I said yes. I wanted to meet all three of them, and when Carl asked me, as usual, if I wouldn't rather have a shot, I said no to his tempting offer for the first time. That made him strangely ill at ease. If it gets too late, he said, I'll come and pick you up. But I said that I was sure I could get home on my own, and he could just go to bed. Well, he said quietly, make sure you cover up your arms. And put some cream on your face, he added, brushing my cheek with his finger. Your skin is still quite dry, and you might not realize it.

During the dinner I sat next to Evelyn Waugh, a small, vibrant, youthful man with a pale face and curious eyes. Friis Møller helped me gallantly over any language difficulties, and he was so attentive and kind in general that it was hard to believe he possessed such a sharp pen. Kjeld Abell asked Evelyn Waugh if they had such young and beautiful female authors in England. He said no, and when I asked what brought him to Denmark, he answered that he always took trips around the world when his children were home on vacation from boarding school, because he couldn't stand them. To excuse my conspicuous lack of appetite, I said that I'd had to eat with my kids before I left home. But I drank plenty, and I had also swallowed a handful of methadone pills before I left, so I was in a happy state and talked at length, making the two famous men laugh again and again. We were about the only guests in the restaurant. It was snowing outside, and it was so quiet that we could hear the thumping from ships' motors far out on the water. While we were enjoying our coffee and cognac, Friis Møller and Kjeld Abell suddenly stared in surprise at the exit, which I couldn't see, since I had my back to it. Who in the world is that? said Friis Møller, patting his mouth with his napkin. It looks like he's coming over here. I turned and saw, to my horror, Carl approaching in his high leather boots, his snow-covered leather jacket, his helmet in his hand, and that shy smile as if it were painted on his face. This . . . this is my husband, I said, confused, because he looked more like a Martian in the presence of these three elegant men, and it struck me that I had never really seen him in the company of others. He walked right over to me and said shyly, I think it's time for you to come home. Let me introduce myself, said Friis Møller, rising and pushing back his chair. Carl shook all their hands without saying a word, and an ironic smile appeared on Kjeld Abell's lips. I stood up, angry and miserable. My eyes were nearly blinded with embarrassment. In silence, Carl helped me put on my coat. When we were outside, I turned to him and said, What do you think you're doing? I said that you shouldn't come and get me. You embarrassed me. But it was impossible to fight with Carl. I wanted to go to bed, he said apologetically, but I couldn't without giving you your chloral. He opened the sidecar for me, and I sat on the seat while he closed the hatch again. During the ride home I cried over my humiliation. When he opened it up for me to get out, he saw my tears and exclaimed, What's the matter? Like in the old days I put my hand on my ear, because now I wanted to be truly comforted. Ow, I cried, this ear has been hurting me all evening. What do you think it could be? It looked like he was really worried. But there was also a faint glint of triumph in his eyes as he gave me a shot in one of the veins that was still open. I thought Falbe Hansen was wrong, he said. He went to bed with me, even more roughly than usual, and afterwards I lay limp and blissful, letting my fingers glide through his thin, reddish hair. He lay on his back with his hands under his head, staring up at the ceiling. We have to do something about this, he said. That bone has to be shaved down. But don't worry. I know an ear specialist who can't stand Falbe Hansen.

The next day he came home with all the fattest books the library had about ear illnesses. He studied them while we drank coffee, mumbling to himself, drawing red lines around the schematic drawings in them, feeling behind and around my ear, and saying that if I kept getting pain there, he would go to the doctor he suggested, and try to get him to do an operation. Is it hurting now? he asked. Yes, I said, making a face. It's hurting a lot. My craving for Demerol had returned with an uncontrollable force. The next day I wrote the last chapter of my novel, packed it in a neat cardboard cover, and wrote on it in capital letters: *For the Sake of the Child*, a novel by Tove Ditlevsen. Then I put it inside the locking cabinet in Carl's room, and I felt as I always did, a kind of mourning over not having the novel to occupy me anymore. I felt physically ill, and I took the bottle of pills from my locked desk drawer, which Carl couldn't open. I swallowed a handful without counting them. I had been very careful with my prescription writing. Sometimes I wrote Carl's name at the bottom and sometimes I wrote John's. He had gotten his degree from Avnstrup Sanatorium. Jabbe and I took turns having the prescriptions filled, and I'm convinced that the naive girl was never suspicious of me or of any of the secretive things that went on in that house. The syringe, the ampoules and the needles were locked inside the cabinet together with my papers, and only once – but that was much later – Jabbe said: That sure is a huge pharmacy bill, when she brought it to me. At that time it was several thousand kroner per month.

The specialist was old, surly and hard of hearing. When the female assistant didn't hand him the instruments he asked for immediately, he threw down whatever he was holding on the floor and yelled: Goddammit to hell, how am I supposed to work with such incompetent help? So, he said, looking in my ear, Falbe Hansen wouldn't operate? Well, we'll see about that. We'll take some X-rays. It could be it's reached the brain membrane. That's what I thought, Carl said. I think she's had a fever once in a while, too. Fever? I said, surprised. How high has it been? asked the doctor. We haven't taken it, said Carl calmly. I didn't want to worry my wife. But she often seems feverish and distracted. A few days later we were there again, and Carl and the doctor zealously studied the new X-rays. There's a shadow there, said the doctor, motionless, without saying anything more. Then he tossed his bald head and said, Fine, we'll operate. I can admit your wife tomorrow to a private room, and we can operate the same morning. When we got home I had a shot and thought, This is how I always want to live. I never want to return to reality again.

When I awoke from my anesthesia, my whole head was wrapped in gauze and then I finally learned what an earache was. I moaned in pain, rolling back and forth. The doctor came in and sat next to the bed. Try to smile, he said, and I formed my mouth into something resembling a smile. Why? I said, resuming my groaning and rolling. We touched the facial nerve, he explained, and that sometimes causes a paralysis, which we have luckily avoided. This hurts so much, I moaned. Can't you give me something for the pain? Of course, he said. You can have aspirin. That's the strongest medicine we give in this ward. We don't turn people into addicts. Aspirin and something to help you sleep at night. Would you call my husband? I said, horrified. I need to talk to him. He'll be here soon, said the doctor. In a little while. For now you need your rest. When Carl arrived he had his brown briefcase and inside it the blessed syringe. And when he gave me a shot in the open vein, I said, You have to come by all the time. I've never felt pain like this in my whole life, and here they only give you aspirin. They might as well give you sugar pills, he mumbled. You have to speak louder, I said. I can't hear you. You're deaf in that ear, he said. You will be for the rest of your life, but at least it won't hurt anymore. When the shot took effect, my pain receded into the background, but it was still there. What am I going to do, I asked sluggishly, when it comes back and you're not here? Try to stick it out, he said. They'll get suspicious if I come too often. He came back in the evening and gave me a shot and chloral. That was after several hours of hell, and I realized that I had never before known what real physical pain was like. I felt like I had been caught in a terrible trap, and where and when it would snap shut on me I couldn't predict. During the night I woke up. It felt as if flames were burning through my head. Help! I screamed out into the room, which was illuminated by the blue glow of the nightlight over the door. A nurse came running in. I'll give you a couple of aspirin, she said. I'm sorry we can't give you anything stronger. The doctor is so strict, she said apologetically. Both his ears were operated on, and he remembers how he endured the pain back then. After she left, I was gripped by wild panic. I couldn't stay there a minute longer. I got up and dressed, making as little noise as possible. Oh, Oh, I moaned quietly to myself, I'm dying, Mother, I'm dying, I can't stand it. When I had put my coat on, I looked out carefully. Across from my room there was another door, which I hoped led to an exit. I ran across to it and soon found myself down on the deserted night street with my bandaged head. I waved for a taxi, and the driver asked me sympathetically if I had been in a car accident. When I got home, I ran up the garden walk and rang the bell like a madwoman. I didn't have my keys. Jabbe came and opened the door. What happened? she asked in alarm, staring at me wide-eyed. Nothing, I said. I just didn't want to be there anymore. I rushed into Carl's room and woke him up. Demerol, I moaned, quick. This pain is making me crazy.

It lasted for fourteen days. Carl stayed home from work

to give me shots whenever I asked for them. I lay motionless and limp in my bed and felt like I was being rocked to sleep in warm, green water. Nothing else in the world mattered to me but staying in this blissful state. Carl told me that lots of people are deaf in one ear, and that it doesn't really matter. I didn't care anyway, because it was worth it. No price was too high to be able to keep away intolerable real life. Jabbe came up and fed me. I almost couldn't get the food down and I pleaded with her to leave me in peace. No way, she said adamantly, not as long as I have any say in it. You're not going to starve to death. Things are bad enough as it is.

One night I woke up and realized that the pain was just about gone. But I was cold and shivering and I was so dehydrated that I had to use my fingers to pry apart my lips. Carl got up, drunk with sleep, and gave me a shot. I don't know what we're going to do, he said, when that vein clogs up too. Maybe we can find one in your foot.

While I was lying there alone in my bed, I realized that it had been a long time since I had seen my children. I walked down the stairs and into their room. I was so weak I had to lean against the wall to keep from falling. I turned on the light and looked at them. Helle was lying with her thumb in her mouth and her curls like a halo around her head. Michael was sleeping with his kitten in his arms; he couldn't sleep without it. And Trine was lying with her eyes open, watching me soberly with a child's inscrutable face. I fumbled my way to her bed and stroked her hair. She still had long blonde eyelashes, which she slowly lowered beneath my caresses. Toys were spread out all over the floor, and there was a playpen in the middle of the room. I almost didn't recognize these children anymore; I wasn't a part of their daily routine. Just like when an old woman thinks back on her youth, I thought how just a few years prior I was a happy and healthy young woman full of vitality and with lots of friends. But the thought was fleeting; I turned off the light and shut the door quietly behind me. It took me a long time to make it back upstairs to my bed. I left the light on, and I lay there, looking at my bony white hands, and I let my fingers move as if they were typing. Then I had a clear thought for the first time in a long while. If things get really bad, I thought, I'll call Geert Jørgensen and tell him everything. I wouldn't do it just for the sake of my children, but also for the sake of the books that I had yet to write.

5

Then time ceases to be relevant. An hour could be a year, and a year could be an hour. It all depends on how much is in the syringe. Sometimes it doesn't work at all, and I tell Carl, who is always nearby: There wasn't enough in it. He rubs his chin with a pained look in his eyes. We have to scale back, he says, otherwise you'll end up getting sick. I get sick if there's not enough in it, I say. Why do you let me suffer like this? Fine, fine, he mumbles, with a helpless shrug of his shoulders, I'll give you a little more.

I lie in bed continuously, and I need Jabbe's help to make it to the bathroom. When she sits down to feed me, her big face is all damp, as if someone spilled something on it. I brush her cheek with my finger and then stick it in my mouth. It tastes salty. Imagine that, I think enviously, to be able to feel sympathy for someone. I pay no attention to the seasons passing. The curtains are always closed, because the light hurts my eyes, so there's no difference between day and night. I sleep; I wake up; I'm sick or I'm well. I see my typewriter in the distance, as if I were looking backwards through binoculars. From the ground floor, where life is actually being lived, the children's voices reach me as through multiple layers of woolen blankets. Faces appear at my side and then vanish again. The telephone rings and Carl takes it. No, I'm sorry, he says, my wife isn't feeling well right now. He eats upstairs in my room, and I watch in wonder, and with a kind of distant envy, at his healthy appetite. Try to get a bite down, he says earnestly. It tastes really good. Jabbe made it just for you. He sticks a small piece of meat in my mouth with his fork, and I vomit it up again. I watch him wipe the spot off the sheet with a wet cloth. His face is close to mine. His skin is smooth and fine, and his eyelids are shiny and damp like a child's. You're so healthy, I say. You will be too, he says, if you could just bear to be a little sick for a while, if you would just let me cut back a little bit. Am I a real addict now? I ask. Yes, he says, with his shy, tentative smile, now you are a real addict. He tiptoes across the floor, pulls the curtain aside and looks at the weather. Won't it be nice, he says, when you can come down into the yard again? The fruit trees are in full bloom. How about having a look? He supports me while I stagger over to the window. Don't you cut the grass anymore? I ask, just to make conversation. Our grass is higher than our neighbor's. It's neglected and full of dandelions, whose tufts are blowing around in the wind. Well, he says, I have more important things to think about. One day he sits down next to me on the bed and asks if I'm feeling good. I am, because there was plenty in the last shot. He says, I have to talk to you about something. At the institute there's a specialist who took 40,000 kroner that he received for scientific studies and spent it on narcotics. I discovered it by chance. I say, I didn't know you even went there anymore. Well I do, he says, when you're sleeping, and he picks up some invisible fuzz from the floor – a new habit of his. So, I say, uninterested, so what do you have to do with that? I was thinking, he says, bending over again and picking up something, of going to a lawyer. At first I was going to go to the police, but don't you think it would be better to get advice from a lawyer first? I guess, I say, indifferently, that's probably better. But don't stay out too long. I need you here when I call you.

My mother comes by and sits by my bed. She takes my hand and pats it. Your father and I, she says, drying her eyes with the back of her hand, are of the opinion that Carl is making you sick. We can't say how exactly, but I don't think he's right in the head. He sounds so strange on the telephone, and he's never here when we come to visit. Jabbe says that he's become quite strange too. Recently he asked her to wash the soles of his shoes so they wouldn't carry germs. She says he frightens her. He's not making me sick, I say calmly. On the contrary, he's trying to make me well. Can you please leave? Talking makes me so tired. But once in a while I myself wonder if Carl's become a bit strange with his fuzz-picking, his tiptoeing and his locking himself in his room when I'm not calling for him. Once in a while I wonder, without any real fear, if I'm dying, and if I should pull myself together and call Geert Jørgensen. But if I do that, I won't get any more shots, that's for sure. If I do that, he'll admit me to the hospital, where they'll only give me aspirin. That's why I keep postponing, and I'm in a state where clear thoughts don't last for very long. Lise visits me and brings her face in close, and her cheek touches mine. I pull my face back with a start, because touching hurts. I can't bear the feel of other people's skin against mine, and it's been a long time since Carl went to bed with me. What's wrong with you, Tove? she asks soberly. You're hiding something, something terrible. Whenever anyone asks Carl, he answers with some nonsense. It's a blood illness, I say, because that's what Carl told me to say, but the worst is over. Now it's going to get better. Would you mind leaving? I'm so tired. Don't you ever write anymore? she says. Don't you remember, how you loved it when you were working on a book? Of course I do, I say, glancing at my dusty typewriter. I remember. It'll come back. Leave now.

Later I think about what she said. Will I ever write again? I remember that time long ago when sentences and lines of verse were always flying around my brain when the Demerol started working; but that doesn't happen anymore. That old blissfulness never comes back, and I know that Carl puts water in the syringe sometimes. One day or night while he's kneeling by my feet and sticking the syringe in a vein down there, I can see that his eyes are filled with tears. Why are you crying? I ask, surprised. I don't know, he says. But I want you to know that if I've done anything wrong I will be punished for it. That's the only confession he ever made. I think you're putting water in it, I say, because I don't care about anything else. Eventually you're going to feel pretty sick, he says, but afterwards you'll feel better, and in the end you'll be healthy again. But you have to stop pestering me, because I have never been able to bear to see you suffer. Everything I'm doing, I'm doing for you, for you to get better, so you can work again and be there for your children. His words fill me with terror. I will not live without Demerol, I shout at him. I can't live without it. You started this and you have to keep it up. No, he says quietly. I'm slowly cutting back.

Hell on earth. I'm freezing, I'm shaking, I'm sweating, I'm crying and yelling his name into the empty room. Jabbe comes in and sits by me. She is crying in despair. He's locked himself in his room, she says, and I'm afraid of him. I put his food outside his door and he takes it inside after I've gone.

Can't you call another doctor? You're so sick, and I can't do anything. When your friends come by, he tells me not to let them in. He won't even see his own mother. He might be going crazy, I say. I know that happened once before. Then I throw up, and Jabbe gets a bowl and dries my face with a washcloth. I ask her to find Geert Jørgensen's number in the telephone book and to write it down on a piece of paper. She does, and I put the note under my pillow. Now I'm unable to sleep, even with chloral. When I close my eyes I see horrible scenes on the insides of my eyelids. A little girl is walking down a dark street, and suddenly a man jumps out behind her. He has a black hood over his head, and he's carrying a long knife. He rushes at her and sticks the knife in her back. She screams, as I do too, and I open my eyes again. Carl comes tiptoeing in. Did you have another bad dream? he says, bending down, picking up fuzz from the floor. We're out of Demerol, he says. I must have forgotten to pay the last bill, but you can have an extra dose of chloral. He pours it into the measuring cup, and I plead with him to give me two. What the hell, he says, it won't hurt you, and he does what I ask. I feel a little bit better, and he pats my hand, which is only half as big as his. It's a question of nutrition, he says with a dopey grin. If you put on twenty pounds, things will be okay. He sits staring into space for a while. Then he starts to sing in a falsetto: We screw our women whenever we want to. That's from Regensen, he says. When I lived there I was a vegetarian. Sometimes I imagine that you're my sister, he mumbles, bending down to the floor again. Incest is more common than people think. Then he tries to go to bed with me, and for the first time I feel afraid of him. No, I say, pushing him away feebly. Leave me alone. I have to sleep. After he leaves, I'm immediately wide awake. He is crazy, I say to the empty air, and I'm dying. I try to focus on those two thoughts, which appear like two vertical strings inside my head, but they get pulled away like seaweed in stormy water. I don't dare close my eyes because of my visions. I wonder if it's night or day. I lift myself up on my elbow, and let myself slide out of bed. I realize that I don't have the strength to stand up. So I crawl on all fours across the floor and pull myself up onto my desk chair. It takes so much effort that I have to lay my head down on the typewriter keys and rest. My breathing wheezes in the silence. I have to take action before the chloral stops working. In my hand I'm clutching the note with Geert Jørgensen's telephone number. I turn on the desk lamp, dial the number, and wait for an answer. Hello, says a calm voice, this is Geert Jørgensen. I say my name. Oh, you! he says. This is quite a time to call and wake me up. Is something wrong? I'm sick, I say. He's putting water in the syringe. What syringe? Demerol, I say. I'm incapable of explaining anymore. Is he giving you Demerol? he says sharply. How long has this been going on? I don't know, I whisper. A few years, I guess, but now he doesn't want to do it anymore. I'm dying. Help me. He asks if I can come and see him the next day and I say no. Then he asks if he can speak to Carl, and I yell Carl's name as loud as I can, while I lay the phone down on the desk. He appears in the doorway in his striped pajamas. What is it? he asks sleepily. It's Geert Jørgensen, I say. He wants to talk to you. Oh, is that it, he says quietly, rubbing his unshaven chin. Then my career is ruined. He says it without reproach, and in that moment I don't know what he means. Hello, he says into the phone, and then he's quiet for a long time, because the other man is talking. I can hear all the way back in the room how agitated and angry he is. Carl just says, Right, tomorrow two o'clock. I'll be there. Yes, I'll explain it all tomorrow.

After he puts down the phone, he gives me a sick smile. Do you want a shot? he says gently. This time I'll put enough in; this calls for celebration. He gets the syringe, and the old blissfulness and sweetness from too long ago return to my blood. Are you angry with me? I say, twisting my fingers in his hair. No, he says, standing up. Everyone has to take care of themselves. Then he looks around the room, studying every single piece of furniture as if he were trying to imprint on himself the room and its furnishings. Do you remember, he says slowly, how happy we were the day we moved in? Yes, I say sluggishly, and we can be that way again. That was silly to call him. No, he says, that was your way out. You'll be admitted and everything will be over. What about the children? I say, remembering them. They have Jabbe, he says. She won't leave them. And what about you? I ask. What is your way out? I'm done, he says calmly. But don't you worry about that. We each have to salvage what we can.

The next day he comes home from Geert Jørgensen's and looks more relaxed than he has been in a long time. You have to be admitted, he says, taking off his motorcycle jacket, for drug rehab. It will start as soon as there's an empty spot at Oringe, and until then you can have all the Demerol you want. Isn't that good? Sure, I say, realizing that that was the same sentence that got me to succumb to the ear operation. And you, I ask, what are you going to do? I'm going to have some trouble with the healthcare authorities, he says with affected dismissiveness, but I'll take care of it. You have enough to deal with just thinking about yourself.

Jabbe is ecstatic when I tell her I'm going to be admitted. Then you're going to get all better, she says. All your friends and your family are going to be so happy. They've been so worried. The day I'm going to be admitted, she carries me down to the bathroom and washes me thoroughly. She washes my hair too, and the water gets filthy. When she carries me back up to bed she says, You don't weigh any more than Helle does. Carl comes in and gives me a shot. This is the last one, he says, but I'll ask them to go slow in there. I'll go with you.

I put my arm around the ambulance driver's neck while he carries me down the stairs. I think he looks worried, and I smile at him. He smiles back, and I see sympathy in his eyes. Carl sits down next to the stretcher, staring out into space. Suddenly he snickers as if he's just thought of something naughty. He picks up a couple of flecks of dust and rolls them between his hands. There's no guarantee, he says flatly, that we'll see each other again. Then he adds: Actually, I never was quite sure about that earache. That's the last sentence I ever hear him say.

6

I'm lying in bed with my head lifted slightly from the pillow, staring stiffly at my wristwatch. With the other hand I'm wiping the sweat out of my eyes. I'm staring at the second hand, because the minute hand won't move, and once in a while I hold the watch up to my good ear, because I think it's stopped. I get a shot every three hours, and the last hour is longer than all the years I have lived on this earth. It hurts my neck to hold up my head, but if I lay it down on the pillow, all the walls start moving in, closer and closer, so there's not enough air in my little room. If I lay my head down, all the creatures come scurrying across my blanket – small, disgusting, cockroach-like creatures by the thousands, crawling all over my body and getting inside my nose, my mouth and my ears. The same thing happens if I close my eyes for a moment. Then they're over me, and I can't stop them. I want to scream, but I can't get my lips apart. Besides, I have slowly been forced to admit that there's no use in screaming. No one is going to come before it's time. I am tied to the bed with a leather belt which cuts into my waist and makes it hard to turn. They don't even take it off when they change the sheets beneath me, which are always full of my excrement. 'They' are something blue and white, which flickers before my eyes with no identity. They're in control now, and it's no use calling out Carl's name endlessly until I get hoarse and my voice becomes an inaudible whisper. The time is five minutes to three. At three o'clock they will come and give me a shot. How can five minutes seem like five years? The watch ticks against my ear in rhythm to my frantic heartbeat. Maybe my clock is wrong, even though they constantly set it for me. Maybe they've forgotten me, maybe they're busy with other patients, whose screams and shouts reach me from the unknown world outside the door to my room.

Well, says a mouth, which to me seems to go from ear to ear in a face that is too large compared to its body, it's time for your shot. I get it in my thigh, and it takes some time before it starts to work. All it does is make me feel a little bit better. I'm able to put my head down on my pillow, and my body stops shaking like a leaf. The face in between the blue and white steps more distinctly closer. It is as pure and gentle as the face of a nun, and I understand that this person does not wish me harm. Talk to me, I ask, and she sits down next to me and wipes the sweat from my face. She says, This will all be over soon. We'll get you back on your feet, but you certainly did get here at the last moment. I ask, Where's my husband? Dr Borberg will come in to speak with you shortly, she says, evading my question. First we have to get you cleaned up a bit. Then I'm lifted up by strong hands while the sheet below me is changed. I'm washed, and then dressed in a clean, white shirt. The worst thing, I say, is all the creatures. I'll get rid of them, she says. Just call me when they come, and I'll chase them away. Now look here. Be a really good girl and drink all of this I have here for you. You're badly dehydrated. Can't you tell? Aren't you thirsty? She lifts my head and puts a glass to my lips. Now drink, she says earnestly. I drink as she asks and I even ask for more. That was good, says the voice. You are a real sweetheart.

Then Dr Borberg comes in, the only human in this world of misery that I perceive clearly. He is a tall blond man in his mid-thirties with a round, boyish face and intelligent, friendly eyes. He asks if I'm able to speak with him for a moment. Then he says, Your husband has been admitted to the National Hospital. He's suffering from a serious psychosis. The Department of Health has brought a case against him, but now it's possible that they will drop it. What about the children, I say, horrified. Jabbe has no money when he's not there. I have to go straight home. You won't be going home for six months, the doctor says firmly, but of course your young housekeeper will need money. I have spoken to her on the telephone, and she will come to see you one day soon. I'll make sure that you're able to talk with her right after you've had your injection. He leaves, and the shot slowly wears off. Then I lie there again, my head lifted off the pillow, staring at my watch, and there is nothing else in the world but it and me.

When Jabbe came, I gave her the bank book, which Carl had placed on the stretcher in the ambulance. Then I asked her to get the manuscript of my novel from the cabinet in Carl's room, and give it to the publisher. I also asked her to stay with the children until I came back home, and she promised she would. She sat observing me with her damp, devoted eyes, patting my hand and asking if I was getting anything to eat. Then she started telling me lots of things about the children, but I couldn't pay attention. Please leave now, Jabbe, I said, while sweat poured out from my whole body. Tell the children I'll be better soon and that I'm looking forward to seeing them so much. Your husband, she said with an anxious look, he's not going to suddenly come back home again, is he? No, I told her, I don't think he will ever be coming back home.

Gradually my miseries lessened. Now I was able to put my head down on my pillow without the walls creeping in around my bed, and I stopped staring at my watch constantly. I was let out of the belt, and I was allowed to go to the toilet supported by one of the nurses. Outside my room, there was a larger room where the beds were so close together that there was only a narrow walkway between them. Most of the patients had belts on, and some of them had large mittens on their hands. They stared at me with empty, glassy eyes, and I pulled closer to the nurse. Don't be afraid, she said. These are just people who are very sick. They won't hurt anyone. But they were yelling and screaming so loud that you couldn't hear your own voice. Why am I here? I asked. I'm not mentally ill. This is a locked ward, she said. You couldn't be anywhere else when you first arrived. When you get better, I'm sure you'll be moved to an open ward. Come here, she said gently, leading me to a sink. Wash your hands. See if you can do it yourself. When I raise my head, I see myself in the mirror, and I put my hand over my mouth to hold back a scream. That's not me, I cry, I don't look like that. That's not possible. In the mirror I see a worn-out, aged, stranger's face with gray, scaly skin and red eyes. I look like I'm seventy, I sob, clinging to the nurse, who leans her head in on my shoulder. There, there, she says. I didn't think of that, but don't cry. When you start getting insulin it will be much better. You'll get more meat on your bones and you'll look like a young woman again. I promise. It happens all the time. When I'm in bed again, I lie there looking at my toothpick arms and legs, and for a moment I'm full of rage at Carl. Then I remember that I carry my share of the blame as well, and my rage disappears.

Early the next morning I got a shot of insulin. I had slept poorly that night, and I dozed off again until I woke at nine-thirty. I felt ravenously hungry. I was shaking, and black dots flickered before my eyes. My whole organism was screaming for food like before it had screamed for Demerol, and I rushed out into the corridor and called for a nurse. Mrs Ludvigsen was her name. I feel sick, I said. Can I have some food? She took me by the arm and led me back to my room. Actually, she said, you don't get your meal until ten o'clock, but I'll bring it to you now. That will be okay just this once. When she came in with the tray, which had on it a plate piled with rye bread with cheese and wheat bread with jelly, I grabbed the food before she even had a chance to put down the tray, and I shoved the food in my mouth, and chewed and swallowed and grabbed for more, while a previously unknown sense of physical well-being spread through my body. Wow, I feel great, I blurted out between two slurps of milk. Can I have all the food I can eat? Mrs Ludvigsen laughed. Yes, she said, even if you eat us out of house and home. It's wonderful to see you eating. She brought more food and I ate like crazy, laughing with bliss. I am so happy, I said. I think I'm finally going to be healthy again. You won't take the insulin away from me again will you? Not before you have reached your normal weight, she said. Later I put on a hospital gown and I sat in a chair by the window. Outside was a large, manicured lawn, and between two low buildings I could see a strip of blue water with white foam. It was fall, and the withered leaves were collected in neat piles on the grass. Some men in striped clothing were raking them, without much enthusiasm. When can I go for a walk? I asked Mrs Ludvigsen while she was brushing my hair. Soon, she promised. One of us will go with you. You're not allowed to go alone yet.

A period followed when I looked at my watch to see if it was time to eat soon. I looked forward to meals, and I ate like a bricklayer. I gained weight, and they weighed me every other day. When I was admitted, I weighed thirty kilos, but now I was up to forty. I could walk without help, and every day I went outside and talked non-stop with the nurse about everything under the sun, because I was in a terrific mood. I realized I felt like I did back in that happy time before I had met Carl. I was allowed to call home every day, and I even spoke on the phone with Helle. She was now six years old and going to school. She said, Mommy, why don't you get married to Daddy again? I don't like daddy Carl. I laughed and said that I might, but that I didn't know if he would want me back. He's not drinking anymore, she said hopefully. He's going to school instead. He was here yesterday with Victor. Victor gave us candy and caramel creams. He was so nice. He asked if I was going to be a writer like my mother.

One afternoon, right after I had eaten, Dr Borberg came to see me. We need to have a serious conversation, he said as he sat down. I sat on the edge of the bed, looking at him expectantly. I'm healthy again, I said. I'm so happy. Then he explained to me that I was regaining my physical health, but that there was much more to it. There would be a stabilizing process, and that was what would take the longest time. I was going to have to learn how to live a bare, unaffected life, and every memory of Demerol would slowly disappear from my mind. It's easy, he said, to feel healthy and happy in this protected hospital room. But when you get home and experience adversity – like we all do – the temptation will return. I don't know, he said, when your husband will be completely well, or even if he ever was, but you must never see him again, no matter what happens, and we will make sure that he never visits you. The doctor asked me if I had ever gone to other doctors, and I told him no. He also asked if Carl had ever given me anything other than Demerol, and I told him methadone. That is just as dangerous, he said. You must never have that again either. Then I told him that I would keep away from it for the rest of my life, because I would never forget all the horrible suffering I'd been through. Yes, you will, he said soberly. You will forget it all soon enough. If you are ever tempted by something like that, you'll think, what harm could it do? You'll think that you can control it, and before you know it, you'll be caught again. I laughed carelessly, You don't think very much of me, do you? We have had very sad experiences with addicts, he said. Only one out of a hundred ever fully recover. Then he smiled and patted me kindly on the shoulder. But sometimes, he said, I think that you are that one, because your case is so unusual, and because, in contrast to so many others we see, you have something to live for. Before he left, he gave me grounds permission, which meant that I could walk outside on the property for one hour every day.

Time passed, and I felt at home in the ward and on the beautiful grounds, where now and again I had a nice chat with one of the other patients who was out walking. I felt so attached to the personnel, that I declined the offer to move to a better ward. Jabbe brought me my typewriter and my clothes, which were in sad shape, since I hadn't bought anything new for years. She also made sure that I had some money, and one day I got permission to travel alone to Vordingborg to buy myself a winter coat. All I had was my old trench coat back from my time with Ebbe, and it wasn't warm. I left for the town late in the afternoon. Twilight was approaching, and a few pale stars emerged in the sky, bleached by the city lights. My mind was relaxed and care-free, and my thoughts kept returning to my time with Ebbe. I thought about what Helle said: Mommy, why don't you get married to Daddy again? I had begun letters to him numerous times, but they always ended up in the trash. I had caused him so much unnecessary misery, and he would never be able to understand why.

After I had bought my coat and put it on, I walked back down the main street without stopping to look in the shop windows. I was hungry and looking forward to dinner. Then my attention was suddenly caught by a well-lit pharmacy window. It radiated a muted light from containers of mercury and beakers filled with crystals. I kept standing there, while the yearning for small white pills, which were so easy to get, rose inside me like a dark liquid. Horrified, I realized while I stood there that the longing was inside me like rot in a tree, or like an embryo growing all on its own, even though you want nothing to do with it. I pulled myself away reluctantly, and kept walking. The wind blew my long hair over my face, and I pushed it aside angrily. I thought about Dr Borberg's words: If you are ever tempted . . .

When I got back I took out a piece of typing paper and looked at it. It would be so easy to cut it with scissors, write a prescription for methadone and walk into the pharmacy and have it filled. Then I thought about how much they had done for me here, and how genuinely people shared my joy over being healthy again, and I felt I couldn't just let them down like that. Not as long as I was here. I walked out to the bathroom, gathered up my courage, and looked in the mirror. I hadn't done that since the day when I had been so horrified by my appearance. I smiled happily to myself and touched my round, smooth cheeks. My eyes were clear and my hair was shiny. I didn't look one day older than I was. But when I went to bed and had been given my chloral, I lay awake for a long time, thinking about that pharmacy window. I thought how well I had worked on methadone; all I had to do was not increase the dosage. Then I remembered the endless suffering during my rehab and thought: no, never again. The next day I wrote to Ebbe and asked if he would come and visit me. A few days later I got his answer. He wrote that if I had called for him a few months prior, he would have come right away. But now he had met another woman, and everything was starting to go better for him. You can't expect, he wrote, to abandon a person for five years and then find him in the same place when you return.

I cried when I read his letter. No man had ever turned me down before. Then I thought about the house on Ewaldsbakken, the neglected yard and my three children, who didn't know their mother anymore, just as I didn't think I knew them. I was going home to be alone with them and Jabbe, and it felt like I wasn't suited for it. For the rest of the time I was at Oringe I never went into town again, so I wouldn't see that pharmacy window.

7

It's springtime when I return to the house on Ewaldsbakken. The gardens are scenting the air with forsythia and golden rain, which drape over our hedge by the narrow gravel road. Jabbe has put out chocolates and a homemade pastry, and the children are all sitting clean and finely dressed around the festive table. At the center of the table, a cardboard sign is leaning against a vase with flowers. Welcome Home Mommy it reads, in crooked capital letters. Helle says she made it herself. She looks at me with her crooked Ebbe-eyes, awaiting my praise. The two little ones are shy and quiet, and when I try to stroke the head of Trine, our little outsider, she pushes away my hand and reproachfully leans in toward Jabbe. I think how it was Jabbe who guided their first steps, Jabbe who talked gibberish with them, blew on their scrapes, and sang them to sleep in the evening. Only Helle shows me any closeness, talking to me as if I'd never been away. She tells me that her daddy has gotten married to a woman who writes poems just like I do. But you are much prettier, she says loyally, and Jabbe laughs as she pours me something to drink. Your mother, says Jabbe, is just as pretty as the day

I first saw her. When the children are in bed later, I sit up chatting with Jabbe. She has bought a bottle of blackcurrant brandy, which we share, while an indefinable longing inside me diminishes slightly. It's better to drink a little once in a while, says Jabbe, whose cheeks are pink and whose eyes are shinier than usual, than all that crap your husband put in you. So, I say, now you want to make me an alcoholic? I'm going straight from the frying pan into the fire! We both laugh, and we agree that she'll have every Wednesday afternoon and every other weekend off. The poor girl hasn't had a vacation in years. She asks me what she's going to do with herself, and I suggest that she put a personal ad in the newspaper. I want to do the same thing. People aren't meant to be alone, I say. I get a piece of paper and a pencil, and we have a lot of fun creating two ads, where we describe ourselves as having every attribute that a man could want. We get rather silly, and it's late before I go up to bed. Jabbe has decorated my room with fresh flowers, but the memories of everything that happened to me here overwhelm me suddenly, and I lie down on the bed fully dressed. I think I can see the shadow of a figure walking around, picking up bits of dust while mumbling to himself. I wonder, where is he now? I walk over to the window, open it, and lean out. There is a clear, starry sky. The handle of the Big Dipper is pointing right at me, and out on the poorly lit road a couple are embracing. They kiss one another under a streetlamp. Quickly I shut the window, realizing I feel like I used to when I was married to Viggo F., when the entire world was filled with loving couples. With a heavy heart I undress and go to bed. Then I realize I forgot to get milk for my chloral. I got a bottle of it from the hospital, and Dr Borberg says that he will send me a prescription for more when this one is used up. He doesn't want me to go to any other doctors. When he said goodbye, he told me to call him if I had any problems, or just so he could know how I was doing. I get milk from the kitchen and go back to bed. I pour myself three doses instead of the two I usually get, and while the deadening effect spreads inside me, I think how it's springtime, and I'm still young, and there's no man in love with me. I embrace myself involuntarily, curl up my pillow, and pull it close as if it were alive.

The days pass steadily and evenly, and I'm always with Jabbe and the children. Being alone in my room makes me sad, and I have no desire to write. The kids get used to me, and now they run to me just as often as they run to Jabbe. Jabbe tells me that I should go out and meet people. She wants me to visit my family and my friends again, but something is holding me back. Maybe it's my old fear that someone will find out what was happening at my house. One morning I wake up particularly depressed. I hear rain falling outside, and my room is filled with a gray, dreary light. The pharmacy window in Vordingborg appears with a clarity in my mind's eye as if I hadn't seen it only once, but a hundred times. I see the pile of paper on my desk. Just two, I think, two every morning, never more than that. What harm could it do? I get out of bed, shuddering with discomfort. Then I sit down at my desk, take out a pair of scissors, and cut out a rectangular-shaped piece of paper. I write it out carefully, get dressed, and tell Jabbe that I'm going for a morning walk. I signed Carl's name, and I'm sure that, wherever he is in the world, he'll cover for me, if it comes to that. When I get back, I take two pills and stand there looking at the bottle. I have allotted myself two hundred. I remember my suffering in rehab, and faintly I hear Borberg's voice inside of me: You will soon forget. Suddenly I become frightened at myself, and I lock the pills inside the cabinet. I slide the key far under my mattress without really knowing why. When the pills take effect, I'm filled with bliss and initiative, and I sit down at my typewriter and write the first couplet of a poem which I have thought about working on for a long time. The first couplet always comes easy. When I'm done and I think the poem is good, I feel a strong urge to talk to Dr Borberg. I call him on the phone and he asks me how things are going. Good, I say. The sky is blue and the grass is greener than usual. There is a pause on the other end. Then he says sharply, Listen, what have you taken? Nothing, I lie, I just feel good. Why do you ask? Forget it, he says with a laugh, it's just my suspicious nature.

I go down to the kitchen and help Jabbe peel potatoes while the children swirl around us. It's Sunday, so Helle is home from school. We have coffee at the kitchen table, and afterwards I go with the children into the nursery, where I read aloud for them from Grimms' Fairy Tales. After lunch I feel so depressed and preoccupied that Jabbe asks me worriedly, Is something the matter? No, I say, I just need a nap. I go up and lie down, staring at the ceiling with my hands under my head. Two more, I think. That couldn't do any harm, compared with how many I used to throw down in the old days. When I go into Carl's room, I see that the key is not in the cabinet. Where in the world could I have put it? I have no idea, and suddenly I'm gripped with panic. An anxious sweat breaks out under my arms, and I turn the room upside down. I'm looking frantically and I realize that it's Sunday. I'm pretty sure the pharmacy is closed. I empty all the desk drawers onto the table, turning them over, knocking their bottoms; but the key isn't there. I need those pills, just two more, and I can't think any further than that. I go downstairs. Jabbe, I say, something terrible has happened. The key to the cabinet is lost, and I have some papers in there that I need right away. It can't wait until tomorrow. Practical Jabbe says that we can just call a locksmith. She did that once when she was locked out of the house. They work around the clock, she says, and she looks in the telephone book and finds me the number. I run upstairs to the telephone and explain to the man that a key to a desk has been lost. Inside the desk there's some vital medicine that I need right away. Then he comes over and picks the lock. There you are, ma'am. Your sorrows are over. That will be twenty-five kroner. After he leaves, I take four pills and think, with the clear, observing part of my consciousness, that now I'm caught again, and that it'll take a miracle to stop me. But the next day I take just two in the morning, like I had originally decided. And when the temptation to take more strikes, it seems to be enough to just hold the bottle in my hand. There it is and it's not going anywhere. It's mine and no one can take it away from me.

A few nights later I'm awoken by the telephone. Hi, says a cottony voice, this is Arne. Sinne is in London, and when she comes back we're getting divorced. But that's not why I called. Victor and I are here at my house having a drink, and we want to come and visit you. It's crazy that you and Victor have never met. Can we come over? No, I say, irritated. I'm sleeping. He continues, Then how about tomorrow, in broad daylight? To get rid of him, I say okay. When I'm back in bed, after having pulled the phone plug out, I remember that tomorrow is Jabbe's day off. Hopefully they won't call back. In the morning I've forgotten all about it. I take my two pills and go down and eat breakfast with Jabbe and the children. After Jabbe leaves, the phone rings again. It's Arne and he's even more drunk than he was the night before. We're sitting here in Green's having a quiet beer, he says. We'll be over in half an hour. After I hung up, I went upstairs and took four pills to help me get through this. Then I dressed the little ones and went for a walk with them down the street. It was July and I was wearing a blue summer dress I had bought one day when I was out with Jabbe. On the way home, a taxi passed us, and in the rear window I saw Arne's drunk, round face next to someone else whom I couldn't make out. The car made it to the house before us, and the two men stepped out, their arms full of bottles. Hi, Tove, shouted Arne. Here I am with Victor. I greeted them, and the man named Victor kissed my hand. He seemed pretty sober, and the sight of him made all my irritation disappear. I let go of the children's hands, and they ran into the house. I couldn't see Victor's eyes because of the sun, but his mouth had the most beautiful cupid's bow shape that I had ever seen. His entire person radiated a kind of disheveled demonic vitality that absolutely fascinated me. I brought them inside, and Arne immediately passed out on Carl's bed. I asked Helle to take care of the little ones for a while, and I took Victor up to my room. He sat down and looked at me without saying anything. I sat in another chair, and my heart was pounding. I was filled with a mixture of happiness and panic at the same time. Panic like when I was a child and my mother was sobbing: I'm leaving; and my brother and I didn't know what would become of us. Victor knelt down in front of me and started caressing my ankles. I love you, he said. I love your poems. For years I've wanted to meet you. I turned his face up toward mine, and I said, Until now I always thought all that talk about love at first sight was a lie. I took his head in my hands and kissed his beautiful lips. Below his tired eyes there were deep smoke-colored shadows, and two wrinkles ran down his cheeks as if they were tracks made by tears. He had a face full of suffering and passion. Don't leave me, I said intently. Don't ever leave me again. It was strange saying that to someone I had just met for the first time, but Victor didn't seem at all surprised by it. No, he said, pulling me close. No, I will never leave you again. Then we went downstairs to the children, who knew Victor from previous visits, while I was at Oringe. Look here, Helle, he said. Here's ten kroner. Now run off and buy red candies for all three of you. After we ate, Helle looked enchantedly at Victor and said, Mommy, can't you marry him so we can have a daddy in the house again? Victor laughed and said, I'll think about it.

I'm head over heels in love with you, I said, when we were lying back in my bed. Will you stay overnight? I will, for the rest of my life, he said, smiling with his blindingly white teeth. What about your wife? I asked. We have the law of love on our side, he said. That law, I said, kissing him, gives us the right to hurt other people. We made love and talked for most of the night. He told me about his childhood, and it was a lot like Ebbe's childhood, but it was still as if I were hearing it for the first time. I told him about the five years of craziness with Carl and about my time at Oringe. I didn't know a person could get so sick from being an addict, he said, surprised. I just thought it was like when the rest of us drink beer. That it's just something you need to be able to cope with life. Eventually he fell asleep, and I lay there observing his face with its elegant nostrils and exquisite mouth. I remembered the time I said to Jabbe: Imagine having feelings for someone. Now I could, and it was the first time since I had met Ebbe. I wasn't alone anymore, and I felt like it wasn't just drunken babble when he said he would stay with me for the rest of our lives. I took my chloral and snuggled close to him. His blond hair had the scent of a child's who had just come home after playing in the grass and sunshine.

8

From then on, Victor and I were almost always together. He only went home when he needed his wife to wash and iron a shirt for him, and I laughed and said that in years to come I might be fulfilling that role. Victor had a four-year-old daughter whom he adored, and he often talked about her. He played hooky from work every other day, and when he did show up, he and I talked on the phone every hour. He was an economics major, just like Ebbe, and he was also more interested in literature, just like Ebbe. Victor would pace back and forth in my room, pretending to be Prince Andrei from Tolstoy's *War and Peace* or d'Artagnan from *The Three Musketeers*. He would fence with an invisible sword and act out huge battle scenes where he played all the roles himself. His lean figure would move around the room while quotations flowed from his lips until he collapsed, exhausted and laughing, onto the bed. I was born at the wrong time, he said – a couple of centuries too late. But if I were born then, I would never have met you. He took me in his arms and we forgot everything in the world around us. Our passion was barely satisfied before it was aroused again, and the children were once more left in

Jabbe's care. That's the terrible thing about love, I said, that you lose interest in other people. That's right, he said, and then it always hurts so damned much in the end. One day he came over happily and told me that his wife had asked for a divorce. So he moved in with me, taking nothing with him but his clothes and his books. He didn't care about material things. About the same time I got a call from a lawyer who had been asked by Carl to arrange our divorce. He explained that Carl wanted the house sold so he could get half its value. Then we'll sell it, said Victor. We can find somewhere else to live.

But a shadow was falling across our happy days, though Victor hadn't noticed it yet. I was taking more and more methadone for fear that I would get sick if I didn't. I lost my appetite and lost weight, and Victor said that I looked like a gazelle who had decided to be eaten by a lion. I took the pills arbitrarily and never really knew how many I needed. Once in a while I wanted to call Dr Borberg and tell him all about it. I was tempted to tell Victor too, but I resisted, for fear that I would lose him.

Early one Sunday morning we rode our bicycles out to Dyrehaven to have coffee in a little out-of-the-way café where we had become regulars. I had taken four methadone before we left, but I forgot to take the bottle with me. We sat there, staring into one another's eyes, and the waiter smiled at us forbearingly. Who knows what he's thinking, I said. Victor laughed. I'm sure you know, he said, that nothing looks as foolish as other people in love. He just thinks we're amusing. Victor placed his hand over mine. You look like an odalisque, he said, and he had to explain to me what an odalisque was. The sky was unbroken blue, and the birdsong had a particular spring joy to it. On the red checkered tablecloth a goldfinch sat eating crumbs, and the moment was planted in my memory like something I could always take out and experience again, no matter what might happen. We took a walk in the woods holding hands, and I told Victor about my marriage to Viggo F., and about how back then I couldn't bear seeing young couples in love. The time flew by and Victor suggested we go back to the restaurant and eat lunch. Suddenly I felt a cold shiver run through me, as if I was being attacked from behind, and I knew what that meant. I dropped Victor's hand. No, I said, I'd rather go home. No, let's not, he said, surprised, and slightly uncomfortable. We're having such a great time; there's no need to rush home. I stood still and put my arms around myself to try and keep warm. My mouth started watering and I felt like I was about to throw up. I blurted out: You know what, I have some pills at home that I really need to get. I can't stay here without them. Can't we go home? Worried, he asked me what kind of pills they were, and I said that the name wouldn't mean anything to him. Then you're still an addict, he said uneasily. I thought that having me would be enough. As we rode home, I told him that I was going to slowly cut back, because I wanted to quit. He was enough for me, it was just a physical dependency that made me need the pills. I also told him, while I was quickly pedaling, that I would call Dr Borberg and ask what to do. Do that as soon as we get home, he said, with an authority that I had never heard from him before. We got home and I took four pills. Then I called Dr Borberg. I'm in love, I said. We're living together and his name is Victor. I certainly hope he's not a doctor, said Borberg. Then I told him about the fake prescriptions and that I wanted to quit, but that I couldn't do it by myself. He was quiet a moment. Then he said flatly, Let me talk to Victor. I gave Victor the phone, and Borberg talked to him for about an hour. He explained to Victor what addiction meant, and what he would have to contend with if he loved me. When Victor put down the phone, he was a changed person. His face radiated a cold, hard will, and he put out his hand towards me. Give me those pills, he said. Scared, I ran and got them and he put them in his pocket. You get two each day, he said, no more, no less. And when there's no more left, that's it. No more fake prescriptions. If I find out that you write even one more, I won't have anything to do with you ever again. Don't you love me anymore? I asked, sobbing. Yes, I do, he said. That's why.

The following days I was miserable. Then it passed and we were both happy again. Now it's over once and for all, I promised Victor. You mean more to me than all the pills in the world. We sold the house and moved into a four-room apartment in Frederiksberg with Jabbe and all the children.

In the middle of fall, Helle was sick one night. She came into our room and crawled up in bed with us, shivering with fever. She had a sore throat, and I took her temperature, which was over 40°C. I asked Victor what we should do, and he said he would phone the night doctor on call. Half an hour later the doctor arrived. He was a tall, friendly man who looked down Helle's throat and wrote a prescription for penicillin. Children get fevers more easily than adults, he said. But just to be safe I'll give her a shot right now. When he opened his bag, I saw syringes and ampoules, and my craving for Demerol, which I thought had been buried far away, returned and uncontrollably consumed my entire consciousness. Victor always fell asleep before I did, and he was a heavy sleeper. The following night I crept out of bed and carefully lifted the phone receiver in the living room. I dialed the doctor on call and then sat down on a stool with my legs tucked under me while I waited. I left the door open so he wouldn't ring the bell. I was half terrified that Victor would find me out, but what compelled me was stronger than my fear. When the doctor arrived, I said I had an earache that was killing me. He looked in the ear that had been operated on and asked me, Can you take morphine? No, I said, it makes me throw up. Then we'll try something else, he said, and he filled a syringe. I prayed to heaven it was Demerol. It was, and I got back into bed next to my sleeping Victor, while the old bliss and sweetness flowed through my whole body. Happily oblivious, I thought I could do this as often as I wanted. There wasn't much risk involved.

But a few nights later, while the night doctor on call was pulling out the syringe, Victor suddenly walked into the living room. What the hell is going on here? he yelled angrily at the frightened doctor. There's nothing wrong with her! Get out of here this instant and don't ever set foot in this house again! After the doctor left, Victor gripped my shoulders so firmly that it hurt. You damned little devil, he snarled. If you ever do that again, I'm leaving you.

But he didn't. He never did. He fought against his terrible rival with a constant vigor and rage that filled me with horror. Whenever he was tempted to give up the fight, he would call Dr Borberg, whose words gave him renewed strength. I had to abandon the night doctors, because Victor hardly dared to sleep anymore. But when he was at work, I visited other doctors and got them to give me shots without much difficulty. To protect myself, I would tell Victor about it in the evening. He called up lots of doctors and threatened to report them to the Department of Health, so I wouldn't be able to go back to them anymore. But in my wild hunger for Demerol I always found new ones. I hardly ate. I lost weight again, and Jabbe was seriously worried about my health. Dr Borberg told Victor that if I kept this up, I would have to be readmitted, but I begged him to let me stay home. I promised I would change and then I broke my promises. Finally Dr Borberg told Victor that the only real solution would be for us to move away from Copenhagen. At the time we didn't have much money, but we got a loan from Hasselbalch Publishing and bought a house in the suburb of Birkerød. There were five doctors in the town, and Victor visited every one of them right away and forbade them to have anything to do with me. So it was impossible for me to get the drug, and slowly I adapted to accept life as it was. Victor and I loved each other, and having one another and the children was enough for us. I started writing again, and whenever reality got under my skin, I bought a bottle of red wine and shared it with Victor. I was rescued from my years of addiction, but ever since, the shadow of the old longing still returns faintly if I have to have a blood test, or if I pass a pharmacy window. It will never disappear completely for as long as I live.

THE FACES

Tove Ditlevsen

Lise, a children's book writer and married mother of three, is increasingly haunted by disembodied faces and voices. She is convinced that her husband, already extravagantly unfaithful, will leave her. Most of all, she is scared that she will never write again. Yet as she descends into a world of pills and hospitals, she begins to wonder, is insanity really something to be feared, or does it bring a kind of freedom?

Tove Ditlevsen's searing, haunting novel portrays a woman on the edge with all the vividness of lived experience.

'Ditlevsen explores the surprising contours of Lise's experience: from her point of view, madness can be funny, soft and secure, and far more enlightening than the "reality" it struggles to evade' *The New York Times*